THE GEOLOGY OF SOUTH AFRICA • FREDERICK AND GEORGE STEUART CORSTORPHINE

※ ※ ※ ※ ※ ※ ※ ※

THE GEOLOGY OF SOUTH AFRICA *190S*

The

Geology of South Africa

BY

F. H. HATCH

PH.D., M.INST.C.e.

PRESIDENT OF THE GEOLOGICAL SOCIETY' OF SOUTH AFRICA, FORMERLY OF THE GEOLOGICAL

SURVEY OF ENGLAND AND WALES, AND LATF. OF THE GEOLOGICAL SURVEY OF INDIA

AND

G. S. COKSTORPHINE

B.St'., PH.D.

CONSULTING GEOLOOIST TO THE "ON-SOLIDATED GOLD-FIELDS OF SOUTH AFRICA

LATE DIRECTOR OF THE GEOLOGICAL SURVEY OF THE CAPE COLONY

ILonion

MACMILLAN AND CO., Limited

NEW YORK: THE MACMILLAN COMPANY

All rights reserved

PKEFACE

Geological investigation in South Africa has in recent years made great advances, and although many gaps remain to be filled, the information already accumulated is sufficiently important to make a condensed account both useful and desirable.

The initiation of a systematic Survey by the Government of the Cape Colony at the close of 1895 marked a new departure in the history of the Geology of South Africa. In 1897 the Transvaal, and in 1898 Natal, followed suit: since then, with the exception of the period 1899-1903 in the Transvaal, every year has seen striking additions to our knowledge of the country.

It must not, however, be forgotten that much has been, and is still being, done by the non-official worker. His contributions are apt to be overlooked as they are not always very accessible, being scattered through the scientific journals of many lands. Further, they lack coherence, partly from the absence of a consistent nomenclature, partly from the want of a proper co-ordination of the results obtained in widely separated districts.

The present work is an attempt to correlate and systematise the valuable results of both official and private work. We recognise the difficulties of the task; but we have been encouraged in undertaking it by the fact that each of us has been engaged in geological work in South Africa for many years—the one first at the Cape and the other in the Transvaal, and now for the past three years both in the latter Colony, where we have had many opportunities of discussing the numerous problems that have forced themselves upon us in the course of our studies. We trust that the following pages will show that our own work has enabled us to appreciate that of others and to remove some of the difficulties that prevent the interesting nature of the geology of South Africa being properly realised.

For the photographs that have been reproduced in some of the illustrations, we have to thank our friends Messrs. E. H. V. Melvill, A. W. Rogers, A. D. Lewis, E. T. Mellor, Nicol Brown, T. N. Leslie and A. Macco. We have also to acknowledge our indebtedness to the Geological Surveys of the Cape, the Transvaal and Natal, and to the Geological Society of South Africa for the use we have been allowed to make of plates that have appeared in their publications. For the figures of fossils we have utilised the recent work of Messrs. Seward, Etheridge, Reed and Lake, and the earlier publications by Krauss, Baily, Sharpe, Salter, Tate, Griesbach and Neumayr. Further, we have to thank the Council of the Geological Society, London, for permission to reproduce figures that have appeared in the *Transactions* and in the *Quarterly Journal* of the Society, and Messrs. Macmillan and Co. for the care with which they have illustrated the book.

In mentioning the names of farms in the Transvaal we have added the numbers given them on Jeppe's map (Pretoria, 1899), and reference to the List of Literature in the Appendix is made by quoting the author's name and the year of publication. Where an author has more than one paper in any year a distinctive letter is added. Two colour-printed maps accompany the volume: one of these forms the frontispiece, and is a geological map of South Africa, on the scale of 1:5,000,000 (78-88 miles to the inch); the other will be found at the end of the book, and is a geological map of the Transvaal, on the scale of 1:1,250,000 (197 miles to the inch).

F. H. H.

G. S. C.

London, *June* 21, 1905.

CONTENTS

Historical

True South African Geology begins with the work of Andrew Geddes Bain; for, though visitors and travellers like Barrow,[1] Lichtenstein,[2] Clarke Abel[3] and Itier[4] noted many interesting geological features, and in some instances even gave detailed accounts of individual localities, none of this work is on the same plane as that of Bain, who, as he himself wrote, "made the first attempt to give the varied formations of the Cape Colony a local habitation and a name, without the shadow of a foundation to commence upon but what his own observation suggested. He had no predecessors whose labour he could avail himself of, nor contemporaries whose assistance he could solicit, but for fourteen years was groping about in the dark, as it were, through virgin fields hitherto quite untrodden, being, as far as geology goes, a *terra incognita*."[5] His incitement to geological work originated from reading Lyell's *Principles of Geology*, which he borrowed from a friend.[1] He was forty years of age when he began, yet before his death in 1864 he had given a correct outline of the geological succession and structure of the Cape Colony.

Bain placed his work before the Geological Society of London in two papers,[2] the second of which included the first geological map of South Africa and a series of sections illustrating his view of the succession of the strata and their structural relationships. He made a very large collection of fossil remains from the east and west of Cape Colony; among these were the first specimens of the peculiar Karroo reptiles that were sent home to be described by Professor Owen.[3] Invertebrate remains from the

Bokkeveld Beds were included, and these afforded the first material for detailed description.[4] About the same time Bain, with his friend Dr. Atherstone, to whom he had imparted some of his own enthusiasm, made a collection of the Secondary fauna from the rocks near Uitenhage, the description of which by Daniel Sharpe[5] is the most detailed account of these fossils published, even at the present day.

Bain's" sequence of the formations of the Cape was as follows:— = Uitenhage Series.

= Stormberg Series.

= Beaufort Series.

Tertiary.

Lias?

Conglomerate.

Wood, Coal, Reptilian

Sandstone. remains.

Fort Beaufort Grit. 1 "Reminiscences and Anecdotes connected with the History of Geology in South Africa," *East. Prov. Man. May.* 1856. Reprinted in *Trans. Gcol. Soc. S. A.* vol. ii. pp. 59-75, 1896. 2 Bain, 1856, 1856 *a.* 'Owen, 1856. 4 Sharpe and Salter, 1856 *a*; Sharpe, 1856 *b*. 5 Sharpe, 1856. 8 Bain, 1856 *a.*

Sandstone And Plant

Remains. Blue Slate.

Claystone Porphyry. = Ecca Shales and Sandstones.

= Ecca or Dwyka Conglomerate.

Carboniferous? Zuurberg Quartzites.

= Witteberg Series.

T. „ I Fossiliferous Bokke-r,,,, r, -i

Upper Silurian?-j veid Beds = Bokkeveld Series.

Unfossiliferous SandLower Silurian? J stone and Con-= Table Mountain Series. (glomerate.

Clay Slate And Gneiss With Intrusive Granite. = Malmesbury Series.

The sections which accompany this paper show that Bain had a clear conception of the relationship of the several divisions, and his map gives a wonderfully correct view of the general distribution of the strata, though not in such detail as is possible to-day.

Practically the only error into which he fell was in connection with a rock which puzzled many of his successors.

His "claystone porphyry" is the much discussed and interesting Ecca or Dwyka Conglomerate, which he held to be the production of an immense volcano supposed to have existed somewhere near the junction of the Vaal and Orange Rivers.1 While offering this explanation, however, he admitted that he was in a dilemma, because he saw some indications that the rock had been produced by water action; but, since he could find no trace of stratification, he felt unable to confirm this view. That Bain did not recognise the true origin of this ancient South African glacial deposit, need not detract from his fame; for men with greater educational advantages, and with a knowledge of recent ice-work as a standard for comparison, have spoken with hesitation, doubt, and even denial, of the glacial origin of the conglomerate.

1 Bain, 1856 o, p. 186.

Like William Smith, "the father of English geology," Bain was a road-maker, and, though he was generously treated by the English Government, his geological work seems never to have received any recognition from his immediate employer, the Cape Government. That body was not, however, unaware of the advantages of geology to the State; for, while Bain was still alive, Mr. Andrew Wyley was engaged from England as Government geologist. Wyley's time was "occupied with purely mineral questions for two and a half years," and he had "the short space of eighteen months for the whole problem of Cape geology "; so that, as he said, those who are acquainted with the history of geology will scarcely feel surprised that he was unable to solve it. 1 His published work, in what may be termed pure geology, consists of a short report with a longer appendix issued a little later.2 He also made a map and sections, which remain in manuscript form in the Surveyor-General's Office, in Cape Town.

In the appendix to his report Wyley gave a tabular view of the succession of Cape strata, in which he was very definite in his correlation of South African with European strata—more so than is justifiable even to-day. Wyley's contribution to South African geology was not an important one: he made no addition to Bain's exposition of the general structure of the country; and his diffuse, rambling observations are lost in a mass of miscellaneous information arranged in diary form.

Almost contemporaneously with Wyley, Dr. R. N. Rubidge, of Graaff-Reinet, and later of Port Elizabeth, wrote several papers on South African geology.3 His observations led him to take a different view of the succession and relationship of the four oldest divisions of the rocks in south-western

Africa from that which Bain set forth. Rubidge was of the opinion that the Malmesbury Slates beneath, and the Bokkeveld Shales above, the Table Mountain Sandstone were the same; and that the Witteberg Quartzites above the Bokkeveld Beds were on the same horizon as the Table Mountain Series. This view was based on erroneous observations made on " two hasty journeys ";1 but, by a curious chance, Rubidge was supported by von Hochstetter, who visited South Africa with the Austrian "Novara" Expedition (1857-59), and made a trip to the country near the Zonder Einde Mountains.2 Owing perhaps to the faulted junctions there exposed, Hochstetter thought that the fossiliferous Bokkeveld Beds underlay the Table Mountain Sandstone; but he is careful to state that he could not have come to this conclusion had not Rubidge given his explanation of the Ceres section. This reading of the succession gained much acceptance, especially on the Continent, and it found supporters even as late as 1897. That it should have existed so long, is the more remarkable from the fact that it was not upheld by the work of Mr. E. J. Dunn, who, on his first map published in 1873,3 after he had been two years in South Africa, adopted Bain's original succession, and, after two additional years' work, confirmed it in a second edition issued in 1875.

In 1884, Professor Rupert Jones, in a paper to the British Association at Montreal, presented the Rubidge-Hochstetter view.4 In the same year, A. Moulle, a French engineer, who had spent two years in South Africa, gave a general sketch of the geology, in which he adopted Bain's succession for the formations in question.5 Dunn, in 1887, in the last edition of his map,6 which may be regarded as a summary 1 Rubidge, 1859, p. 196. 2 Hochstetter, 1866. 3 Dunn, 1873 a.

Rupert Jones, 1884. 8 Moulle, 1885. 6 Dunn, 1887. of his fifteen years' work in South Africa, retained for the oldest formations the succession which he had first presented. In the same year Professor Cohen, now of Greifswald, published the second part of his sketches of South African geology.1 In dealing with the Ceres section, Cohen states that the Malmesbury Slates and the grey wackes of the Bokkeveld are different formations; but, not recognising the true character of the Witteberg Quartzite on the north of the Warm Bokkeveld, places the Table Mountain Quartzites above the Bokkeveld Series, and agrees with Rubidge and Hochstetter as to the identity of the two quartzite series.

In 1888 Professor A. H. Green, who visited South Africa in 1882 to report to the Government of the Cape on the coals of the Colony, published *A Contribution to the Geology and Physical Geography of the Cape Colony,* in which he adopted Bain's succession for the above beds.2 Dr. A. Schenck, in the same year, came to the conclusion that the Table Mountain Sandstone (with which he classed the Zuurberg and Witteberg Quartzites) was contemporaneous with the Bokkeveld Beds, his view being that the former was the shore equivalent of the latter.3 In the following year, 1889, Dr. G. Giirich published a convincing paper on the relationship of the disputed series, which he had studied in the neighbourhood of Ceres: in this he assigns them to the positions advocated by Bain, Dunn and Green.4

The Geological Survey of the Cape Colony which was begun in 1895 proved the correctness of Bain's original succession, and demonstrated the individuality of the Malmesbury Beds, the Table Mountain Sandstone, the Bokkeveld Beds and the Witteberg

Quartzites as distinct series in ascending order, with a marked unconformity beneath the Table Mountain Sandstone. The Survey retained the name "Malmesbury Series" for the oldest quartzites, slates and schists in the south of the Colony, including outcrops at Worcester and George which Dunn 1 had named "Namaqualand Schists." The old rocks at Cango near Oudtshoorn, also included by Dunn in the Namaqualand Schists, were in 1898 found to consist in part of conglomerates containing well-rounded boulders of granite. It is probable therefore that these beds, though older than the Table Mountain Series, are younger than the Malmesbury Slates. Two years later Messrs. Rogers and Schwarz2 discovered in the divisions of Calvinia and Van Rhyn's Dorp a hitherto unrecognised series of slates and quartzites, for which the name "Ibiquas Series" was introduced.

The work of the Survey showed that the Table Mountain Series plays the chief part in the structure of all the mountains of southern Cape Colony northward to the Karroo; further, that the Bokkeveld Beds occupy a large portion of the country between the Karroo and the south coast; and, finally, that the uppermost member of the Cape System has but a small share in the composition of the Groote Zwartebergen, these consisting chiefly of the Table Mountain Series. As a result the name "Zuurberg, Zwartberg and Witteberg Sandstones" adopted at first by the Survey, in consonance with the usage of previous workers, was reduced to "Witteberg Series" as more suggestive of the distribution of the uppermost sub-division.

In comparison with the progress made in the south and west, little has been done in regard to the Pre-Karroo rocks of the north of Cape Colony. Up to the present the Geological Survey has only been able to devote six 1 Dunn, 1873.-Rogers and Schwarz, 1901 b. months to the northern portion of the Colony, this work being confined to the interesting country forming the basin of the Orange River, in the Hopetown and Prieska districts. The earlier accounts of the northern geology deal with special localities, and scarcely suffice for a comprehensive picture of the region as a whole. Namaqualand, on account of its copper-mines, has naturally been frequently reported upon. An account of the mines and their immediate neighbourhood was given in 1854 in a Government report by the then Surveyor-General of the Cape, Mr. C. D. Bell. 1 In the following year Mr. Richard Bright,2 in his later years magistrate at Stellenbosch, gave a lecture on "Namaqualand and its Mines," which he had himself visited. He speaks of the granite, syenite, gneiss, schists and quartzite as extending from the coast to the mines; and, in one locality, Schaap River Mountains, he recognised certain quartzites as " Table Mountain Sandstone." In the same year Delesse3 wrote a paper based on Bell's report and on specimens which had been sent to Europe; but his geology cannot be regarded as specially authentic, since he placed Jurassic rocks — the Uitenhage Series— somewhere on the Orange River. In 1856 4 Wyley reported *Upon the Nature and General Character of the Copper Districts of South Namaqualand,* but this contains little of geological interest.

One of Dunn's earliest reports to the Cape Government deals with Namaqualand and Bushmanland.5 He describes the gneiss of the Orange River valley and certain schists which he considered to lie above it. He also describes the "Namaqualand Schists (metamorphic)" of the Doornberg as consisting of jasper rocks rich in magnetite, schists, gneiss 1 Bell, 1855. 2 Bright, 1855. 3 Delesse, 1855. Wyley, 1856. Dunn, 1873. and schistose conglomerates. The old rocks near Prieska he states to be "identical in character with, and evidently a portion of, the same formation as the old metamorphosed stratified rocks of Klein Namaqualand," although "their precise relation to the Malmesbury Beds underlying the Table Mountain Sandstone remains yet to be worked out." 1 On each of his three maps Dunn gives a different interpretation to these rocks in the north of Cape Colony: on the first they are shown as Namaqualand Schists; on the second, partly as Namaqualand Schists and partly as Malmesbury Beds; while in the last edition they are given as a portion of the Lydenburg Beds, which, according to him, is a division above the Malmesbury Beds comprising, not only the rocks of Lydenburg, but practically the whole of the old rocks of the southern Transvaal, including what we now know as the Witwatersrand Series, the Black Reef, Dolomite and Gatsrand or Pretoria Series.

Much detailed and accurate work was done in the north of Cape Colony by G. W. Stow. Self-taught like Bain, Stow devoted his attention to the Province of Griqualand West especially, but also to the Uitenhage district. He was for a time geologist to the Government of Griqualand West, and, at a later date, to that of the Orange Free State. No official reports of Stow's Griqualand West work appear to have been published, but two small reports for the years 1878 and 1879 were issued by the Free State Government.2 A portion of his Griqualand West work was published in the *Quarterly Journal of the Geological Society,* London, in 1874,3 giving various sections and much valuable information. He describes the granite and gneiss of the district, as well as the other Pre-Karroo rocks, and when the Cape Survey came to deal with these rocks in the territory adjoining that 1 Dunn, *loc. cit.* p. 8. 2 Stow, 1878, 1879. 3 Stow, 1874. described by him, his classification was found to be a proper presentation of the facts,1 and was accordingly adopted. It is as follows:— 1. Granite and gneiss. 2. Keis Series—Quartzite and mica schists. 3 Doornberg Series Griqua Town Series—Magnetic jasper rocks.

I Campbell Hand Series—Limestone and quartzite. 4. Matsap Series— Quartzites and conglomerates.

The Survey also found that a large portion of northern Cape Colony in the vicinity of Griqualand West is composed of volcanic rocks of both acid and basic types.

Owing to a clear natural division, there has been no uncertainty, from Bain's time onward, as to the separation of the older rocks of South Africa from those that make up the Karroo and younger systems; but there has been much interesting discussion as to the origin and meaning of the strange conglomerate which lies at, or near, the base of the Karroo System. Bain, as already stated, considered the conglomerate to be due to the activity of some great volcano. Wyley adopted the same explanation, but, laying more stress than Bain on the included boulders, named the rock a "trap conglomerate." 2 Atherstone was also a supporter of the igneous theory. He described the rock as having "a felspathic fusible base, and assuming the appearance of a conglomerate or breccia, the included pebbles of granite, gneiss, quartz, slate and sandstone being sometimes angular, sometimes rounded, whilst in some parts of the Zuurberg it is vesicular, *i.e.* containing gas-bubbles which have been filled up with zeolites, agates, etc." He adds: "It is not a true porphyry, although the base is porphyritic, but appears as if the molten lava in bursting up through the lower beds had broken up and mixed in its liquid paste the fragments 1 Rep. Geol. Com. for 1899, p. 68. 2 Wyley, 1859, p. 7.

of the different rocks it had passed through." 1 Dr. P. C. Sutherland, of Natal, who was later to arrive at the true explanation, at first also took the rock to be a lava-flow, and thought the striations underneath it were due to the movement of the igneous mass.2 Ralph Tate, after stating that the rock as exposed "on the flanks of the Zuurberg is decidedly a dolerite containing angular and rounded fragments of quartzite and granite," curiously enough names it a "trap breccia." 3

It was in 1868 that Sutherland, while describing the Natal occurrence, first published what is now known to be the true explanation of the origin of this peculiar conglomerate:—" The deposition of this formation cannot be accounted for except by reference to glacial action. It is by the action of glaciers, coast ice and icebergs, and by them alone, that fine silt and boulders of many tons weight can be deposited simultaneously

on the same sea or lake bottom. The great Scandinavian drift is precisely the same in mechanical composition as the boulder clay of Natal with which we are now dealing. Professor Ramsay has assigned certain breccias of Permian age to glacial action; there is, therefore, no reason why our *quaestio vexata* should any longer remain unsettled.... The sandstone on which this boulder formation rests is highly grooved and striated, as if clay or some semi-plastic substance containing hard fragments had passed over it with considerable pressure." 4 Two years after Sutherland's lecture C. L. Griesbach5 ascribed the peculiar appearance of the boulders to weathering. Moulle, writing fourteen years later, confirmed Griesbach's description, but named the rock a melaphyre breccia.6 1 Atherstone, 1857, p. 587.
2 Sutherland, 1855. 3 Tate, 1867, p. 142, footnote.
Sutherland, 1868, pp. 18 and 17. 5 Griesbach, 1871.
6 Moulle, 1885.

G. W. Stow knew the conglomerate in Griqualand West, but appears to have been unable to view the glacial striae as having originated in Palaeozoic times.1 In 1875 R. Pinchin, repudiating both glacial and igneous theories, described the conglomerate as metamorphic.2

Dunn during his stay in the country wrote much about the conglomerate: in the end he confirmed the correctness of the glacial view for all the outcrops in the Cape Colony. He seems to have first come across the rock in the north of the Colony, east and west of Hopetown, in 1872. There, and at once, he had no doubt as to its glacial origin, but stated that very scant material had been met with for determining its age. He considered it "probably older than the upper drift of Pniel classed as *P. Pliocene.*" Professor Cohen, who, accompanied by Stow, saw some of these outcrops in 1872, but did not describe them till 1887, was of the opinion that they were of Pleistocene age, though he did not see sufficient evidence for adopting the glacial view.4

On his first map (1873) Dunn showed

the northern outcrops as " Glacial Conglomerate" at the top of his sedimentary sequence, but represented the whole band along the south of the Karroo as an igneous rock, under Wyley's name of " Trap Conglomerate." In the second edition (1875) Dunn still kept the two occurrences separate, but introduced the name "Dwyka Conglomerate" for the outcrops in the south of the Karroo as well as for those in Natal. In a report published in 1879, he discusses the origin of the rock, and gives his reasons for introducing the non-genetic term, "Dwyka Conglomerate," from the "characteristic occurrence near the river of that name." In this report he gives up the igneous explanation of the southern occurrence, stating that

"the so-called trap conglomerate is as much a sedimentary rock as the sandstones above and below," and that, with the dark arenaceous shales beneath, it must be included in the Ecca Beds.1 In a later report (Camdeboo and Stormberg, 1883) Dunn reverts to the older and more suitable name Ecca Conglomerate. The crowning stage of Dunn's investigation of this rock was reached in his *Report on a supposed extensive Deposit of Coal underlying the Central Districts of the Colony.2* On the sketch-map accompanying that report, Dunn showed the northern glacial conglomerate of his former maps and the southern "Dwyka" as one continuous outcrop: in the text he assigns a glacial origin to both. In the last edition of his separate map, published in the following year (1887), the same view is presented, and in the legend the "Dwyka Conglomerate" is described as glacial.

Dunn's work—conclusive though it was—did not at once find general acceptance. Other geologists, who visited South Africa without seeing the definite evidence of ice action that Sutherland and he had shown to exist, were either unable to accept such an explanation, or denied altogether that the aspect of the rock was that of a glacial conglomerate: thus Cohen stated that it was of clastic origin and not a product of volcanic activity;3 while Green thought it was a coarse shingle formed along a retreating coast-line, but with the reservation that if he had found the rock in a known glaciated country his attitude might have been very different.4 Microscopic examination of the specimens taken home by Green led to the suggestion that the rock was a volcanic breccia. This determination would almost invariably be given from an examination of hand-specimens, and perhaps even of microscopic sections, of the hard, compact, dark rock characteristic of the southern outcrops. It is only the striations on the included boulders that suggest the real nature of the rock, and these can rarely be recognised on the smaller pebbles of an ordinary hand-specimen. The difficulty in determining the southern rock as glacial, and not volcanic, is shown in the fact that both Sutherland and Dunn maintained its igneous origin before being convinced of its true character.

Dr. A. Schenck, now of Halle, writing in 1888, held the Dwyka to be glacial, but considered that its identity with the outcrops of conglomerate in the north of Cape Colony was still doubtful.1 F. M. Stapff entered into the controversy in the following year (1889), and gave an anti-glacial explanation for all the southern conglomerate outcrops, accepting, but only to a limited extent, glacial action for the northern rock.2 Schenck replied, and, more definitely than in his earlier paper, adopted a glacial origin for the Dwyka as well as for the northern conglomerate, and was also disposed to admit their identity.3 In 1893 A. R. Sawyer, in reporting to the Cape Government on the geology and mineral resources of the division of Prince Albert, described the Dwyka as a "sedimentary rock." From its occurrence in the field, and from an examination of the matrix in thin section under the microscope, he held it to be "undoubtedly a volcanic ash mixed no doubt in part with other fragmentary materials derived from the operation of moving water." 4

The next observation of the southern Dwyka was recorded by E. H. L. Schwarz,5 of the Cape Survey. Mr. Schwarz, in 1896, obtained in a small basin

of the 1 Schenck, 1888. Stapff, 1889. 3 Schenck, 1889 a. Sawyer, 1893, p. 4. 5 Schwarz, 1897 o.

conglomerate that lies north of the Gydo Mountains, near Ceres, faceted and striated boulders which are now exhibited in the South African Museum, Cape Town. In the following years glaciated boulders were found at various localities along the southern boundary of the Karroo. In fact, the glacial theory was the only one to which, from the beginning, the results obtained by the Cape Survey gave any support. As, however, all the outcrops investigated in the south showed that the conglomerate and its occasional shale beds were conformably interbedded between the Witteberg Quartzites and the Ecca Shales, the question as to the source of the ice-worn stones could not be answered from the evidence there obtainable.

In the northern portions of the country, however, evidence had been slowly accumulating to prove the correctness of Sutherland's view. Penning, in 1891, saw the conglomerate at the base of the coal-formation at Boksburg in the Transvaal, and described it as a product of Palaeozoic glaciation; he did not, however, suggest a correlation with the southern rock.1 In 1893 A. R. Sawyer suggested that the breccia beneath the coal at Viljoen's Drift, near Vereeniging, might correspond to the Dwyka of the southern Karroo.2 An important stage was reached when Schmeisser, in 1893, saw on the farm Modderfontein, Boksburg, a rock resembling an indurated boulder-clay, which he recognised as agreeing with Schenck's description of the Dwyka Conglomerate of Cape Colony and Natal. By the discovery of *Schizoneura* and *Glossopteris* in some of the Transvaal collieries, Schmeisser was further enabled to correlate the coal-measures of the Transvaal with the Ecca Beds of the Cape, thus leaving no doubt as to the position of the Transvaal conglomerate.3 1 Penning, 1891. 2 Sawyer, 1893. 3 Schmeisser, 1895.

Confirmatory evidence of the correctness of Sutherland's view was also obtained by Molengraaff in 1897 from the Vryheid district, where he found the

glacial conglomerate resting unconformably on old slates and quartzites, which, where exposed, show undoubted *roches moutonnees* marked by glacial striae.1 In 1899 further evidence of the morainic nature of the conglomerate was obtained by Messrs. Rogers and Schwarz during a survey of the Prieska and Hopetown divisions in the north of the Cape Colony.-' There the old rocks are exposed in a manner similar to that described by Molengraaff in Vryheid, and the *roches moutonnees* and the glacial striae are perhaps even more distinct. The work carried out in 1904 near Balmoral by E. T. Mellor,8 of the Transvaal Geological Survey, has given the same results; and similar evidence has been obtained by Anderson in his survey of Natal and Zululand.4

Since the early investigations of Bain and Wyley, the ordinary sedimentary rocks of the Karroo and their fossils have been described and classified by Tate, Rupert Jones, Dunn, Green, Feistmantel and Seeley.

The interest of the stratified rocks of the Karroo is palaeontological rather than geological. North of the area which has been implicated in the great foldings that produced the Zwartebergen there is a series of horizontal or gently dipping sandstones and shales without any marked structural features. Even the palaeontological interest is limited to scattered localities: extensive areas and considerable thicknesses of strata may be examined without any trace of organic remains being found; in fact, the sparseness of fossil localities—quite as much as the absence of fossil horizons—is a characteristic of South African geology.

1 Molengraaff, 1898.

3 Mellor, 1904.

2 Rogers and Schwarz, 1900 d. Anderson, 1901, p. 16; 1901 c, pp. 88-91.

Rupert Jones gave, in 1867, a sequence for the Karroo strata in a paper by Ralph Tate1 on certain species of South African fossil plants which had been collected and presented to the Geological Society, London, by Atherstone, Rubidge, Sutherland and others. The various divisions are named from below upwards, thus:— 1. Ecca Beds, in an "upper and lower series separated by, and lying conformably with, the remarkable band of igneous rock which extends across South Africa " i.e. the Dwyka Conglomerate.

2. Koonap Beds. 3. The Beaufort Beds. 4. The Stormberg Beds.

In 1883, and again in 1888, the late Professor A. H. Green[2] discussed the Karroo Beds, separating them into five groups:—

Stormberg Beds,

Karroo Beds,

Kimberley Shales (great unconformity),

Ecca Beds,

Dwyka Conglomerate (unconformity).

He considered the northern shales to be distinct from the southern, placing them under the name Kimberley Shales unconformably above the Ecca Beds. Green correlated his Kimberley Shales with Stow's Olive Shales, and regarded Stow's "Ancient Conglomerate" at the base of these shales as distinct from the Dwyka, with which he suspected it had been confounded. This, however, is incorrect, for the Kimberley Shales and the underlying conglomerate are identical with the Ecca Beds and their basal conglomerate.

A valuable discussion of the Karroo System, with a description of its fossil flora, was published by Ottokar Feistmantel in 1889.[3] Feistmantel begins his paper with a catalogue raisonne of the chief literature; he next deals 1 Tate, 1867. 3 Green, 1883, 1888. 'J Feistmantel, 1889.

C critically with various authors' views of the classification and sequence not only of the Karroo but also of the underlying systems, and then gives what—until Mr. Seward began his work on South African fossil floras—was certainly the best account of the Karroo plants. Feistmantel's views are particularly interesting in virtue of his experience in India and his knowledge of the Australian fossil floras. In an earlier paper[1] he had dealt with the comparative geology of the three regions, and it is to be regretted that he did not live to

complete his description of the South African fossil plants. Feistmantel arranged the Karroo Beds in three groups: a lower, including the Dwyka Conglomerate and the Kimberley-Ecca Shale—the best classification for these lowest beds; a middle, including the Beaufort Beds; and an upper, comprising the Stormberg Beds. From his determination of the plant remains Feistmantel concluded that the Stormberg Beds were probably equivalent to the Lias and Rhaetic; the Beaufort, to the Trias; and the lowest division, to the Permo-Carboniferous of the Northern Hemisphere.[2]

Professor H. G. Seeley, in his series of papers on the Karroo Reptilia, has incidentally given a division of the system into zones in accordance with the distribution of the remains of those peculiar vertebrates. He proposed, in 1892, a five-fold division of the entire system from above downwards, thus[3]:— 5. Zone of the Zanclodonte. 4. Zone of the Specialised Thecodonts. 3. Zone of the Dieynodonts. 2. Zone of the Pareiasauriana 1. Zone of the Hesosaure.

In 1904 A. C. Seward described certain of the fossil plants collected by the Cape Survey in the lowest and 1 Feistmantel, 1887. 2 Feistmantel, 1889, p. 75. 3 Seeley, 1892.

uppermost divisions of the Karroo System: as a result, he confirms Feistmantel's tentative correlation of the Stormberg Beds with the Rhaetic of Europe.[1]

A marked geological feature in South Africa is the comparative scarcity of rocks corresponding to the later Secondary and Tertiary Systems of other parts of the world. With the exception of a considerable variety of superficial deposits—the origin of some of which certainly dates back to Tertiary times— there are no rocks other than those occurring, over comparatively limited areas, at Mossel Bay and the neighbouring inland districts of Oudtshoorn and Worcester, at Uitenhage, and on the Pondoland, Natal and Zululand coasts, to represent the great lapse of time indicated by the Jurassic, Cretaceous and all the Tertiary formations of other parts of

the world. The earliest account of these coastal deposits was given in 1837 by Hausmann,[2] who described a suite of fossils sent him from Enon and Uitenhage by a Mr. Hertzog. As a result of his determination of these fossils, Hausmann correlated the formation with the Lower Greensand of Europe. In 1843, and again more comprehensively in 1845, Ferdinand Krauss[3] of Stuttgart gave the geological results of a visit he had made to the eastern portion of Cape Colony, where these beds occur. He also said that the rocks "probably belong to the Lower Greensand." Bain described the beds which occur near Uitenhage, and came to the conclusion that they had more of an " Oolitic than a Liassic character." [4] Sharpe, who described the Secondary fossils collected and sent home by Bain and Atherstone, stated that "the forms which they most nearly resemble are those which are found in the middle and lower part of the Oolitic Series." He considered that Bain placed the beds too low, in comparing them to the Lias, but Krauss' view that they were Cretaceous " seemed to rest on still weaker grounds." [1]

The Uitenhage Beds were described and classified by Atherstone[2] in 1857. In 1867 Ralph Tate[3] adopted Atherstone's classification of the beds and introduced the name "Uitenhage formation." He concluded that "the fossil fauna of the Sunday's River and Zwartkop River limestones represents that of the Oolitic rocks of Europe, and approximates to that of the Great Oolite." [4] Stow, in his minute, careful manner, gave in 1871 an account of the "Jurassic Formations." [5] He described a series of sections with the fossil contents of each zone, and showed conclusively that there is great variation in the sequence of the beds. In a paper published in 1881 Neumayr, after describing various new mollusca from the Uitenhage formation and reviewing the work of his predecessors, supports the view that the Uitenhage formation is Cretaceous, and places it parallel with the Neocomian." On his 1887 map Dunn shows the distribution of these beds, under the name

"Enon Conglomerate and Sunday's River Beds, Jurassic," at Worcester—their most westerly occurrence—at Oudtshoorn, Mossel Bay and Uitenhage.

Bullen Newton, in describing in 1896 7 a specimen of *Ahctryonia ungvlata* found by Mr. David Draper at Sofala, gave a critical review of the previous descriptions of the Uitenhage fossils, concluding that these are of Lower Cretaceous or Neocomian age.

During its first years the Cape Survey found that the Uitenhage Beds are well represented in the south 1 Sharpe, 1856, p. 202. 2 Atherstonc, 1857. 3 Tate, 1867.

4 *Loc. cit.* p. 167. 6 Stow, 1871. 8 Holub and Neumayr, 1881. 7 Newton, 1896. western districts from Worcester to Mossel Bay. Their unconformable relation to the older rocks in everywhere apparent — an especially fine section being afforded at Cape St. Blaize, where they lie almost horizontally on steeply dipping Table Mountain Sandstone.1 The Uitenhage Series is now known to cover a considerable area in the south of Cape Colony, and to show great divergences in its sedimentation. The fossil plants collected from this formation during the progress of the Geological Survey have recently been described by Seward, who confirms the earlier determinations of the age of the series as Lower Greensand.-'
On the coast of Pondoland, south-west of the mouth of the Umtamvuna River, are certain outcrops of Cretaceous rocks, that have been known and recognised as such since 1855. Fossils collected by R. J. Garden were described by W. H. Baily, who concluded that the Beds were probably the equivalent of the Upper Greensand of England.3 Griesbach,4 in addition to the localities where Garden found these beds, mentions "a small stream flowing into the St. Lucia Bay, in the Zulu country."5 He uses the somewhat impossible name "Izinhluzabalungu" Beds for the Pondoland occurrence, this, according to Garden, being the native name for certain caves in the formation. Griesbach describes the rocks as lying unconformably on the Karroo Beds, and con-

siders that there are five distinct fossil zones. Among the fossils he finds considerable resemblance to those occurring in Indian rocks of the same age. Dunn, on his 1887 map, shows two patches of these rocks, on the Pondoland and Natal coasts: he names them "Umtamvoona Beds," and classifies them as Cretaceous.

In 1901 Rogers and Schwarz described the Pondoland Cretaceous rocks; but no complete description of the fossils has yet been published. In the first report of the Geological Survey of Natal and Zululand, Anderson describes the Cretaceous rocks from three localities in Zululand: one on the south bank of the Umfolosi River, close to Lake Isitesa; another on the Umsinene River, which he identifies with Griesbach's St. Lucia Bay locality; and a third in the bed of a stream, "about two miles east of Crossly's store, Bombeni, near the southern end of the Lebombo Range." 1

In the Transvaal, geological inquiry has had the same history, as in Cape Colony: first the observations—sometimes of scientific value, sometimes purely casual—of the passing traveller; then the work of those with more opportunity for thorough study, whether as local amateurs or as professional visitors to some area of real or supposed economic value; then finally the systematised work of a State Survey. The geology of the Cape Colony being comparatively well known when that of the Transvaal began to be studied, most writers have naturally been tempted to draw comparisons between the two regions, with much resulting confusion, but with little scientific profit. It is, of course, since 1886 that most attention has been given to Transvaal geology; but before that time the gold-fields of Lydenburg and De Kaap, and the coal deposits of the southern Transvaal, had given occasion for the visits of such men as Cohen and Penning, who both made contributions toward the elucidation of the stratigraphy of the country.

Of the earlier travellers who have added to the knowledge of the Transvaal, Mauch2 and Hiibner3 may be men 1 Anderson, 190U, p. 47. 3 Mauch,

1872. 3 Hiibner, 1872.
tioned. Mauch has many scattered geological observations in the story of his wanderings; and Hubner, in giving a sketch of his route from Potchefstroom to Inyati and thence north to Tati, describes the old granite and its associated rocks.1

After Hubner, Penning seems to have been the next to attempt the solution of the stratigraphical problem. In 1884 and 1885 he read two papers before the Geological Society of London dealing respectively with the *High-level Coalfields* and the *Gold-fields of Lydenburg and De Kaap.* He described the coal formation as resting on rocks of " probably Upper Palaeozoic age, the Megaliesberg *(sic)* Beds." To the shales forming the lower part of the coal formation he applied the name Kimberley Beds.2 In his second paper Penning gave, for the district with which he dealt, the following sequence3:— 4. High Veldt Beds

3. Devonian (?) rocks
2. Silurian (?) rocks.
1. Granite (?) rocks.

E. J. Dunn, on his map of 1887, to a much greater extent than in either of the previous editions, presents a distribution of the rocks of the Transvaal and their correlation with those of Cape Colony, but in both respects this portion of the map has not the same value as his representation of the geology of the latter colony. Schenck discusses Transvaal stratigraphy in his paper of 1888/ and to a less extent in one on the *Occurrence of Gold in the Transvaal* written in the following year.'' He classifies the Transvaal rocks in the same main groups as those of Cape Colony, namely:— 1 *Loc. cit.* p. 224.

2 Penning, 1884, p. 659. Penning, 1885, p. 670 *et seq.* Schenck, 1888. 5 Schenck, 1889. = the coal formation. = Magaliesberg Beds, including the dolomite,

which he called chalcedolite.
3. Karrooformatioii.
2. Kapformatioii.
1. Sudafrikanische Primarformation.
In the first group Schenck places the granite and gneiss and his "Swasi Beds," the latter including clay-slates,

quartzites, and striped magnetite slates. He unites the rocks of the Magaliesberg with those of the Witwatersrand, and correlates both with the Table Mountain Sandstone and Bokkeveld Beds, which in his opinion are equivalent facies. Schenck's classification of the Transvaal rocks has been more or less followed by subsequent writers.

Dr. G. A. F. Molengraaff, to whose work Transvaal geology owes much, first visited South Africa in 1890, in which year he published, in Dutch, a non-critical *resume* of the then existing views regarding South African stratigraphy.1 The results of his own visit, which lasted some two months, were briefly given in a lecture to the Third Congress of Naturalists and Chemists at Utrecht in 1891,2 and three years later, in more complete form, as a paper in the *Neues Jahrbuch*. In the latter, Molengraaff bases his classification on that of Schenck, but gives more detail. The lowest Witwatersrand Beds are separated from the upper as the " Old Schist Formation," with an unconformity above and below, and to this series the magnetite quartzites and slates of the Magaliesberg are assigned—a grouping which Schenck had also given. The classification presented in this paper was abandoned by its author, when later, as State Geologist, he had had opportunity for more extended and more systematic stratigraphical investigation.

A further addition to his previous classification was made by Penning in 1891. One of his main groups, the " Megaliesberg formation, Permian," includes the Witwatersrand Beds 1 Molengraaff, 1890.

1 Molengraaff, 1891. 3 Molengraaff, 1894. and his "Klipriver Series," the latter embracing the Black Reef, the Dolomite (which he called "Chalcedolite") and the Magaliesberg Quartzites. He recognised that the only Transvaal formation that could be approximately classified was "the High-level Coalfields of South Africa," which he regarded as of Oolitic age. In his 1885 paper, Penning speaks of an unreliable report of graptolites having been observed in his " Silurian "(?) rocks,1 and in the

1891 paper he states that he believes his provisional De Kaap Valley Beds "to be of Silurian age, although there is no fossil evidence except that of a few obscure Corals." 2

In 1892 Mr. Walcot Gibson3 contributed a paper to the London Geological Society on *The Geology of the Goldbearing and Associated Rocks of the Southern Transvaal*. In this paper, which was based on his personal observations in South Africa, he stated that the Witwatersrand conglomerates, quartzites and slates formed a definite geological series, of which both summit and base were missing. He was unable, however, to decide whether the apparent succession of the strata was the true order or not, but pointed out that if the observed order was correct it had been much disguised by faulting, folding and thrust-movement. From the apparent dip, the whole group of strata "would seem to be at least three miles thick." His subdivisions (in descending order) are:—

2. Quartzite and Conglomerate Series (Main Reef Series and associated rocks).

1. Lower Quartzite and Shale Group.

Pie considered that these divisions are separated by a fault; consequently, although they evidently form portions of a larger series, "the exact sequence and relationship of the beds cannot be fully made out."4 1 Penning, 69, p. 452. 2 Penning, 1885, p. 571. 3 Gibson, 1892. 4 *loe. HI.* p. 423.

In 1894 Mr. David Draper gave a geological description of south-eastern Africa,1 including Natal, Zululand, Swaziland, the south-eastern Transvaal, and the eastern portion of the Orange Free State and Basutoland. The bulk of the paper gives an account of the Karroo Beds found in south-east Africa, including the Dwyka Conglomerate, which the author was inclined to believe showed as much evidence of igneous as of aqueous origin. He quotes the opinion of Dr. Molengraaff, who had "studied the rock both *in situ* and by means of microscope sections," to the effect that it is " a volcanic tuff (a probably Permian diabase tuff), full of fragments of older rocks." 2 The old beds are de-

scribed as " Primary Rocks," consisting principally of Table Mountain Sandstone resting unconformably on Malmesbury Schists, the latter comprising schists, slates, quartzites, granite and gneiss. The general classification which Draper gives is interesting, in that he regards the Bokkeveld Beds as wanting in the Transvaal, but he indicates their position as being underneath the " Malmani Limestone (Dolomite)." Two years later 3 Draper gave a. description, classification and correlation of the *Primary Systems of South Africa*. He amplified his previous sequence by the insertion of the Lydenburg Beds (Dunn) and Swazi Beds (Schenck) above the Malmesbury Beds, and by the adoption of the correlation, suggested by Professor Rupert Jones in a foot-note to the previous paper, of the Magaliesberg and Gatsrand Quartzites with those of the Zwartberg and Witteberg of the Cape. Mr. Draper places a slight unconformity beneath these, another beneath the Dolomite, and a great unconformity beneath the Table Mountain Sandstone, with which he correlates the Witwatersrand Series. In a lecture given in London in the same year, 1896, Draper1 classified the older Transvaal rocks, from above downward, thus:— . (Gatsrand Beds.

In 1898 F. H. Hatch published *A Geological Survey of the Witwatersrand and other Districts in the Southern Transvaal*.2 In his classification he also adopted the divisions introduced by Schenck: (1) Archaean; (2) Cape System; (3) Karroo System. The Archaean System comprises the granite and the crystalline schists; the Cape System includes five series of beds, from the Hospital Hill Series to the quartzites of the Magaliesberg and Gatsrand, with a division, into upper and lower, between the Klipriversberg Amygdaloid and the Witwatersrand Beds. In this paper Hatch shows that the Magaliesberg Beds, as originally pointed out by Penning, are the same as those of the Gatsrand and not identical with the Witwatersrand Beds as had been maintained by Schenck and Molengraaff. The paper gives the succession, though not the grouping, which is now accepted. The Klipriversberg Amygdaloid is shown correctly as a flow lying unconformably beneath the Black Reef: at that time the author had not seen evidence to prove its unconformity upon the Witwatersrand Beds, but the evidence for this was furnished by himself at a later date. 3

Molengraaffs work as State Geologist of the Transvaal began in September 1897, his first report giving the results of his work for the remainder of that year.1 In this publication, a *Preliminary Report on the Succession of the Formations in the Southern Half of the South African Republic* is given. The author adopts, for the lowest subdivision, the name "South African Primary Formation or Barberton Formation," which includes:— 1. Granite and schists.

2. Hospital Hill Series, including Hatch's Hospital Series and Gibson's

Lower Quartzite Group, as well as a large portion of Schenck's Swazi Schists.

3. The Witwatersrand Series—the exact position of which in the general system has not yet been satisfactorily determined.3

He approved of Schenck's term, "Cape System," as applied to the Black Reef, Dolomite and Magaliesberg or Pretoria Beds, correlating them respectively with the Table Mountain Sandstone, the Bokkeveld Beds and the Witteberg Beds of the Cape. In this report the Magaliesberg Beds are placed in the position to which Penning and Hatch had previously assigned them. Of the Karroo System in the Transvaal, only the coal-bearing sandstone is dealt with: it is placed parallel with the Stormberg Beds of the Cape Colony. The second and last report3 of the Transvaal State Geologist gives the results of the work carried out in 1898—results bearing conspicuous testimony to their author's energy and enthusiasm. In this the South African Primary System is presented virtually as in the previous report, but the author states that absolute certainty regarding the relation of the schists to the Barberton Formation has,

however, not been established.4 The Cape System is enlarged by the provisional inclusion, in ascending order, of the " Red Granite" and the "Waterberg Sandstone." The "Red Granite" had generally been confused with the " Old Granite," 1 MolengraaiT, 1898 *a*. 2 *Loc. cit.* p. 123.

11 Molengraaff, 1899. Molengraaff, *loc. cit.* p. 3. though Hiibner had recognised that the red rock of Pilandsberg was much younger than the latter;1 while the sandstone embraced under the name Waterberg Sandstone had been mentioned by Cohen2 and briefly described by Harger.3

The work of the Transvaal Geological Survey under the Republican Government was cut short in 1899 by the war; but in 1901 Molengraaff published the results of his previous work, with an accompanying map, in the *Bulletin, de la Societe ge'ologique de France*. The sequence given in this paper is not essentially different from that presented by the author in his 1898 report. He takes the Barberton Series, of which the Hospital Hill and Witwatersrand Series are held to be local modifications, as the oldest formation, into which he considers the old granite to be intrusive. The "Red Granite," with its associated norite and porphyritic rocks, is now classified as the "Plutonic Series of the Bushveld," and regarded as a great laccolite, once covered by Waterberg Sandstone, instead of as a flow intermediate in age to the Pretoria and Waterberg Series. Towards the end of 1904 an English translation of Molengraaff's paper by Mr. J. H. Ronaldson was published under the title of *The Geology of the Transvaal:'*

In November 1902 the Geological Society of South Africa resumed its meetings, after an interval of two and a half years, and the Government Survey was reorganised in 1903 under the direction of Mr. H. Kynaston. As a result of the activity of both institutions, considerable advance has been made in our knowledge of the detailed geology of various portions of the Transvaal, several important stratigraphical facts having been brought to light. Early in 1903

attention was directed to the fact that in certain portions of the country there lie, between the Black Reef and the Witwatersrand Series, beds of conglomerate, grit and banded chert, associated with volcanic flows, tuffs and breccias, all of which have been grouped together in the following pages as the Ventersdorp System. The existence of various members of this series—for instance, the Klipriversberg Amygdaloid and the coarse conglomerates at Hartebeestfontein, west of Klerksdorp and at Kromdraai, Krugersdorp—has been known for some years, but their true position in the stratigraphical sequence has only lately been recognised.1 In the same year the correlation of the coalbeds in the Orange River Colony, the Transvaal, and Natal came under discussion, and it was shown that the entire central South African coal-field was of Ecca age.2

The relation of the Waterberg Series to the older rocks has been worked out independently by Messrs. Dorffel,3 Jorissen,4 110111168''' and Mellor,' who all agree that it is unconformable to the Pretoria Series, while in the northern Transvaal it has been found to compose the Zoutpansberg and to rest directly on the old granite.7 The position of the Witwatersrand Series relatively to the old granite has also been reinvestigated, the evidence adduced favouring 'the view that the granite is not intrusive in, but is older than, the auriferous series, and forms the floor on which the latter was laid down.3 The view, originally put forward by Schenck, that there is a series of slates and schists beneath the Witwatersrand Series, into which the old granite was intruded, has also been supported by recent work at Marabastad, Abelskop, Swaziland and elsewhere in the Colony." 1 Molengraaff, 1903 *a*; Hatch, 1903 *c,* 1904: Corstorphine, 1904. 2 Corstorphine, 1903. 3 Dorffel, 1904. *4* Jorisseu, 1904 a.

''Holmes, 1904. 6 Mellor, 1904 *a.* 7 Corstorphine, 1904 *b*. 8 Corstorphine, 1904 o. 9 Hatch, 1904 *c*; Jorissen, 1904 *a.*

Natal stratigraphy has, as indicated in

the foregoing, been outlined chiefly in the papers of Sutherland, Griesbach, Schenck and Draper. The Government Survey was begun in 1898, and two reports, each covering a period of two years, have been published by Mr. William Anderson, the Government Geologist. In Natal the old slates and schists with intrusive granite are overlaid unconformably by a series of quartzites, which Anderson, in his last report, has recognised as the Table Mountain Series, a confirmation of the correlation which had been made by most of the earlier writers. He has also confirmed the unconformity beneath the Dwyka and come to the conclusion that the Natal coal is of Ecca age.1

Ehodesia has, up to the present, not received much attention from the geologist. In 1895 Messrs. Chalmers and Hatch published a paper entitled *Notes on the Geology of Mashonaland and Matabeleland,3* and since then Mr. F. P. Mennell has written on *The Geology of the Country round Bulawayo,* and given a more extended account of *The Geology of Southern Rhodesia.* The sedimentary beds, more especially the coal-bearing series, have been described by Mr. A. J. C. Molyneux.5

Systematic

The stratigraphical scheme adopted in the following pages for the South African formations represents an attempt to systematise the facts in the light of. our present-day knowledge. Here, as elsewhere, stratigraphical features do not coincide with political divisions; and whether a purely geographical, or a purely stratigraphical 1 Anderson, 1904. 2 Chalmers and Hatch, 1895. Mennell, 1902.

4 Mennell, 1904. 5 Molyneux, 1903. scheme be adopted, difficulties are bound to arise. So far as the older rocks are concerned, there are two geological provinces in South Africa: one comprising the southern portion of Cape Colony and Natal; the other the Transvaal, Rhodesia and the northern portion of Cape Colony. Could these two provinces be treated quite independently, the arrangement for descriptive purposes would be easy; but there are at

least two periods during which the geological history was the same for both. The oldest rocks——the Malmesbury Series of the south and the Namaqualand and Swaziland Series of the north and east——are on the same geological horizon; while the Karroo System is a common component from the extreme west of the Karroo plateau across Cape Colony, Orange River Colony, the Transvaal and Natal. It is the Pre-Karroo rocks of the north and the south that render common treatment difficult, if not impossible: in the north we have rocks——the Witwatersrand Beds——that are not represented in the south; moreover, an important southern division—— the Cape System —is but partially represented in the north. In short, the geological history of the two regions is not identical.

The problem has been to some extent obscured, at least for those who are not familiar with the country, by the diverse nomenclature and the various and ill-defined groupings of the strata which have been introduced. The vast extent of country, and the fact that only during a comparatively few years have systematic surveys of the various colonies been carried on, are of course responsible for much of this: it is no reflection on any of the earlier workers that their results often suffer in value from the want of co-ordination and due recognition of the meaning of the work of others in distant parts of the country. Probably in no part of the world have more divergent attempts at a correlation of the strata in different areas been given——rarely with any presentation of a reasoned-out basis for the attempt: any new scheme is in consequence subject to the criticism that it is but adding another to the many that have been weighed and found wanting. In Part V., however, the arguments in favour of the correlation adopted in the following pages are given at length. In this respect at least it differs from most of its predecessors.

Presented in tabular form, the formations known to occur in the several South African colonies are then as shown on Plate I.

In the following pages the Pre-Kar-

roo formations have, in order to afford a connected view of the geology of the Cape and Transvaal, been treated in two sections: the one deals with southern Cape Colony and, so far as the Table Mountain Series is present, Natal; the other with northern Cape Colony, Bechuanaland, Rhodesia, Transvaal and Natal, in so far as the Swaziland Schists are there present. By this means the series characteristic of the Cape and of the Transvaal respectively are described consecutively, brief references sufficing to show the connection which is believed to exist. The Karroo rocks are treated as one throughout the entire country; and with regard to the Post-Karroo formations there is no room for confusion.

PART I PRE-KARROO ROCKS

SECTION I

SOUTHERN CAPE COLONY; NATAL (FOR TABLE

MOUNTAIN SERIES)

CHAPTER I ARCH.EAN SYSTEM—MALMESBURY SERIES AND INTRUSIVE GRANITE

The oldest rocks in the south-west and west of South Africa are the slates and fine quartzites to which E. J. Dunn gave the name Malmesbury Beds. The beds are generally highly tilted—in many places they dip at an angle of 70 to 90 degrees—and their upturned edges are covered unconformably by younger formations. Since no petrographical characteristics distinguish the different horizons, and no organic remains have as yet been found, the true base and top of the formation are unknown: consequently the thickness remains undetermined. The outcrops in all cases bear evidence of longcontinued denudation: as a rule the slates and quartzites form low ground, or they outcrop in valleys; only rarely, as at Signal Hill in Cape Town, do they give rise to any conspicuous feature. The series consists essentially of fine clay-slates and quartzites, both of which tend to be micaceous. The slates show little variation over wide areas, except where they have been invaded by granite. They are close-grained, finely laminated rocks, composed of minute quartz particles and clayey matter, with many fine micaceous scales which are often only visible under the microscope. The quartzites are very compact and fine-grained, breaking with a curved or even conchoidal fracture; scales of mica are generally conspicuous on the fractured surface. Both slates and quartzites

Fig. 1.—Malmesbury Slate Outcrop, Green Point, Cape Town.

generally present two sets of cleavage planes, which cut obliquely across the bedding: in consequence there is a tendency to sharp, jagged outcrops where, as on the sea-shore, the softer debris is continually being removed. Both slate and quartzite tend, where exposed, to assume a yellow, brown, or reddish colour, and weathering generally reveals the presence of a good deal of clayey matter even in the compact quartzites.

In spite of their fine-grained character these rocks have hitherto yielded no trace of organic remains. Possibly such remains will be discovered when the beds come to be opened up to a greater extent than has yet been the case; but it is certainly striking that no evidence of fossils has been found in spite of much careful examination. One cannot imagine that the waters by which the fine sand and mud were deposited were utterly devoid of life: yet the rocks themselves are not so metamorphosed as to lead to the complete obliteration of such organic remains as must once have been present; in fact these rocks show fewer signs of metamorphism than do most of the Pre-Cambrian or even Cambrian rocks of Great Britain, in both of which welldefined fossils have long been known.

The slates and quartzites which predominate in the vicinity of Cape Town give place to phyllites, sericite schists and mica schists in the Tulbagh valley and in the Worcester district. North of the town of Worcester, crystalline limestone occurs and the slates themselves are very calcareous, a condition which also prevails farther east, between Ashton and Swellendam. There is an ottrelite schist between Hex River and Swellendam; and a beautiful andalusite-mica schist outcrops conspicuously on the road along the coast west of the Zwart River in the George district. In the Van Rhyn's Dorp division crystalline limestone w"ith interbedded clayey bands occurs in the basin of the Troe Troe River. Conglomerate beds are found near Vogel Vlei and in various portions of the French Hoek valley.

Structurally the beds of the Malmesbury Series present little of interest: over wide areas they occur in isoclinal folds; although the crests of the anticlines are rarely visible. In the vicinity of granite intrusions where good exposures of the junction are available, there is an intimate intermingling of slate and igneous rock (see Fig. 2); but the mass of the rock appears unaffected.

Granitic invasions of the Malmesbury Series occur at the following localities: Cape Peninsula, Saldanha Bay, Malmesbury, Stellenbosch, Paarl, Worcester, Robertson, Bruintjes River, North of Cape Agulhas, and George and neighbourhood.

The commonest type is biotite granite, but biotitemuscovite and muscovite granite are also found. The predominant felspar is orthoclase, but microcline and plagioelase also occur. With regard to structure, the porphyritic type predominates—large crystals of orthoclase felspar being scattered through a coarsely crystalline aggregate of quartz, felspar and mica. Both coarse pegmatite veins and finegrained segregations are of frequent occurrence. The Stellenbosch intrusions are much sheared, and at George muscovite is more abundant than in any of the other localities. Tourmaline is by no means rare in portions of individual masses; while of alteration minerals, epidote is conspicuous at Paarl and pinite on the slopes of Table Mountain.

In many cases dykes of quartz-porphyry or of microgranite are associated with the normal granite. On the Cape Peninsula and elsewhere the granite is pierced by dykes of normal diabase; while at Gordon's Bay and at George there are sheared dykes in the slates themselves. It is not unlikely that the normal diabase dykes are of an age approximating to that of the Karroo intrusions; while the sheared and uralitised dykes (epidiorites) are much older, being anterior to the uptilting of the sedimentary series, since they share in the metamorphism consequent thereon.

Distribution of the Malmesbury Series

The Malmesbury Series is particularly well developed throughout the division from which it takes its name. The main outcrop stretches from the shores of False Bay northward to beyond the Berg River, and forms a great portion of the low coast region east of the range known as the Drakenstein, Limietberg and Olifants River Mountains. The Malmesbury Beds extend over the surface of this area except where broken through by the granite intrusions of the Cape Peninsula, Stellenbosch, Paarl, Worcester, Malmesbury and Saldanha Bay, or where covered by outliers of Table Mountain Sandstone.

Where slates and quartzites predominate the entire area presents a gently undulating surface; but the presence of granite intrusions or of overlying Table Mountain Sandstone imparts a more broken character to the landscape.

Petrologically this clay-slate and quartzite area presents little of interest. The rocks in the vicinity of Cape Town may be taken as typical. They consist exclusively of darkblue compact quartzite and fine-grained slate. At Cape Town they stretch from the sea up the lower slopes of Table Mountain, till cut out by the granite. Signal Hill and the Lion's Rump are composed of the slates, which thence pass northward to the shore of Table Bay. The entire base of Lion's Head, however, consists of granite which has also cut out the slates along the slope of Table Mountain. To the south of Cape Town the slates form the base of Devil's Peak and the slopes and lower ground of the Peninsula southward as far as Newlands, where they give place to granite. The southern portion of the Peninsula from Wynberg to Cape Point shows no slate outcrops, granite being directly covered there by the Table Mountain Sandstone.

The stretch of low land between False and Table Bays, which connects the

Peninsula with the mainland, though much covered by laterite and blown sand, consists of Malmesbury Beds; while towards the east, beyond Durban Road, granite predominates. The strike of the beds over this area varies from some degrees west, to several degrees east, of north, the former being the more persistent: the dip is generally high, often exceeding 70 degrees. In the extreme north there is a stretch of quite fifteen miles covered by a succession of these steeply dipping beds; and across the centre of the area the width of outcrop is not much less. It is, however, impossible to say what the true thickness is.

Contact phenomena are well developed around most of the granite bosses, notably on the Cape Peninsula, at Stellenbosch and at Paarl. On the Peninsula the best examples are to be seen on the line from the Platte Klip, just above Cape Town on the slope of Table Mountain, across the eastern base of Lion's Head to the beach at Sea Point. This contact zone was described in 1818 by Clarke Abell; Darwin in his *Geological Observations* mentions it in an account of his investigations during his stay at Cape Town with the *Beagle* in 1832[2]; A. G. Bain described it, and 1 Clark Abel, 1818. -Darwin, 1844.
gave a section of Lion's Head to show the relation of granite to slate[1]; while in more recent times Professor Cohen has furnished a detailed petrographical description of the more notable phenomena.[2] The line of the granite intrusion, as now laid bare, rises from the beach at Sea Point to a height of over a thousand feet on Lion's Rump, falling again on the slope of Table Mountain to about half that elevation.

The beach at Sea Point presents a typical example of a granite and slate contact (see Fig. 2). The slates stand nearly vertical, and the first intimation of the presence of the granite, to one approaching from the east, is a fine-grained dyke about three feet wide trending seaward through normal slates and quartzites. Farther west a considerable thickness of granite has penetrated the slates, and these, on a fresh surface,

show numerous dark alteration spots; they weather easily, leaving a much-pitted rind. Over the next fifty yards of beach there is a small sandy bay with normal slate as the underlying rock. The western side of this bay, however, shows the outcrop of an intimate mixture of slate and granite. The granite is here coarsely porphyritic, and large orthoclase crystals are seen projecting from the slaty matrix into which they have been forced. The slate is drawn out into vertical bands through which the granite constituents are so dispersed that no distinct separation of the two rocks is possible. In some places large fragments of slate are to be seen completely enclosed in granite (see Fig. 3): in other places granite veins of varying width cut the slate and connect separate masses of typical granite. A marked feature of this junction is the absence of fine-grained granite, the coarsely porphyritic type being developed even in closest proximity to the slate. The outcrop of mixed slate and granite extends along the shore for a distance of over a 1 Bain, 1856 *a*. 2 Cohen, 1874.
hundred yards, passing then into pure granite, which, however, in places still shows an occasional slate fragment. Over the Lion's Rump this contact zone is covered by soil and vegetation; but the slate outcropping along the ridge presents in the vicinity of the granite the spotted character noticeable on the beach. The southern slope of Lion's Rump

Fig. 3.—Enclosures of Malmesbury Slate in Granite, Sea Point.
and the northern portion of the slope of Table Mountain show no outcrop of the junction till Platte Klip is reached, where a small stream rising near the top of the mountain has laid bare the contact zone in a gorge; a series of fine veins of granite ramifying through the slate can be seen at this place. Farther south on the slopes of the Devil's Peak the slate is often spotted, indicating that the granite cannot be far below the surface.

South of the Devil's Peak the Malmesbury Slates have no very conspicuous outcrop, and the granite does not show at the surface until Newlands

is reached. The stones known as the "Hen and Chickens" are the weathered outcrops of granite on the top of a mass which projects eastward from the slopes of the Peninsula. Out on the flats at Claremont and Kenilworth granite again appears, while the road westward from Wynberg past Constantia to Hout's Bay is also on it. Along the whole of the lower portion of the north-western corner of the Peninsula, from Sea Point round to Hout's Bay, the granite is capped by Table Mountain Quartzite: it is only at the Hout's Bay neck that the latter has been removed by denudation.

In the southern portion of the Peninsula there is no granite at the surface from Muizenberg to Fish Hoek, the Table Mountain Sandstone extending down to sea-level. On the western shore, however, the basement granite is exposed right along the coast. Good exposures of the granite are seen on the eastern side from Fish Hoek to Smitswinkel Bay; but there are sandstone outcrops at two or three points on this coast-line. At Smitswinkel Bay the Table Mountain Sandstone is faulted down, forming overhanging sea-cliffs, which continue to Cape Point.

In the Stellenbosch district the Malmesbury Series is composed chiefly of gritty slates striking from N. 40 W. to N. 15 E., and dipping at high angles. The slates are invaded by two granite masses. The most westerly intrusion stretches from the railway, between Durban Road and Kraaifontein, southeast towards the Helderberg, where it is covered by the Table Mountain Series, and separated from the Somerset West mass by a belt of slates; it has an outcrop of some eighty square miles. Like that of the Cape Peninsula it is composed of a coarsely porphyritic biotite granite, and shows the same variations in composition and structure; in a few places, moreover, it can be seen to have a similar relation to the slates. At Bosman's Siding veins of granite penetrate the slates, and on the railway about two miles from Eerste River station the same phenomenon is observable. Near the contact the slates are spotted and knotted *Knotenschiefer)*. The town of Stellenbosch stands on the slates, but immediately to the east and north another granite intrusion, in which the Jonker's Hoek valley lies, is exposed. This mass extends to the north-west for a distance of four miles, forming three broad bands, trending with the strike of the slates. Shearing is very conspicuous, the rock being quite schistose in places: this is especially well seen immediately north of Stellenbosch, and also in the lower part of Jonker's Hoek, where the granite outcrops in dyke-like ridges; the schistose rock grades into the normal type, and is not limited to any particular zone. Towards Pniel the granite is covered by an outlier of Table Mountain Sandstone, forming the Simonsberg. The junction with the slates runs east and west at Pniel, and thence the granite outcrop stretches north-west, almost in contact with the Paarl mass.1

South-east from Stellenbosch granite is exposed between Somerset West and Sir Lowry's Pass, where it passes under the Table Mountain Series of Hottentot's Holland.

A narrow band of slate separates the northern extension of the granite near Pniel from the Paarl Mountain intrusion. The latter forms the most typical mass of the whole area, as it is not overlaid by the Table Mountain Sandstone, and, except at the base of the mountain, has been freed from its once-overlying slates. The summits are great bare tors, whose shape and glittering appearance have secured for them the name Paarl (Pearl) Mountain.

The mass at Paarl is less porphyritic than the other 1 Schwarz, 1!»00«. intrusions described, and the biotite occurs in more or less regular lines. On the ridge of the mountain, south-west of the town of Paarl, the rock is a fine-grained hornblende granite: epidote is a frequent alteration product in the veins exposed in the quarries at the base. Dykes of quartzporphyry occur on the western border of the mass.

On the east side of the Berg River another exposure of granite stretches from the south of Paarl to the north of Wellington, for a distance of over fif-teen miles. It lies under the Table Mountain Sandstone of the Drakenstein and Limietberg. The lower portion of the famous Bain's Pass, leading from Wellington over the mountains to the Breede River valley, has been cut through this granite.

In the picturesque valley of French Hoek there is an interesting inlier of the Malmesbury Series and its intrusive granite, surrounded by mountains of Table Mountain Sandstone. The rocks consist of phyllites, slates and quartzites; while much-sheared conglomerates also occur. Mr. E. H. L. Schwarz has described the latter as identical with those occurring at Cango.1

Quartz-porphyry outcrops beneath the sandstone escarpments of Klipboschberg, Middenberg and Dassiesberg. At, the first-named locality the rock consists of red felspar crystals and rounded quartz phenocrysts, imbedded in a grey matrix. This rock is almost certainly an apophysis from an underlying or neighbouring granite mass.

The granite at Malmesbury calls for no special mention. On its western side, and separated from it by a band of slate, lies the most extensive boss in this part of the country— the Saldanha Bay mass. This intrusion forms the underlying rock along the shore from a point south of Dassen Island northward to St. Helena Bay; it is much covered by blown 1 Schwarz, *he. cit.* sand and old compacted sand-dunes. Dykes of quartzporphyry are common in it at Saldanha Bay.

To the east of the Winterhoek the Malmesbury Series forms the bottom of the Tulbagh valley: it trends as a narrow strip southward into the Breede River valley, and finally southeastward to beyond Swellendam. The higher declivities of the Tulbagh valley consist of the Table Mountain Series; beyond Worcester, only on the northern side of the Breede River valley, do the Malmesbury Beds pass under this series; on the south side a great fault brings the Ecca Series down to the same level as the Malmesbury Beds. This fault continues for over ninety miles, dying out east of Swellendam. Along its course southwards the strip of Malmesbury Beds is bounded in turn by beds of the Ecca, the Witteberg, the Bokkeveld and the Table Mountain Series, the last-named gradually assuming its normal relation to the Malmesbury Beds as the fault dies out.

North of Worcester the slates are calcareous; in one or two places lenticular masses of crystalline limestone led at one time to some fruitless quarrying for payable marble. There are thin veins of granitic rock among the slates in one of these old quarries, and also in a neighbouring shaft. As the slates are more than usually spotted and altered, one may reasonably infer the presence of a mass of granite not far below the present surface. From Worcester to Ashton the Malmesbury Series forms the foothills under the Langebergen, but it is often difficult to distinguish it from the Witteberg, Bokkeveld and Table Mountain Series on the south side of the fault. Slate, phyllite and ottrelite schist are the common types of rock; quartzite occurs near the granite at Robertson, limestone between Ashton and Swellendam, and graphitic slate at Dassies Hoek east of Robertson. West of the latter village a granite boss constitutes a conspicuous hill: the rock is coarsely porphyritic; in places around the boss there is a mixture of slate and granite, recalling that on the beach at Sea Point. A similar but smaller intrusion occurs thirty miles farther east at Bruintjes River.

The most southern exposures of Malmesbury Beds are those in the Caledon and Bredasdorp districts near Cape Agulhas. Three small outcrops occur. The most westerly, in the valley known as Hemel-en-aarde, consists of granite only. An inlier of schists, slates, quartzites and conglomerates is found at Elands Kloof: these beds include a band of chlorite and ottrelite schist, striking from north to northeast, and dipping at 70 or more; granite and quartzporphyry also occur. The third small outcrop is in the Zondag's Kloof, where sandy and sericitic slates outcrop, together with intrusive granite: the slates are of the same type as those near Malmesbury, and strike north-west; the granite is much sheared.1

The main outcrop of the Malmesbury Series in this area is in the neighbourhood of the village of Elim. On the east it probably extends for some distance towards the shore at Struys Bay, beneath a thick covering of blown sand and dune limestone. The rocks are the typical quartzite and slate striking from east to north-east. Granite appears on the farms Avoca and Uilen Kraal River: it is a coarse biotite-granite with pegmatite veins. The slates near the granite are quite micaceous. On the coast at Groot Hagel Kraal a small detached granite outcrop appears from under the blown sand.

The most easterly outcrop of Malmesbury Beds occurs between Mossel Bay and Knysna. The rocks there developed are mainly slates, phyllites and mica schists, quartzite being 1 Rogers and Schwarz, 1900.

less abundantly present than in the other exposures. On the Knysna Road, immediately east of the Zwart River, there is an outcrop of andalusite-mica schist, in which the andalusite occurs in crystals often over one inch long and a quarter inch in section. Granite dykes penetrate this schist, and west of George the road section shows numerous fine veins

Flo. 4.—Caiman's River; Gorge in the Malmesbury Series, east of George. ramifying through the slates. On the east a deep gorge cut by the Caiman's River shows the slates associated with quartzite (see Fig. 4). The granite is first seen to the east of Mossel Bay: the great Brak River flows over it, and on its banks shows many fine examples of shearing, folding and plication. The granite extends eastward as far as the Robinson Pass, a distance of some thirty miles.

E. J. Dunn described the rocks of George as showing the same characteristics as those of Namaqualand, and on his map he represents them, with the beds exposed near Worcester and Oudtshoorn, as "Namaqualand Schists." But the Geological Survey has shown that in these districts the rocks into which the granite is intrusive are of essentially similar type and occupy the same strati-graphical position as the slates of the Cape Peninsula or of the Malmesbury Division.

The only ore-deposit known in any of the granite areas is the tin-stone on and around the farm Annex Langverwacht, near Kuils River. The mineral occurs as a dissemination through the granite and, in association with wolframite, in quartz veins.

At Cape Town and Paarl the granite is quarried for use as a building stone.

CHAPTER II
Cango And Ibiquas Series
The Cango Series

In the portion of the Oudtshoorn district known as Cango, there are certain rocks older than the Table Mountain Series that do not coincide in character with the Malmesbury Beds as developed elsewhere. They consist of:— 4. Slates.

3. Dolomitic Limestone. 2. Quartz-felspar-grit. 1. Sheared Conglomerate.

The series forms an outcrop of a rudely lenticular shape, extending from Wilgenhout River farm, on the west, to Kruis River on the east, a distance of over seventy miles, while its maximum width north of Oudtshoorn is ten miles.

The conglomerate consists of large pebbles or boulders of quartz, quartzite, slate, diabase and granite, lying in a greenish chloritic matrix. A distinct eye-structure has been produced by the matrix being sheared and drawn out around individual pebbles. In the transverse river gorges, such as Coetzee's, Potgieter's, and Schoeman's Poorts, three to four miles of conglomerate is exposed, but this thickness is almost certainly exaggerated by folding (see Fig. 5).

The quartz-felspar rock is well seen at many places along the Grobelaar's River valley. It has a compact, dark-coloured matrix in which lie blebs of quartz and angular pieces of fresh felspar. Under the microscope the felspar is seen to be plagioclase and microcline as well as orthoclase; it lies, together with the quartz grains, in a fine sericitic matrix. The rock is one of the so-called " porphyroids," and is probably an ancient arkose.

The dolomitic limestone is a dark crystalline rockshowing externally and internally the same appearance and structure as the non-cherty variety of dolomite found in the Transvaal and Bechuanaland. It has the typical elephanthide surface, but in Cango no chert bands occur. Here and there, throughout even the thickest bands, as for example that in which the Cango cave occurs, there are thin slaty seams. Near the dolomite outcrops there is always a good deal of recently formed calc-tufa. Beds of white limestone also occur, together with the dark dolomitic variety.

The slates are black and massive, the cleavage tending to produce rhomboidal blocks rather than thin plates. There are often thin dolomite layers among them.

Throughout the series there appear small and large dykes of diabase. On the road from Cango to Oudtshoorn several can be seen in the sheared conglomerate. Their intrusion was anterior to the shearing; for they also have shared in it, with the result that their igneous character is almost unrecognisable. A large dyke runs for a distance of eight miles from the west of Coetzee's to the east of Potgieter's Poort, forming a distinct ridge among the foothills west of the southern slope of the Zwartberg Pass. On the east the Nels River flows over many small dykes which are all sheared and altered to uralitic diabases or even to hornblende schists.

Distribution of the Cango Series

The conglomerate occurs on the farms Wilgenhout and Vaartwell east of Amalienstein, and continues as a narrow band eastward as far as Welgevonden, whence a belt six miles wide trends southward, dying out farther west at Nels River. With its associated rocks, the conglomerate is well seen in Coetzee's, Potgieter's and Schoeman's Poorts. In the firstnamed the series consists of sheared phyllites, with crushed clay pebbles, passing into more quartzitic rocks. The dip is 33 south. In Potgieter's Poort silky phyllites and coarse conglomerates are cut through for a distance of four miles. In Schoeman's Poort, along the valley of the

Grobelaar's River, a good section of the beds is exposed. They all dip to the south, and appear to lie above the Table Mountain Series. This, however, is a result of the inversion which, in this portion of the country, affects all the beds up to the middle of the Ecca. The conglomerate appears at the southern end of the Poort, and is followed on the north by slate, dolomitic limestone, quartzite and quartz-felspar-grit. The entire section suggests a repetition of the beds by folding; but the area is very complicated, and its tectonic features can only be made clear by more accurate mapping than is possible with the topographical maps now used by the Cape Survey. In the main band of dolomitic limestone, which extends from the farm Nooitgedacht to Rust-en-vrede, a distance of fifteen miles, the much-spoken-of Cango Cave occurs. The cave is on the farm Grootkraal, on the right bank of a small stream, the Dongka Gat, which flows into the Grobelaar's River. It extends for a distance of over 700 yards, the greatest width being 200 feet. The walls and roof show numerous stalactites, and the floor is covered with a considerable thickness of stalagmite (see Fig. 6). It was discovered by a farmer, Van Zyl, in 1780.

The Cango rocks are younger than the Malmesbury Series, but older than the Table Mountain Sandstone. Though they appear to overlie the latter, this is not their true stratigraphical position, but is a result of over-folding. Between Gamka Poort and Meiring's Poort the entire conformable sequence, from the Ecca down to the Table Mountain Series, dips south and has been inverted, so that each member passes under the one geologically beneath it. That the Cango Series is younger than the Malmesbury, may be inferred from the fact that it contains boulders identical with the granite that is found intrusive in the Malmesbury Beds of George. Its unconformable relation to the Table Mountain Series can be seen at the south end of Meiring's Poort.

In the Eastern Province at Maitland, along the Loerie River to Hartley, and in the Gamtoos River, there is, according to Atherstone, a dolomitic limestone identical with that of Cango. In the limestone, copper, argentiferous and lead ores were formerly opened up at the Maitland Mine. Above the limestone, as can be seen at Maitland, Van Stadens River, and at the Loerie River, there is a hard, coarse, pebbly sandstone, used, in the neighbourhood, for making millstones. Conformably below the limestone there are quartzose sandstones, micaceous shales and schists.[1]

The Ibiquas Series

In the Van Rhyn's Dorp division on the west of Cape Colony there is a series of sedimentary rocks intermediate to the Malmesbury and Table Mountain Series. Its existence was detected by Messrs. Rogers and Schwarz in 1900, and in the report of the Survey for that year the term Ibiquas Series was adopted to designate this hitherto unrecognised stratigraphical division.[2]

The series is found in the north-eastern portion of Van Rhyn's Dorp from the slope of Kobe's and the Bokkeveld Mountains westward, and in the lower valleys of the Kromme, Kransgat, Hantam, and North Doorn Rivers in Calvinia. The formation is inclined to the east-north-east, so that the lowest beds are exposed on the west, where considerable disturbance and folding is apparent, while eastward it is almost horizontal. The lowest beds consist of variously coloured slates and argillaceous sandstone, with grit, arkose and conglomerate in less abundance; while the upper beds are composed of dark-coloured micaceous shales and sandstones, not unlike those of the Bokkeveld Series. The sandstones show false-bedding, ripple-marks, wormcasts and tracks of animals; but as yet no determinable organic remains have been found.

[1] Atherstone, 1857. -Corstorphine, 1901: Rogers and Schwarz, 1901.
On the farm Diep Kloof, Van Rhyn's Dorp, beds of conglomerate from one to ten feet thick are interstratified with slate, grit and arkose; these extend from the northernmost cliff of Kobe's Mountain to the Oorlog's Kloof River. The pebbles in the conglomerate consist of granite, quartzporphyry, crystalline limestone, slate and vein-quartz. The grit and arkose are generally associated, and extend west several miles from the Kobe escarpment.

The escarpment of the Bokkeveld Mountain is composed of Ibiquas slates overlaid by Table Mountain Sandstone. The latter, however, dies out on the Door n River and leaves the Ibiquas Series to form the hills that, under various names, continue the Bokkeveld Mountain plateau northwards. Over this area the beds dip generally at under 25, and rarely over 45.

The unconformity between the Table Mountain and the Ibiquas Series is well seen on the Bokkeveld escarpment at Keizer's Fontein, where, in a nearly vertical cliff, the Table Mountain Sandstone rests almost horizontally on Ibiquas sandstones and slates, dipping 50' east-north-east. At the north end of the Bokkeveld Mountain, south of the Door n River, the unconformity is again visible; but the western escarpment does not show the unconformity well, since there the Ibiquas and Table Mountain Series have the same strike.

The Ibiquas Series is well exposed on the road from Bokkefontein to (North) Doorn River, which makes a descent of 1200 feet from the top of the mountain to the river valley: it consists of sandstones and shales of a purplishbrown colour. Between this road and Karreboom's Geberge the series lies horizontally, forming a number of flat-topped hills of varying elevation up to 300 or 400 feet.

West of Stinkfontein Poort, through which the Doorn River flows, the Ibiquas Shales form the lower slopes of the hills and the bottoms of the river valleys, and are overlaid by Dwyka Conglomerate; the unconformity is, however, not well marked. On the north the Ibiquas Series is faulted against the granite of Bushmanland. The faulted junction was seen in Calvinia by Messrs. Rogers and Schwarz at two localities separated by seven miles of Dwyka Conglomerate.

No observations have yet been made by which the thickness of the series can be determined. Where the top is visible, as on the plateau of the Bokkeveld Mountain, the formation has been reduced by Pre-Dwyka denudation: in no case has the base of the series been discovered.

Rogers, in 1908, found in the Verloren Vlei, in the northern part of the Piquetberg division, two outcrops of reddish sandy shales and thin beds of sandstone which he classed as Ibiquas Beds. One patch occurs on the west bank of the Verloren River, on the farm Witte Drift, at the foot of a sandy slope; it dips westward at from 15 to 30". A conspicuous ridge of Table Mountain Sandstone separates this outcrop from those at Van Rhyn's Dorp. The second patch is on the east bank of the river, on the farm Afgunst, and on the north-west lies in direct contact with Malmesbury Beds.

CHAPTER III THE CAPE SYSTEM

The term Cape System is here applied to an enormous thickness of sandstones, quartzites, shales and slates which, in the south of Cape Colony, rest unconformably upon the Malmesbury Series, and are followed conformably by the basement beds of the Karroo System. The name Cape formation (*Kapfovmatiou*) was introduced by Dr. A. Schenck in 1888, since which time it has been very generally used. Schenck, as well as later writers, extended the term to the Transvaal; but in consequence of the difference of opinion as to which, or how many, of the northern series should be grouped under this name, its application to the Transvaal succession should be given up.

In 1852 Bain gave the correct stratigraphical sequence of the three members of the Cape System under the names Lower Silurian, Upper Silurian and Carboniferous formations. A few years later, the fossils which Bain collected from the Warm and Cold Bokkeveld having been determined as Devonian by Salter and Sharpe, Wyley grouped the same three formations as Lower Devonian, Upper Devonian and Carboniferous Limestone, at the same time using Table Mountain Sandstone as the local name for the lowest member. For the middle and uppermost members of the group, the names Bokkeveld Beds and Zuurberg, Zwartberg and Witteberg Sandstones, were introduced by Dunn on the first edition of his map. As a result of the work of the Cape Survey, the name Witteberg alone has been retained for the youngest division. Consequently the Cape System, as now understood, consists of the following three conformable divisions:— 3. The Witteberg Series— sandstones, quartzites and slaty shales often showing the pseudo-fossil *Spirophyton,* with stems and other plant remains. 2. The Bokkeveld Series—sandstones, quartzites and shales, all containing abundant marine inveHebrate fossils of Devonian type. 1. The Table Mountain Series—conglomerates, sandstones and quartzites, with several slate bands; resting unconformably on the older rocks.

While the base of the system, except in a few localities, is sharply separated from the underlying Malmesbury or other older rocks, there is no sharp line of demarcation between the individual members, nor even, in the south of Cape Colony, between the top of the Witteberg Series and the base of the Karroo System. There is also in many places a considerable resemblance between the quartzites of the Witteberg and those of the Table Mountain Series: in such cases the only safe distinction is their respective stratigraphical relation to the fossiliferous Bokkeveld Series. All three members of the group have shared alike in the great folding movements of the region. A feature of the mountain chains is the frequent outcrop of the Table Mountain Quartzites as anticlinal ridges, while the Witteberg and Bokkeveld Beds, having been denuded from the summits, appear only on the lower slopes.

Throughout the entire system, igneous rocks play a very subordinate part: the few dykes which cut through the sediments, especially in the north-western districts of Cape Colony, belong to the later Karroo period.

The Cape System may be said to form a natural barrier between the coastal region and the arid table-land of the interior. Where mountain chains occur, these are to a very large extent composed of its lowest member— the Table Mountain Series; and the dominant strike of this series has determined the present coast-line of South Africa, except between Algoa Bay and the southern portion of Natal.

The Table Mountain Series

The Table Mountain Series is composed essentially of quartzites. Though the name sandstone is often applied to them, the rocks are rarely typical sandstones, being generally indurated by pressure, frequently hardened by secondary silicification and much jointed and sheared, even when, as on the Cape Peninsula, they are horizontally bedded. The quartzites are of a white or bluish colour when fresh, but red or brown when weathered. They are invariably marked by the presence of gritty and pebbly patches or lenticular bands; numerous individual pebbles may also occur irregularly interspersed throughout the beds. The pebbles are chiefly of vein-quartz, but quartzite, slate and quartz-porphyry also occur. In general the lamination is not conspicuous, and there is a tendency to a rounded or almost conchoidal fracture. Current-bedding is seen in most localities. Some of the beds on the Cape Peninsula, as at Lakeside and Fish Hoek, have been quarried for building-stone, while a much laminated outcrop at Palmiet River, near Caledon, has been worked for the same purpose; but even the least indurated of these beds is not a freestone, and it is only at a most disproportionate expense that the stones can be got in any other form than "rough dressed." In some of the newer buildings of Cape Town the quartzite has been used: though not suitable for fine tracery or ornamental cornices, it has been effectively adapted to simple and substantial constructions.

Under the microscope the quartzites are seen to contain

Flo. 7.—Alternate Hard and Soft Sandstone in the Table Mountain Series, South Side of the Zwartberg Pass.

scales of mica and granules of tourmaline, magnetite and zircon in addition to the predominating quartz grains.

The beds, especially where they lie horizontally, weather into most fantastic shapes. On the top of Table Mountain and throughout the Cape Peninsula, as well as on the plateau mountains in the north-west of the Cape Colony, subaerial weathering has reduced the rock to the most grotesque shapes. Weathering may begin as a series of cracks in the hard rind; these widen out, becoming circular so as to resemble pot-holes, which may ultimately combine, and boulders of the quartzite are in this manner frequently reduced to a mere shell.

On Table Mountain the quartzite often contains considerable quantities of infiltrated milnganese and iron oxides, sometimes in botryoidal masses. Near Goudini Road, in the Breede River valley, and at Du Toit's Kloof, near Paarl, pyrolusite and manganite occur in vein-like deposits which in past years led to unsuccessful mining operations.

Shales and slates are found throughout the series. On the lower portion of the escarpment of Table Mountain the quartzites are distinctly argillaceous, passing into a reddishbrown shale or slate. In the Ceres district there are two well-marked slate bands, an upper find a lower; at the Pakhuis Pass, Rogers found the upper band represented by a mudstone containing glaciated boulders.1

On the Montagu Pass, over the Langebergen, between George and Oudtshoorn, a contorted slate band is exposed in the uptilted quartzites. This rock, which is dark green in colour, is a sheared phyllite, and represents the lower slate band of other localities.

Distribution of the Table Mountain Series

In the extreme west of Cape Colony the Table Mountain Series occurs as a number of horizontally bedded outliers resting on Malmesbury Beds or on the Granite. Of these the best known and most typical is that of the Cape Peninsula, with its conspicuous northern escarpment forming the precipitous wall of Table Mountain. The higher ground of the Peninsula is composed of two main masses of the series, separated by an outcrop of granite at Constantia 1 Rogers, 1902.

Nek. The northern mass is the plateau of Table Mountain; it dominates Hout Bay on the south and Table Bay on the north and north-west, while its eastern escarpment, above the Cape Flats, faces the interior. In the extreme.

Fig. 8.—Lion's Head from Sea Point: the Summit is Table Mountain Sandstone, and the Lower Outcrops are Granite.

north of the Peninsula there is the small outlier which forms the upper portion of the well-known Lion's Head (see Fig. 8), and the north-western corner is occupied by another more extensive outlier forming the hills separating Hout Bay from the Atlantic. In this northern area the sandstone is confined to the highest ground of the Peninsula, except on the west side of Hout Bay, where it reaches sea-level. The general feature made by the beds of quartzite right round the Peninsula is a steep escarpment of bare rock, in many places over 1000 feet high, the numerous ledges of which are brightened by a little vegetation. Both horizontal bedding-planes and vertical joints are quite conspicuous features, and impart a distinctive character to the mass. Here, as elsewhere, the outer crust of the rock is reddish brown, and, when illuminated by the rays of the rising sun, the vivid colouring of the mountain sides is quite comparable to that of the dolomite peaks of southern Europe.

The southern portion of the Cape Peninsula, from Constantia to Cape Point, has a much lower elevation, averaging less than 1000 feet above sea-level. On the north side of False Bay the sandstone reaches sea-level, and no granite appears north of Fish Hoek. On the coast near Simon's Town beds of quartzite outcrop on the beach, dipping at a high angle—70 to 90—an effect probably of local faulting. South of Simon's Town the Table Mountain Series becomes much thinner, and the basement bed rests, as was noted by Clarke Abel in 1812, directly on the granite:

the same phenomenon may be seen, though not so clearly, on the slope of Table Mountain, west of the Kloof Nek near Cape Town, and also near the summit of the Lion's Head.

On the top of the plateau, either on Table Mountain itself or in the southern portions of the Peninsula, the weathering of the horizontal beds has given rise to a series of irregular terraces, from which stand out numerous fantastically carved blocks. The surface is either bare or covered by a thin layer of light sandy soil, with many loose, pebbles. Between Simon's Town and Cape Point the top of the plateau is very barren, being in many places covered with a deep layer of disintegrated sand, often heaped up into dunes.

Other western outliers of the Table Mountain Series are to be found in the Malmesbury district. Of these the largest forms the hills known as Riebeek's Kasteel, which attains a height of 3000 feet above sea-level; a smaller one occurs at Honig Nest on the Berg River, and there are others at Joostenberg and Klapmuts Hill. There can be no doubt that just as the several masses of Table Mountain Sandstone on the Cape Peninsula were once connected, so all these others on the west were originally one with the main mass of the formation that now forms the mountain chains between the coast and the interior.

In the more extended outcrops on the mainland the Table Mountain Series appears over so wide an area, and in such a manner, as to indicate that it must extend inland, underneath the younger formations, at least as far as the western and southern boundaries of the Karroo. It is only on the west, from False Bay north to beyond the Berg River, and along the narrow strip of country from Tulbagh down the Breede River valley to Swellendam, that denudation has exposed, by the removal of the Table Mountain Series, a surface of older rocks. The western portion of the country has certainly been subject to more denudation than the southern: for throughout the former there remains little or none of the two upper members of the Cape System, and even the Table Mountain Series has in places disappeared; whereas in the south the main outcrops are of the Bokkeveld Series, under which the presence of the Table Mountain Quartzites may in all cases be assumed.

The most northerly point of the outcrop of the Table Mountain Series is on the Bokkeveld Mountain, south of the junction of the Kromme and northern Door n Rivers, on the boundary of the Calvinia and Van Rhyn's Dorp divisions. The series takes part in the formation of an escarpment on the farm Stinkfontein, being there represented by a thickness of some five feet of sandstone, resting upon Ibiquas Beds and overlaid by Dwyka Conglomerate. Passing southward the sandstone is over fifty feet thick at Van Reenen's Pass; on the Matsiekamma Mountain, a projection from the main escarpment, it is nearly 1000 feet thick; while on Kobe's Mountain, to the westward, it is at least 2000 feet. The level of the top of the escarpment does not vary much, the increased thickness of the Table Mountain Series being the result of a lowering of the old rocks on which its basement beds rest.1

At Matsiekamma Mountain the outcrop of the Table Mountain Series begins to widen considerably, and a little south of the southern Door n River it stretches from the coast eastward to the summit of Nardouw Mountains and the Cederbergen. South of Matsiekamma and the Giftberg the southern Door n River pierces the chain, its gorge being the only break from the Bokkeveld Mountain, Calvinia, to Mitchell's Pass near Ceres. At Lambert's Bay the outcrops of the Table Mountain Series are particularly interesting, as the beds contain pebbles of red and brown banded jasper, similar to that of Prieska and Griqualand West.

On the high plateau of the Cederbergen the Table Mountain Series is bent into a wide anticline, with a north-north-west axis; while near Clanwilliam a series of north-west folds appears, the Olifants River flowing for part of its course along one of the synclinal

troughs. Southward the folds tend to assume a more northerly direction and gradually increase in intensity, the southern portion of the Cederbergen forming elevations of over 6000 feet above sea-level. At the point where the Leeuw River cuts across the axis of the Cederbergen, 3000 feet of the Series are exposed. The southern extension of the Cederbergen is known as the Cold Bokkeveld Mountain and the 1 Rogers and Schwarz, 1901 il.

F

Schurftebergen, and in these the Series is even more folded than is the case farther north. The folding has given rise on the west side of the Cold and Warm Bokkevelds to an intervening chain known as the Witzenbergen, which culminates in the great Winterhoek. In their northern portion the Witzenbergen and Schurftebergen are separated by a synclinal valley of Bokkeveld Beds; but towards Ceres the two folds of the Table Mountain Series merge together, and the entire thickness is crossed by Mitchell's Pass, which leads from the Malmesbury Beds of the Tulbagh Valley over the quartzites to the shales of the Ꭺvarm Bokkeveld (see Fig. 9).

To the west of the Cederbergen and the Olifant's River valley, where the outcrop of the Table Mountain Series extends as far as the coast, a series of gentler folds has produced the range which is known, in its northern extension, as the Olifant's River Mountains: this range under various names—Twenty-four Rivers Mountains, Vogel Vlei Mountains, Limietberg, Drakenstein, Hottentots' Holland—extends southward to the eastern shore of False Bay. As the folds pass southward the individual ridges tend to curve off to the east, giving rise to the main mountain chains of South Africa.

At the point where the mountain chains begin to turn eastward, namely, in the Hex River complex south of the Warm Bokkeveld, the folding of the Cape System is both intense and wide spread. The tectonic features have been somewhat obliterated by the prolonged denudation to which the country has

been subjected: still the various ranges, though they show but the remnants of their original grandeur, are clearly true mountains of elevation. There are two main lines of folding, which may be regarded as radiating from the Hex River *massif*. The southern one trends southeastward as the beginning of the Langebergen, continuing, under various names, as an unbroken chain to the shores of St. Francis Bay; the northern one, passing through the Anysberg, becomes the great Zwartebergen chain, which bounds the

© ©' eastern portion of the Great Karroo on the south and then continues eastward to Algoa Bay. Minor spurs are the ridges constituting the Zonder Einde Mountains and the series of elevations that form the greater portion of the coast and occur throughout the adjoining country from Hangklip to Cape Agulhas; they may be regarded as forming a subsidiary but imperfect range terminating at Mossel Bay.

In all these ridges, or mountain chains, the Table Mountain Series plays the chief part. In the frequency with which the beds of this series are seen on end or bent and twisted within a small area into sharp anticlines and synclines, the intensity of the folding to which the region has been subjected is revealed. The quartzites invariably form a central anticlinal ridge in the mountain chains, or at least one limb of a broken or denuded anticline, overlaid on its slopes or in the synclinal valleys by the younger Bokkeveld, or, in places, by the Witteberg Series.

In the northern range, trending east from the Hex River Mountains, the Table Mountain Sandstone appears first in the Anysberg, the intervening hilly area being still covered partly by Bokkeveld and partly by Witteberg Beds. Geologically the Anysberg is the commencement of the Zwartebergen. It consists of an anticlinal ridge which

D O increases in elevation as it trends eastward. Between the Buffel's River and the Gamka the chain is known as the Klein Zwartebergen; but east of the latter river the name Groote Zwartebergen is applied. East of Toverwater Poort the names Antonies Berg, Baviaans Kloof Mountains and Elandsberg Mountains are used; but physically there is only one range. which throughout its entire length presents similar geological features. In complexity the structure of the chain increases from the Anysberg eastward. In the Buffel's River Poort and the Seven Weeks Poort, the Table Mountain Series is greatly folded, and the Bokkeveld Beds are faulted down against it on the south. Between Gamka Poort and Meiring's Poort the chain shows an inversion, each of the formations, from the Ecca Series downward to the Bokkeveld,

Fig. 10.—Contorted Table Mountain Quartzite, Zwartberg Pass, Groote Zwartebergen.

dipping successively under the one geologically older: the Table Mountain Series, which, here as elsewhere, makes up the bulk of the chain, thus appears to dip under the rocks of the Cango south of the Zwartberg Pass. In the gorge at the entrance to the pass the quartzites stand vertical; and higher up numerous sharp bends and folds are met with within quite small areas (see Fig. 10).

The whole country between the Zwartebergen and the Langebergen has been much plicated, the folding involving all three members of the Cape System. In several places denudation has laid bare the Table Mountain Sandstone —such mountains as the Paardeberg, the Roodeberg, the Amalienstein Mountain, and the Touwsberg being partial or complete anticlines which protrude through the overlying series. Touwsberg is an isolated anticline with a nearly eastwest axis; it is covered on all sides by conformably lying Bokkeveld Beds. Warm Waterberg is of similar structure; but on its south side the Bokkeveld Beds are faulted against the Table Mountain Series, the latter showing a slickensided fault-face of considerable height.

N. *Wagenbooms Berg Riethook Mis-Langebergen* s

Flo. 11.—Section from tho Langebergen to Wagenbooms Berg: 4. Witteberg Series; 3. Bokkeveld Series; 2. Table Mountain Series; 1. Malmesbury

Series. Scale: 1 inch=3 miles. (From *Cupe Geo). Survey Hep.* 1897.)

Eastward, the Paardeberg, Roodeberg and the Amalienstein Mountain are made up of a continuous outcrop of the Table Mountain Series, faulted against the Cango rocks that lie to the north, and covered on the east by the Uitenhage Series of the Olifants River valley. East of the Gouritz River the Table Mountain Series of the Roodeberg becomes, by an increase in the number of folds, continuous with the Langebergen on the south.

At the Hex River *massif,* on the south side of the Hex River Pass, there begin also the Kwadow's and Keeroin Bergen, from which a northern anticlinal ridge of Table Mountain Quartzite, known as Wagenbooms Berg, passes eastwards under the Bokkeveld Series. Immediately to the south of the latter is the main southern chain, the Langebergen, which here appears as a prolongation of Keerom Berg. The folded structure is well seen in Kogman's Kloof, which passes through the mountains from the Breede River valley at Montagu. In this Kloof the Table Mountain Quartzites have been bent into a series of sharp folds, which being now much denuded are represented mainly by vertical walls of rock, while in many places there is evidence of horizontal thrust. The general structure of the chain in this locality is that of a broken anticline, of which the northern limb alone remains, *Photo A. W. Rogers.*

Fig. 12.—View of the Langebergen, looking west from the Robinson Pass.

dipping north above and away from the Malmesbury Series; while on the south there is a fault of such great magnitude that Ecca Sandstones are brought down to the same level as the Malmesbury Slates. The fault dies out to the east of Swellendam, at the point where the Table Mountain Series begins to dip normally under the Bokkeveld Beds. The southern face of the Langebergen, from the Breede River valley in the west to the termination near Cape St. Francis, is nevertheless a prolonged escarpment. Farther east the folding is more intense, and several subsidiary outcrops

of the series appear. In the Gouritz River section the folds are thrust over so that the entire formation has acquired a southerly dip and consequently appears to pass under the granite (see Fig. 12). East of the Gouritz River the complex folding to which the series has been subjected is well exhibited in the Robinson Pass. North of this point

Fig. 13.—Gouritz River Poort, through the Langebergen.

the folding has brought up several anticlines, so that there is, as has been mentioned, a continuous outcrop of Table Mountain Series from the southern Langebergen to the northern Zwartebergen. This comprises the Roodeberg and the mountains near Calitzdorp.

At George the Table Mountain Series of the Langebergen, which arc known there as the Outeniqua Mountains, approaches the coast, and a few miles farther east it forms the actual coast-line as far as Cape St. Francis.

At Millwood, near Knysna, the Table Mountain Series contains conglomerate beds and quartz veins, in the vicinity of which small quantities of alluvial gold are found. Some of the quartz veins have been worked, but up to the present without success. The conglomerates have often excited the interest of prospectors by their resemblance to the Witwatersrand banket: unfortunately, mere petrographical resemblance has no economic value. At Knysna the series is folded along an east and west axis.

The extreme outcrop of Table Mountain Series on the south coast occurs between St. Francis Bay and Algoa Bay, and is geologically, if not geographically, the continuation of the Groote Zwartebergen. This Eastern Province outcrop comprises the Baviaans Kloof Mountains, the Great Winterhoek, with the Cock's-comb Peak and the Elandsberg.

South of the Langebergen there are several less important outcrops of the Table Mountain Series trending eastward, suggesting that beneath the overlying Bokkeveld Series and the dune deposits of the coast the quartzites form a series of hidden anticlines. The Zonder Einde Mountains are the chief of these subsidiary ranges, and the outcrop of Table Mountain Sandstone, which reaches the coast at Mossel Bay, may be regarded as a prolongation of this line of folding.

Southward, between Cape Hangklip and Agulhas, the quartzites form a considerable part of the coast and of the adjoining country. From Agulhas to Cape St. Blaize there are several patches, but much of this stretch of coast-line is hidden by dune deposits.

In the south-eastern corner of Cape Colony the regular trend of the old formations parallel to the coast is interrupted, and they disappear, in succession from the Table Mountain Series upwards, under the sea, so that there is a considerable stretch of coast from the Gualana River to Port St. Johns, composed of outcropping Karroo Beds. North of Port St. Johns, after a stretch of coast covered by Dwyka the Table Mountain Series reappears, but is not accompanied by the other divisions of the Cape System.

At Port St. Johns the Table Mountain Series constitutes an inlier some eight miles loner and five wide, surrounded by the Ecca Series and cut through by the St. Johns River. About twenty miles north-east the Table Mountain Series appears on the Pondoland coast, whence it continues northward through Natal into Zululand. The series as there developed consists of variously coloured sandstones with a few interbedded shales and a very coarse conglomerate at the base. The sandstones become quartzites at the contact with igneous rocks. The pebbles contained in the basal conglomerate are chiefly quartz and quartzite, but occasionally jasperoid rocks occur; in places felspar is present in such quantity as to give rise, by weathering, to an impure kaolin. Fossils are practically unknown, the only recorded find being by Griesbach, who in some shales, which he considered interbedded in the series at Kranz Kop, near Greytown, found some small bivalves and a finely striated *Patella,* both too indistinct for determination. Anderson, who visited the locality, during the period covered by his first report, was

unsuccessful in his search for additional organic remains.

The beds are almost invariably horizontal, resting unconformably on Archasan Schists and Granite: in many cases they form the capping of the table-top mountains and isolated hills that are so typical of Natal scenery. The outcrops occur mainly between the uplands and the coastal belt of unconformable Dwyka Conglomerate. Intrusions of basic rocks are frequent. Quartz veins and reefs occur in considerable abundance, the former auriferous to a slight degree; gold has also been found in the basal conglomerate, but so far never in payable quantity.

There has been some divergence of opinion as to the correlation of these Natal sandstones. Sutherland and Griesbach described them as Table Mountain Sandstones; but they were mapped by Dunn as Zuurberg and Witteberg. In the first report of the Natal Geological Survey, Anderson called them Palaeozoic Sandstones; but in his second report he has decided, as a result of an extended tour in the Cape Colony, during which he found opportunities for a close examination of the Table Mountain Sandstone, to support the original correlation of Sutherland. The recognition by Rogers and Schwarz of the sandstone at Port St. Johns, and farther north at Cape Grosvenor, as Table Mountain Series, affords additional confirmation for this correlation.

BOKKEVELD SERIES

Over a large area in western and southern Cape Colony, the Table Mountain Series is overlaid conformably by the shales and sandstones grouped together as the Bokkeveld Series. This series has not been found elsewhere in South Africa—not even in Natal, where the Table Mountain Series is so well represented. It has a high importance in the South African succession, for it comprises the oldest rocks in which until now recognisable organic remains are known to occur. Fossils from the beds of the Cederbergen, near Clanwilliam, were sent home to Hausmann, and described by him in his paper of 1837. Others were obtained by Itier, and men-

tioned in his *Journal d'un voyage en Chine,* in 1848. But the first detailed account was published in 1856 by Salter and Sharpe, from the specimens collected and sent home by A. G. Bain to the London Geological Society. Bain named the series Upper Silurian, but Salter and Sharpe determined his fossils as of Devonian age—a determination which has always been supported, and has received renewed confirmation by the work of Reed and Lake on the fossils collected by the staff of the Cape Geological Survey.[1]

Though the occurrence of the beds on the Warm and Cold Bokkevelds was known and described by many of the earlier writers, it appears that Dunn, who systematically introduced local names for the South African stratigraphical divisions, first used the term "Bokkeveld Beds," as the distinctive name of the series, on his map of 1873.

The series has no special petrographical interest: it consists entirely of shales and sandstones, the latter being felspathic or clayey towards the base, but siliceous and hard towards the upper part.

The junction with the Table Mountain Series, though a conformable one, is generally distinctly marked: the hard quartzites of the older formation stand up as conspicuous ridges, while the position of the basal beds of the Bokkeveld Series is indicated by the presence of gently undulating low ground. In the upper part of the series the quartzites are harder, and, owing to their interstratification with shales, often form conspicuous escarpments or *kranzes.*

In the west and south of Cape Colony the Bokkeveld Beds cover an area equal to, if not greater than, that occupied by the Table Mountain Series. They generally appear on the flanks of the mountains, and also in the synclinal valleys between the various ranges.

From the Warm Bokkeveld, the series is continuous over the Gvdo Pass northward to the Cold Bokkeveld, whence it 1 Reed, 1903 and 1904; Lake, 1904.

extends as a band on the west side of

the Cederbergen as far north as the Oorlog's Kloof River. The Warm Bokkeveld, although, broadly speaking, a plateau, is in reality a basin like hollow, bounded on the west and south by a rugged dipslope of Table Mountain Quartzites which form the northern side of the Waai Hoek and Hex River Mountains, and on the north by a conspicuous escarpment of Witteberg Quartzites. The entrance to the Warm Bokkeveld from the west is by Mitchell's Pass. At the summit an extensive view of the area is obtained. The high ridges surrounding the basin on the west and south dip directly under the shales and sandstones. Towards the south the actual passage is not well seen, but near the Gydo Pass the junction is visible, being emphasised by the petrographical difference between the upper hard quartzites of the Table Mountain Series and the soft bottom shales of the Bokkeveld, but mainly by the presence of numerous invertebrate fossils in the latter. *The Fossils of the Bokkeveld Series*

The fossils hitherto found in the series are almost exclusively invertebrate, only one remnant of a fish having been found by Schwarz at Gamka Poort. The Trilobites indicate, according to Lake, a Lower Devonian horizon. Reed, in his recent description of the Brachiopods and Molluscs, agrees with previous writers as to the close resemblance between the South African, American and Falkland Island Devonian faunas. From a study of these two invertebrate groups, however, he is unable to say to which division of the Devonian the Bokkeveld Series belongs.

The Bokkeveld Trilobites include many interesting forms: *Phacops pupellus, P. arbuteus, P. crista-galli = Encrinurus crista-galli* of Woodward), *P. africanus, P. occellus, P. impressus, P. caffer* (Fig. 14 *b*), *Dalmanites lunatus, TypMoniscus baini* (Fig. 14 *c*), *Proetus malacm* (Fig. 14 *d*), *Homalonotus herschelli* (Fig. 14 *a, a'*), *H.*

Fig. 14.—Trilobites from the Bokkeveld Beds. *a* and *a'*, *Homalonotus herscJielli*, 4 nat. size (after Salter); *b*, *Phaeop caffer* (after Salter); *c*,

Tjphloniscus baini (after Salter); rf, *Proetus malacus* (after Lake). *quernus, H. colossus*, the last-named being a new species represented by a portion of the left cheek and several fragments of the thoracic segments from Uitkomst, on the Warm Bokkeveld. Lake considers that this species attained a length of twenty inches.

Fig. 15.—Cephalopoda and Gasteropoda from the Bokkeveld Series. *a, Orthoceras gamkaensis* (after Reed); *b, Conularia africana* (after Sharpe); *c, Bcllcrophun*, lji nat. size (after Reed).

Fig. 16.—Lamellibranchs from the Bokkeveld Beds. *a, Cleidophorus africanus*, left valve (after Sharpe); *b, Xueulites*, internal cast of right valve, 1J nat. size (after Reed).

Bokkeveld Series: the Cephalopoda by two distinctive species of *Orthoceras, 0. gamkaensis* (Fig. 15 *a*), and *0. bokkeveldensis*, occurring in considerable numbers at Gainka Poort; the Gastropoda by *Pleurotomaria*, five species of *g*

Fig. 17.—Brachiopnds from the Bokkeveld Series. *a, Spirifer antarcticui* (Morris and Sharpe) =.S". *orbignyi* according to Reed: *b, Spirifer orbignyi* (after Sharp?): *c, Chomtes falklandicus* (after Reed); *d, Orthotctes sulirani* (after Reed); *e, Levtoaelia flabellites*, dorsal valve exterior (after Sharp?); *l, Lcptocalia flabellites*, brachial valve, H nat. size (after Reed); *g, Orthis*, brachial valve (after Reed).

Belh'rophoa (Fig. 15 *c*), and a *Loxonema*; the Pteropoda by *Tentaculites crotalinus* and *T. baini, Conularia africana* (Fig. 15 *b*), with three other species, and *Theca subaiqualis*;

the Lamellibranchs comprise the genera *Cleidophorus*, e.g. *C. qfricanus* (Fig. 16 *a*), *Leda (L. inornata), Sanguinolites, Nuculites* (Fig. 16 *b*) *(X. abbreviatus, N. africanus, N. brauneri, N. capensis,' N. colonicus, N. martialis), PalcBoneilo (P. antiqua = Soleneila antiqua*, Sharpe), *P. subantiqua, Modiomorpha (M. baini)*.

The Brachiopoda include two species of *Lingida*, one being closely allied to *L. densa*, Hall; *Orbiculoidea baini, Orthotetes sulivani* (Fig. 17 (/) (= *Stropliomena baini* of Sharpe); *Choneten falklandicm* (Fig. 17 *c*), and three other species; three species of *Rensselaeria; CryptoneJla baini* (= *Terebratula baini* of Sharpe); *Spirifer orbignyi* (Fig. 17 *b*), to which Reed also assigns the specimens which Sharpe determined as *S. antarcticus* Fl-i»--*ophioerimi$ stangeri*, twice nat. size (after Salter). (Fig. 17 *a*), this species not being represented with certainty by any of the specimens from the Bokkeveld Beds; *Spirifer ceres, Leptoealia flabellites* (Fig. 17 *e* and *f*) (= *Orthis palmata* of Sharpe); *Orthis* (Fig. 17 *g*), and *Vitulina pustulosa*.

Crinoid stems and joints are of frequent occurrence, and Ophiuroids are also found; the latter have not yet been determined, but Salter described one of the Crinoids as *Ophiocrinus stangeri* (Fig. 18). Worm-tubes, which have been referred to *Serpulites*, also occur.

Phota E. H. f. Mddll. Via. 19.—Bokkeveld Sandstone with Trilobites.

Distribution of the Bokkeveld Series

In working out the series as it exists on the Warm Bokkeveld and the Hex River Mountains, Schwarz 1 found in 1897 that there is a definite sequence of shale and sandstone beds: shales or thin sandstones occur at the base; these are overlaid by more massive sandstones, followed in turn bv shales—these three bands being the chief fossil-carriers. The upper more barren portion consists of three other alternations of sandstone and shale. The Warm Bokkeveld is composed of the three lower fossiliferous bands, — shales, sandstones, and shales,— and it is only towards the north that, under the escarpment of Witteberg Beds, the upper less fossiliferous portion of the series outcrops.

Fossils are found in the lower shales, near Ceres, on the south-west of the Warm Bokkeveld, Lamellibranch genera being 7'Ai.lo E. H. V. MdviU.

Fui. 20. — l'iece of Bokkeveld Fossil Lferous Sandstone, showing Casts of

Spirifer, Leptocielia, etc.

1 Schwarz, 1897 *a.* especially abundant in the exposures at the brickfields just east of the village. The road from Ceres to Hottentot's Kloof and Karroo Poort passes over numerous fossiliferous outcrops, and on Van Wyk's Farm at Karroo Poort the fossiliferous sandstone is full of casts of Brachiopods, especially *Spirifer* and *Leptocadia.* On the road northward across the Gydo Pass to the Cold Bokkeveld, and its immediate vicinity, there are many exposures of sandstones and shales which are particularly full of trilobite casts, *ffomalonotus herschelli* being especially abundant.

Fig. 21.—Section across the Warm Bokkeveld: 4. Witteberg Series; 3. Bokkeveld Series; 2. Table Mountain Series; 1. Malmesbury Series. Scale: 1 inch = Ii miles. (From *Cape Geol. Survey Rep.* 1897.)

The Gydo Pass rises over a narrow outcrop of Bokkeveld Beds exposed by the denudation of the Witteberg Series. Above the pass the outcrop of the former is in places so narrow and so much covered that it appears almost as if the Witteberg were faulted against the Table Mountain Series. The Bokkeveld Beds, however, trend northward as a narrow strip along the Cold Bokkeveld on the east side of the Cederbergen. They widen out northward at Bosch River, the Dwyka Conglomerate resting directly and unconformably upon them. The Bokkeveld outcrop finally disappears south of Oorlog's Kloof River, where the Dwyka comes to rest directly on Table Mountain Sandstone. To the west of the outcrop just mentioned, the Bokkeveld Series lies between the Table Mountain Sandstone of the Schurftebergen and the Witteberg escarpment of the Gydo Mountain, and between the Schurftebergen and the Witzenbergen it constitutes the valley as far as Rosendal. At Wagen Drift the narrow valley coming from the Gydo Pass widens out to form the Cold Bokkeveld plateau. The western side is bounded by the continuation of the Schurftebergen, while on the east there is the southern extension of the Cederbergen.

A good section of the Bokkeveld Series, together with a portion of the underlying and overlying series, is seen on the east side of Tafel Berg on the Cold Bokkeveld. North of Tafel Berg, as far as Whupperthal, the Bokkeveld outcrop is a narrow band bounded by the eastern outcrop of the Table Mountain Sandstone and the western boundary of the ʌVitteberg Series, which in parallel lines trend northwards. The Bokkeveld Beds forming this strip dip at a high angle. At Whupperthal the outcrop widens; and the hills east of the Cederbergen are formed of the series, with, however, a frequent capping of Witteberg Beds. Boter Kloof has been cut through the Bokkeveld so as to expose the underlying Table Mountain Series.

In the valley of the Olifant's River, Clanwilliam, there are several outliers of Bokkeveld Beds. The largest of these begins at the farm Keerom, and continues northward for thirty miles to the Hex River, a tributary of the Olifant's River. A smaller outlier extending north-west occurs near Clanwilliam village.1

In the south between the Langebergen and the Zwartebergen, west of the Gouritz River, the series outcrops extensively over the rough arid country known as the Little Karroo. A thin strip of much-folded Bokkeveld rocks runs north of the Langebergen, west of Montagu, where, at the north end of Kogman's Kloof, the junction with the Table Mountain Series is visible. The country from the north of the Langebergen to the Anysberg, the western 1 Rogers and Schwarz, 1901. end of the Zwartebergen, consists mainly of Bokkeveld Beds, being interrupted only by the inliers of Table Mountain Quartzites that form the anticlinal ridges of the Warm Waterberg and the Touws Berg. Over a considerable portion of this area the two lowest sandstone bands of the Series can be traced, being seen on the southern flank of the Anysberg, and on the north of the Zwartebergen cast as far as Gamka Poort. To the north of Naugas Hills near

Triangle Station, the upper beds are well developed and are full of fossils. Plant remains are there associated with Trilohites; while in some beds *Conularia africana* is very abundant.

From the Breede River at Worcester a long narrow valley of Bokkeveld Beds trends southward. It is bounded to the west by the Table Mountain Quartzites of the outlying folds of the Drakenstein, and on the east, first by Witteberg Beds, and still farther south by the Table Mountain Quartzites of the Zonder Einde Mountains. At the north end of the valley is the hot spring known as Brand Vley, which issues at a temperature of 140" F. Near the middle lies the village of Villiersdorp. The beds there are much sheared, and do not show the usu&l differentiation into shale and sandstone.

In the south-west of Cape Colony there is an interesting outlier of Bokkeveld Shales at Houw Hoek. It lies in a hollow surrounded by Table Mountain Series. On the Caledon Road, near the Houw Hoek Hotel, much sheared specimens of the typical Brachiopoda occur in a greyish weathered shale. South of the Langebergen, as far east as the Gouritz River, a considerable extent of country is composed of the Bokkeveld Series. North of the Zonder Einde Mountains it forms the greater part of the Breede River valley, while south of the range the undulating country of the Caledon and Swellendam divisions consists largely of the same beds. South of the Zonder Einde Mountains, throughout Caledon, Bredasdorp, Swellendam, and Riversdale, eastward to the Gouritz River valley, the Series forms the country known as the " Rumens." The area west of the Breede River is cut across by the Zout or Salt River, on each bank of which there is a ridge of high ground serving as the startingpoint for innumerable other ridges trending in all directions. East of the Breede River the same type of scenery prevails, but the Bokkeveld outcrop is considerably narrower, owing to extensive sand belts along the coast, and the presence on the north of the Uitenhage Series under the Table Mountain summits of the Langebergen. A good many of the flat-topped hills are there covered by a recent limestone. Throughout the Ruggens the present rivers have cut their beds into a surface which appears to have been an ancient plain, and the valleys of to-day lack the escarpments which are elsewhere so typical a feature of the Cape landscape.

Over the entire area the rocks are slaty and sheared, sometimes grey in colour, sometimes passing into a black carbonaceous variety, well seen at Napier and at Port Beaufort. Fossils are not abundant throughout this area, but *Cleidaphorus* has been found near the former village.

Detached outcrops of the Bokkeveld Series occur at Knvsna, on the south coast, where Schwarz1 found five separate outliers, occurring mainly in the valley of the Keurboom's River. The rock from these localities is a much sheared light-grey shale or slate, and the numerous fossils in it are crushed and distorted. On the east bank of the river the junction with the Table Mountain Series is exposed on the Humansdorp road. Among the fossils are *Orthoceras, Spirifer, Phacops* and *Cleidophorus.* 1 Schwarz. 1900 *c.*

The Witteberg Series

The uppermost member of the Cape System plays a minor *rôle* in the structure of southern Cape Colony, and is altogether less interesting than the two older series. Bain, although he did not use the name, recognised the individuality of the Witteberg Series at Karroo Poort. His observations were afterwards borne out by the work of Dunn, who, on the first two editions of his map, used the name "Zuurberg, Zwartberg and Witteberg Sandstones," altered on the third edition to "Witteberg and Zuurberg Sandstones." In the Report of the Cape Geological Survey for 1897 the name was further reduced to "Witteberg Quartzites."

In the Witteberg Series there is little petrographical variety. Over wide areas a hard blue micaceous quartzite, weathering white and not unlike the Table Mountain Quartzite, prevails, but in places red or brown outcrops occur.

Often the hard quartzite is replaced by a felspathic micaceous rock of dull olive-green colour, passing in many localities into a shale or slate. None of the Bokkefeld fossils have

Piece of Witteberg Quartzite with *Spirophyton* marking.

yet been found in these upper beds, which are almost as barren as the Table Mountain Series. Plant stems allied to Lepidodendron occasionally occur; but the most widespread marking in the series is the pseudo-alga *Spirophyton caudagalli* (see Fig. 22). This curious marking is persistent throughout the series over wide areas. Specimens have been examined by Mr. A. C. Seward of Cambridge, who concludes that it is a purely inorganic structure.

The passage from the Bokkeveld Series upward to the Witteberg is a gradual one, and there is more difficulty in defining the upper, than there is in fixing the lower limit of the former series. In mapping, a purely conventional boundary must be assumed. Even in the well-exposed section at Gamka Poort there is no definite line of demarcation. 1 On the Warm Bokkeveld, Schwarz found a micaceous sandstone with numerous worm-tubes in the passage beds, and since the characteristic black shales of the Bokkeveld do not occur above this bed, it was adopted by the Survey as the base of the upper series.

Distribution of the Witteberg Series
The Witteberg Quartzites, as already mentioned, form an escarpment bounding the north of the Warm Bokkeveld. This is the southern edge of the main outcrop of the series, which continues as a band of varying width along the western and southern boundaries of the Karroo (see Fig. 23). The outcrops south or west of this band are comparatively few and small, the chief lying in the Breede River valley.

North of the Bokkeveld the Witteberg Series runs in 1 Schwarz, 1900 *b.* much the same line as the already described Bokkeveld Beds, but its outcrop finishes in the basin of the South Door n River, where the Dwvka Conglomerate begins to rest on the lower members of the Cape System. Over this

Fig. 23.—The Witteberg Series, as seen in the Wittebergen, south of Matjesfontein.

area the Witteberg Series is generally seen capping hills whose lower portions are composed of Bokkeveld and Table Mountain rocks. On the Tafel Berg in the Cold Bokkeveld, for example, the Witteberg Series is at least 1200 feet thick, and contains the characteristic *Spirophyton:* SECTION II NORTHERN CAPE COLONY; BECHUANALAND; RHODESIA TRANSVAAL; NATAL CHAPTER I ARCHAEAN SYSTEM—SWAZILAND SERIES, NAMAQUALAND SERIES
The oldest rocks of northern South Africa, here grouped together under the name Swaziland Series,1 show a greater variation of type than those in the south. They consist of slate, quartzite, occasional conglomerates and a variety of schists, with large masses of intrusive granite and gneiss. In the Transvaal the slates and other sedimentary rocks occur chiefly in the east and north (Swaziland, Barberton district and Pietersburg), although they are also known in the west near the Bechuanaland border. They were described by Cohen and Gotz 2 as well as by Schenck,3 the latter classifying them with similar rocks from other parts of South Africa, under the name *Siid-Afrikanische Primarformation.*

These old rocks are well developed near Pietersburg, at Mont Mare, south of Marabastad, an old Kaffir town, and consist of normal slates, magnetite-quartzite-slate, phyllite, ottrelite and andalusite slate. The magnetite-quartzite-slate, known to the miners as "calico-rock," is very conspicuous at 1 Hatch, 1905. '-' GOtz, 1886. 3 Schenck, 1888. the summit of the ridge. It consists of alternating bands of white granular quartzite and dark bands of magnetite with some hematite and limonite. These bands are sometimes straight, sometimes bent, folded and faulted within small areas. This rock also builds up the Ijzerberg west of Eersteling, where the iron was formerly exploited by the natives. The phyllites consist of quartz and mica, with which chlorite and rutile are constantly associated. Apatite and tourmaline are present in some types. The most interesting rocks of the series are the ottrelite-slate and andalusiteslate. There appears to be a gradation between the two types. The ottrelite-slate is white and silvery in appearance, and the crystals of ottrelite are often visible to the naked eye. The other minerals present are quartz and mica, while rutile and tourmaline also appear. Under the microscope the ottrelite is nearly always fresh, and shows its characteristic shape—the ends of the crystals being rarely complete; its peculiar twinning and growth in starshaped aggregates are also noticeable. The andalusiteslate appears more quartzitic than the phyllite or ottreliteslate, and is dark in colour with conspicuous grey crystals of andalusite ("knotted schist"). It consists of quartz, muscovite, andalusite, accessory rutile, and a little ottrelite. The quartzites are generally very micaceous, and some contain much tourmaline.

The minerals found in these schists are characteristic of a granite contact zone, and this, taken in conjunction with the fact that the granite occurs in close proximity to them, leaves little doubt that the latter has been intruded in the old sediments, and is accountable for their present degree of metamorphism.1

Mr. E. Jorissen has described a number of localities 1 Hatch, 1905. where the old rocks are exposed, and where evidence is available that they have been invaded by the granite. The localities which Jorissen 1 describes are so widely separated, and the evidence so consistent, that he considers he may safely generalise and apply his conclusions to the whole country. On Abels Kop (No. 152) and Goudplaats (No. 318), south-west of Schweizer-Renecke, the slates and schists strike N. 10 E. magnetic, and dip from 75 to 90"'; the granite is sheared in the same direction as the schists, and is in places distinctly gneissose. The alternation of gneiss with sericiteschist and talc-schist may be studied at the homestead of the farm De la Reys Kraal (No. 226). On the Harts River, near the south-east corner beacon of Abels Kop, a broad outcrop of a highly quartzose chlorite-schist occurs, striking N. 12= E. magnetic, and dipping 75 E. On the main road between Abels Kop and Goudplaats, chlorite and cklorite-limestoneschists, underlying the granite, have been exposed by the river for a distance of half a mile. The schists nearest the granite contain intrusive veins of aplite. Jorissen is of the opinion that the chlorite and calcite are original elements in the rock, both from their mode of occurrence and from the fact that the rock passes into a granular limestone on another part of Goudplaats. A large zone of banded raagnetitequartzite-slate, "calico rock," crosses the river, and can be traced from south-east of the Abels Kop to the hill on Goudplaats. It is much folded and contorted, and the individual laminae are also crumpled and plicated. With the granite on Goudplaats and Grasplaats (No. 321) much hornblende-schist is associated. On Nooitgedacht (No. 365), in the Pretoria district, at the ford across the Moos River, there is an outcrop of much sheared and contorted mica-schist and quartzite traversed by veins of old granite. A fine-grained gneiss 1 Jorissen, 1905. occurs in the Brood Koppies, two small hills on Zwartkoppie (No. 262), on the western side of the Vredefort granite. A few hundred yards east of the hills, and appearing to overlie the gneiss, there is a broad belt of actinolite-, talc-, and micaschist and amphibolite, traversed by dykes of granite and by veins of pegmatite, both of the latter being gneissose in structure. This complex of schists can be traced almost to Vredefort Road Station. The farm Nalik's Kraal (No. 400), in the Lydenburg district, consists of hornblende-schist micaschist and an amphibolite with magnetite, striking from N. 10 W. to N. 30 W. Near Embabaan or M'babane, in Swaziland, there are many localities where outcrops of micaschist, talc-schist, chlorite-schist, amphibolite and quartzite, with intrusive granite veins, occur. Jorissen states that at one place near the waggon road the actual contact between granite and quartzite can be seen, the latter showing welldeveloped contact metamorphism. Under the microscope minute veins of granite are seen to pass into the quartzite, while both rocks are highly epidotised. In a cutting on the hill at the back of the Constabulary Camp, pieces of schist are enclosed in the granite.

The obvious conclusion deducible from the phenomena described at such widely separated localities is that the schists, into which the granite is intrusive, are distinct and separate from the Witwatersrand Series and must be considered as representatives of an older (Archaean) group. According to Jorissen, they were denuded down to a peneplain, and the intrusive granite was laid bare, long before the deposition of the succeeding Witwatersrand Series. The granite may be exposed, as it is north of Johannesburg, without any of the sedimentary rocks into which it is intrusive being visible; but the phenomena in the eastern, western and northern Transvaal render it clear that, before the granite appeared, these old beds existed. Their relation to the Witwatersrand Series has unfortunately been obscured by the grouping and classification adopted by Molengraaff. As a result of his work as State Geologist in 1897 and 1898, this author thought that he was justified in classifying the oldest rocks of the Transvaal and the Witwatersrand Beds in one group, which he termed the Barberton Series. The enormous development of conglomerates and quartzites on the Witwatersrand he regarded as a purely local facies of his series. There is no doubt that the magnetite-quartzite-slate of Marabastad and elsewhere has the closest resemblance to the contorted band of the Hospital Hill Slate, but these two petrographically similar bands are each accompanied by totally different rocks, which furthermore have a different relationship to the gi"anite. On the Witwatersrand and in the neighbourhood of Heidelberg, the Witwatersrand Series rests upon the granite, which is there the basement and older formation; but in those places where the old slates and schists appear, evidence for the intrusive nature of the granite is usually forthcoming—a proof that these slates and schists belong to an older period than that of the Witwatersrand Series.

There are four main areas covered by eranite in the Transvaal—one between the Witwatersrand and the hills south of Pretoria, a second to the east of Heidelberg, a third in the basin of the Vaal River, in the neighbourhood of Vredefort, while the fourth is practically continuous over the entire northern and eastern Transvaal, passing eastward into Swaziland, Zululand and Natal, and northward into Rhodesia, Bechuanaland and Namaqualand. In all these granite areas there are schistose rocks differing from those into which the granite is intruded. The granite itself passes in many places into banded or normal gneiss: a frequent phenomenon is the appearance of distinct veins or patches of hornblende-schist; while elsewhere basic intrusions in the granite have been sheared into chlorite-or talc-schists.

Of the bosses in the southern Transvaal and Orange River Colony. that of the Witwatersrand is well exposed to the north of Johannesburg, where it underlies the lowest or Orange Grove quartzites of the Witwatersrand Series. It has a rudely circular outcrop, and covers an area of some 400 square miles. On the north-west, north and east it is overlaid by the Black Reef, while its extreme south-eastern boundary passes under the Ventersdorp Series. The geological margin of the boss is nowhere exposed. At the surface it shows many undulations, and has in places been deeply cut into by the streams which flow northward to join the Crocodile River, of which the Yokeskey and its tributaries are the chief. On the north it is limited by the outcrop of the Black Reef and Dolomite, and on the west and south by that of the Witwatersrand Beds; while on the east it disappears under the dolomite and coal formation, which, in that part of the country, constitute a monotonous plain. There are many structural and mineralosfical variations in this granite mass. The normal rock is a fairly coarse aggregate of orthoclase, biotite and quartz. Veins are numerous: some being pegmatitic intergrowths of

felspar and quartz; some, fine-grained aplites; while others are composed mainly of hornblende. Masses of pegmatite occur in places, as for instance on the farm Syferfontein, just off the Pretoria Road, about 4 miles north of Johannesburg. Aplite is exposed at Mulder's Drift, where its horizontal jointing and fine-grained character have led to its being mistaken for quartzite. Hornblende veins are particularly well seen in the bed of the Crocodile River on the farm Zwartkop (No. 101), also where the Johannesburg-Moddeifontein Road crosses the Yokeskey, and again at the junction of the Yokeskey and Crocodile. Under the microscope the predominant felspars are seen to be microcline and plagioclase; biotite is by far 'the commonest ferromagnesian constituent; muscovite is rare. In many localities the rock is a biotite-hornblende-granite, and in individual cases the hornblende and plagioclase become so abundant that it may be termed a quartz-diorite. When hornblende is a conspicuous constituent, there is generally much green epidote present, as for instance in the small quarries north of Sans Souci, at Johannesburg.

The Heidelberg boss is exposed to a much smaller extent than the one just described. It is, however, of exactly the same character as the Witwatersrand mass, showing similar variations in structure and composition. On the farm Kuilfontein it has a distinctly banded appearance. On Brakfontein it occurs as a large outcrop of fine-grained rock which is not unlike a grit, especially when weathered.

The granite at Vredefort has been described by Molengraaff as intrusive in Witwatersrand Beds. It is possible, however, that the contact phenomena which he describes are confined to a small development of schists belonging to the Archaean System, and that the relation of the Witwatersrand Series to these has been obscured by the overtilting or overthrusting which there prevails.

Granite bulks largely in the northern Transvaal: it extends across the Limpopo into Rhodesia, westward through

Bechuanaland into Namaqualand, as well as eastward through the low country into Zululand and Swaziland. Throughout this extensive area the granite is in places overlaid by outliers of younger rocks, especially of the Waterberg and the Ecca Series. Much of the granite shows a gneissose structure and contains numerous veins of hornblende schist. The schist often occurs in dyke-like masses, which under the microscope are seen to consist of crystals of fresh hornblende, felspar (both orthoclase and plagioclase) and quartz; garnets being frequently associated with these minerals. In other places the hornblende rock appears in irregular patches among the normal granite, much as if the two had been stirred together. Aplite, with or without garnet, may be seen in immediate proximity to the hornblende veins.

At numerous localities throughout all these exposures there are basic intrusions which fall into two distinct classes: some are typical dolerites, as fresh as those found in the Karroo Beds, to which in age they are probably allied; while others are much older and so altered that their original character is only recognisable from their field relation to the granite. The latter appear as chlorite and talc schists, or as serpentine rocks, sometimes in small bosses, sometimes in dyke-like prolongations in the granite. Both types of intrusion may form low hills or ridges in the granite landscape.

The geological features that prevail in the northern Transvaal are continued across the Limpopo into Rhodesia, the granite area of southern Rhodesia being characterised by a slightly undulating bush-country, dominated by granite koppies or "tors." A more broken country is formed by the schists, which are quite comparable with the oldest rocks of the Transvaal. At various places it can be seen that the granite is intrusive into them. Mennell,1 for instance, describes dykes of granite traversing these slates at Gwelo, and he states that near Figtree the junction of the Matopo granite with the slates is quite comparable with the classic contact at Sea Point,

Cape Town, while at other localities andalusite, fibrolite, cordierite, and idocrase are developed in the 1 Mennell, 1904.

H magnetite-quartzite-slates where the latter have been invaded. These old rocks, styled by Mennell the Bulawayo Schists, are altered sedimentary rocks containing much igneous material, and forming a series of synclines dipping away from the granite. The oldest are mica or talc schists and gneisses with which are associated later basic intrusions, transformed now into epidiorites or hornblende and chlorite schists.1

Banded magnetite-quartzite-slate occurs also in Rhodesia, where it alternates with sheared conglomeratic and arenaceous beds, slates and gneissic bands. According to Mennell,2 these banded ironstones, as they are styled in Rhodesia, are best developed in the Sebakwe district and between Gwelo and Selukwe, but are also seen near Bulawayo along the Tuli road, and in the Belingwe, Hartley and Victoria districts. In correlating the banded ironstones of Rhodesia with the Hospital Hill Series of the Transvaal and with the Griqua Town Series of the Cape, Mennell makes a double error. The two latter series do not occupy the same stratigraphical position, and, moreover, the banded ironstones of Rhodesia cannot be correlated with either. The entire series of rocks associated with them has the closest resemblance to the rocks of Marabastad and Swaziland, and as they show an identical relationship to the granite, there can be little doubt that they belong to the Archaean System.

The old rocks pass from Rhodesia and the northern Transvaal through Bechuanaland into the north of Cape Colony, and thence into Namaqualand. Along the Bechuanaland railway granite is abundant, and it shows the same tendency to pass into gneiss which has been observed in the Transvaal Archaean granite. Passarge describes central Bechuanaland as consisting of granite and gneiss. Only at one locality, Aasvogelkop, did he discover clayslates dipping 1 Chalmers and Hatch, 189;".-*Loc. cit.* north-east at a high an-

gle, and overlaid unconformably by conglomerate and quartzitic sandstone. He mentions three regions where the Archaean rocks appear: the district between Ramathlabama and Sandpits; the granite area of Gaberones, which has an extension from east to west of some sixty miles and is probably continuous with the granite gneiss-area of Marico; and the basin of the Makalapsi (Mahalapsi), whence the outcrop, according to Hübner, continues to the Bamangwato Mountains.

Similar old rocks are found on the Cape Colony side of the Orange River, extending from the Hopetown district to the ocean. These were first described by Dunn1 in 1873; and in 1899 a portion of them was examined by Rogers and Schwarz. The latter authors state that the gneiss and granite area is fifteen miles wide at Draghoender; while at the Brak River, Dunn found its width to be twelve miles. Much of the area is occupied by schists, but where these have been denuded, Dunn found gneiss or granite as the underlying rock. The character of the granitic gneiss varies greatly: at times it is a true granite, at others a hornblende gneiss, or again an aggregate of quartz and felspar only. As in the northern Transvaal, the rock is often much epidotised, and garnets are abundant, sometimes in dodecahedra and icositetrahedra over an inch in diameter, sometimes in innumerable small crystals of the first-named form. Two and a half miles south-east of Olyvenhouts Drift there is a group of tors, about 40 feet high and 100 feet long, which has been named Tourmaline Kopje. Fully 40 per cent of the rock composing this kopje consists of brown tourmaline in short stout crystals. Southward to Kenhardt the granite plain is broken by many kopjes from 20 to 200 feet in height. The strike of both gneiss and schist varies from north-west to 1 Under the name Namaqualand Series.

north-east. At the Great Falls the Orange River has cut a channel 200 feet deep in the compact granite-gneiss. In addition to ordinary white quartz veins, others of rosecoloured, amethystine and

flinty quartz are found in this area. Near Kahamas graphic granite covers "acres of country," and on the bank near the Great Falls there are veins of a bluish-green felspar and rose quartz.1

Rogers and Schwarz found, associated with the granite of Hopetown and Prieska, altered sedimentary rocks, such as quartzite and hornstone and other metamorphic rocks, the last being of two types—the one characterised by much hornblende, the other by an abundance of almandine garnet. On the farm Grenaats Kop they observed micaschist traversed by a large vein of granitic rock, and on Uitzigt the same rock veined with pegmatite. The granite is much better exposed than the old sediments, but large areas are covered by the Keis Quartzites or by the glacial conglomerate. It is generally a medium-grained biotite granite with coarse veins of the muscovite variety; in some localities a red felspar is present. Quartz-porphyry and felsite dykes. are not infrequent: they are probably segregations. In Kenhardt there is also much sheared granite, often with the appearance of true granulite, and hornblendic segregations are abundant.

Little Namaqualand is essentially a granite area, in which the rock has a marked banded and schistose structure. The Archaean rocks form a broad belt along the coast, and, according to recent observations of Mr. J. Kuntz,-consist of granite and gneiss, changing locally by loss of the felspar, or of both felspar and mica, into mica-schist and "quartzite" respectively.

In Natal the Archajan rocks cover considerable areas in 1 Dunn, 1873. 2 Kuntz, 1904.

the lowest parts of the river valleys and near the coast, generally appearing from beneath the Table Mountain and Ecca Series. Anderson has found that granite, gneiss and schist form a narrow belt stretching from the Mapamulo district on the Tugela, through Nonberg, Inchanga, and MidUlovo, to near the mouth of the Umtamvuna River. In the Umzinto district and in the lower parts of the Buffalo and Tugela River valleys there is a series of metamorphic schists, gneisses and limestones associated with the granite. These rocks are overlaid unconformably by Table Mountain Sandstone and Dwyka Conglomerate. Hornblendic and micaceous gneisses and schists with occasional heavy basic crystalline rocks are the chief types. They all show vertical or highly inclined cleavage planes. Similar gneisses and schists occur in the southern part of Zululand. Where the road from Nkandhla to Melmoth crosses the Umhlatuzi River, Anderson found old quartzites, jasperoid rocks and conglomerates into which the granite was intrusive.

Throughout the whole area occupied by the rocks of the Archaean System three different types of schist occur. There are first the schists, slates, quartzites, crystalline limestones and conglomerates, into which the granite was intruded, producing in many localities typical contact metamorphism; then, secondly, there are the various schists, which were either developed as differentiations from the granite, or, like the gneisses, became banded and schistose by differential movement during the solidification of the original magma; while, finally, there are the ancient intrusions in the granite which, partly by earth-movements, partly by pneumatolytic processes, have become so altered as to have lost their original structural and mineralogical characteristics.

The first type is perhaps the least easily distinguished: it has often been confused with the lower members of the Witwatersrand Series; but there can be no doubt that it is represented sporadically from Natal on the east, through the northern Transvaal, Rhodesia, Bechuanaland and northern Cape Colony, to the Atlantic Ocean on the west, and in the south of Cape Colony by the Malmesbury Series.

The differentiations from the granitic magma are to be found wherever there is a fair exposure of the granite. They occur as hornblendic and micaceous veins or patches, which are often garnet-bearing.

The old intrusions, often metamorphosed beyond recognition, are also abundant. They are especially interesting in Rhodesia, as there they are frequently auriferous.

Gold Occurrences in the Swaziland Series

Gold is found in the Swaziland Series in the most diversified deposits: it occurs as a constituent of basic igneous intrusions and of the hornblende and chlorite schists into which these igneous rocks have in many cases been changed by earth-movements; it is found in the banded and plicated quartzite-magnetite-slates (calico rock) which are a feature of the series; it is known as a constituent of quartzitic sandstone; and it occurs in quartz veins which may have been formed either by "replacement" of the slates in which they occur, or by the in-filling of rents in the plicated schists, or again by a slow re-cementing of the fissures produced by fault and crush movements. In few instances only have auriferous quartz veins been found to occur in the granite. In the following description brief reference is made to all these types.

In the neighbourhood of Barberton (Moodies range, Victory Hill, Sheba range, etc.) quartz veins have been worked for gold with varying success since the year 1884. As a rule, they follow the stratification of the beds in which they occur, both as regards strike and dip. Consisting chiefly of quartzites and slates, these beds are tilted almost to the vertical, and the quartz veins appear to have been formed in many cases by the mineralisation (" replacement") of the slates along zones of crushing and differential movement, which often coincide with the original beddingplanes that separate the quartzite from the slate. In the case of the Sheba, a quartzite "bar" forms the hangingwall of the vein, the latter being in part only a mineralised portion or "replacement" of the slate that underlies the quartzite. In consequence, there is no defined footwall, the mineralisation of the slate becoming gradually less as progress is made from the quartzite hanging-wall into the slate. Although continuous along the strike, the vein does not carry gold in payable quantities outside a limited area, which in quartz-mining is termed a "chute." The Sheba chute in its biggest section measures 120 feet across the lode by 300 feet along the strike. It has been worked for 1200 feet in the direction of the dip. The Ivy mine on Moodies range is a fine example of a quartz lode developed along a well-defined fault-plane, one of the containing walls being as true and smooth as a billiard-table. In this mine also the gold is confined to chutes. Gold in quartzitic sandstone is worked at Piggs Peak in Swaziland.

Auriferous quartz veins occur in the Swaziland Beds near Marabastad, south of Pietersburg (Eerseling, Mont Mare, etc.). These deposits were worked for gold before the discovery of the Rand—the district being then known as the Marabastad gold-field. The veins occur in the slaty beds of the series, which have been more susceptible to crushing and differential movements than the harder quartzites; both in strike and dip they roughly follow the direction of bedding. At Palmietfontein (No. 101), six or seven miles south of Pietersburg, a quartz vein in the old granite has been worked. At Abelskop and Goudplaats, in the Harts River valley, south-west of Schweizer Reneke, in the Bloemhof district. gold has recently been found in a striped and contorted rock, consisting of ferruginous banded chert and quartzitic schist ("calico rock"), which is associated with chlorite schist. The mineralisation appears to be most pronounced when the rock is most plicated, the numerous rents produced by the folding having been favourable for the deposition of secondary quartz. The whole formation is highly tilted and lies between granite outcrops, at the contact with which hornblende schist and amphibolite is developed: from Jorissen's description it must be considered as a member of the Swaziland Series. At the present moment developments are being pushed to prove the commercial value of the discovery.[1]

In the Murchison district auriferous quartz veins, usually of limited extent, are of frequent occurrence in the hornblende and chlorite schists. In some cases the gold is found in the schists themselves. At Coblentz, three miles from Mabina, it is found in a crushed and plicated zone of ferruginous quartzitic schist enclosed in chlorite and hornblende schists, which microscopic examination shows to have been derived from sheared basic igneous rocks.2

In Rhodesia the auriferous veins are confined almost entirely to the schists belts. These consist of chlorite. hornblende, talc and sericite schist, and are, for the most part, the result of the metamorphism of basic igneous rocks.3 In the majority of cases the veins follow the strike 1 Jorissen, 1905; and Heneage and Hoi ford, 1905.
-Hcncage and Holford, 1905. 3 Chalmers and Hatch, 1S95.
of the country rock and, in consequence, have generally a lenticular character which is in close genetic relation to the foliation of the schists. Gold also occurs in some of the dyke rocks: for instance, the Ayrshire mine has been opened in a dyke of augite-diorite traversing the granite; and recently in the Lomagunda district gold has been found in a schistose dyke (probably a quartz-diorite), which, on account of the presence of numerous pebble-like enclosures of granite, was at first taken for a conglomerate similar to the "banket" of the Witwatersrand. Chemical analysis shows that a portion of the gold in the Lomagunda rock occurs as telluride associated with mispickle.

Economically the auriferous quartz veins of Rhodesia are divisible into two types: (1) small veins averaging, say, three feet in width with ore chutes (carrying fairly rich ore) from 400 to 500 feet in length; about thirty-five mines have been opened on veins of this type; (2) large veins of considerable width (up to thirty feet) which, although low grade, carry sufficient gold to repay working, the payable areas extending; in the direction of the strike for a considerable distance—in some cases between 2000 and 3000 feet.1 1 Curie, *The Economist,* December 17, 1904, p. 2045.

CHAPTER II THE WITWATERSRAND SYSTEM

The Witwatersrand System embraces a group of sedimentary rocks which is clearly separated by great unconformities from the Archaean below and from the Ventersdorp System above. Where the base of the Witwatersrand Beds is visible, it is found resting immediately on the old granite or on schists associated with the granite (see Fig. 24). No organic remains have been discovered, although concretionary nodules of unusual shape, which are occasionally found in the beds, have sometimes been mistaken for fossils. Lithologically, the series consists of conglomerates, grits, quartzites and slates, the proportion in which these occur varying locally. All these rocks, when we except the size of the components, are of the same nature. Thus the conglomerates consist of rounded to sub-angular fragments of quartz and quartzite, the former greatly preponderating, in a matrix of quartz grains, the whole being cemented to a hard and compact rock by secondarily deposited silica. The quartzites, which were originally deposits of quartz sand, owe their quartzitic character to metamorphism by pressure and the deposition of secondary silica. The slates, originally fine slime or mud, are found under the microscope also to consist largely of minute fragments of quartz.

The Witwatersrand System has been divided1 into an i Hatch, 1898. Upper and a Lower Division — the Upper embracing quartzites, grits and numerous conglomerates, with little slate; the Lower being characterised by many slates and few conglomerates. The division is conveniently made at the horizon of the Main Reef; but since the whole series is quite conformable, the separation is of course arbitrary, and is not intended to convey any want of geological continuity: it is

Fig. 24.—Witwatersrand Beds resting on Granite, Uitkyk (No. 97), Heidelberg, Transvaal.

true there was at one time an inclination 1 to introduce an unconformity at this point in the series; subsequent investigation, however, has not yielded any evidence in favour of this view.

The Lower Division
The Lower Witwatersrand Beds are well exposed in the range of low hills that forms the northern boundary 1 Molengraaff, 1894.
of the gold mines from Boksburg to Krugersdorp. These hills are the highest portion of the elevated tract of country known as the Witwatersrand, or briefly as the Rand, and constitute the water-parting between streams tributary to the Limpopo River on the north, and those tributary to the aal River on the south: the former discharging into the Indian Ocean; the latter first into the Orange River and finally into the Atlantic. The range has an abrupt escarpment on the north, but slopes gradually southward to the outcrop mines. Johannesburg and the numerous outlying townships that extend east and west along " the reef" have been built on this slope. A section taken across the beds immediately to the north of Johannesburg shows four or five small ridges of quartzite, alternating with broader belts of slate, which, on account of their inferior resistance to agencies of denudation, generally form shallow depressions or valleys. The beds dip southward at angles varying from 45 to 85, the total width of the outcrop from the granite to the Main Reef conglomerate being a little over two and a half miles. The thickness of the Lower Witwatersrand Beds may be estimated at from 10,000 to 12,000 feet.

The first quartzites, which rise abruptly from the granite to a height of three hundred feet, have been called the *Orange Grove Quartzites,* from Orange Grove, a holiday resort near Johannesburg. They consist of two thick bands of quartzite separated by a slate band. The outcrop of the lowest quartzite forms a noticeable escarpment facing north, and commanding an extensive view over the oraiiite country.

The Orange Grove Quartzites are followed by a belt of slates rich in iron-ore, especially magnetite. Persistent in these slates is a strongly magnetic hard band, forming in Parktown, a northern suburb of Johannesburg, a con spicuous outcrop, on which stand the two service Water Towers. The entire belt has, therefore, been conveniently termed the *Water Tower Slates.1*

The Water Tower Slates are followed in upward succession by quartzites, which are, however, of much less thickness than those at the base of the series. This second belt of quartzite is marked by a peculiar mode of outcrop: owing to the relatively rapid weathering of the slates that lie above it, a somewhat rugged dip-slope has been formed which has the appearance of a rudely built retaining-wall sloping away from the lower beds. The wall-like outcrop enables one readily to recognise this particular band of quartzite. Another, though a less reliable distinction, is the presence of occasional ripple-marks, which are best seen on fresh exposures. This phenomenon has suggested the name *Ripple-marked Quartzite* for the bed in question. The Ripple-marked Quartzite is well developed in the northern townships of Johannesburg — Parktown, Berea, Yeoville, Bellevue, Bellevue East and Observatory. On the last-named township, as well as to the northeast of Bezuidenhout's homestead east of Johannesburg, its outcrop is thrown back by a series of small reversed faults.

Next in order to the Ripple-marked Quartzite is a very considerable thickness of somewhat soft ferruginous slate, generally reddish at the outcrop, but sometimes with a black surface film of manganese or iron oxide. From their prevalent colour these beds have been called the *Red Slates*. The Red Slates are separated from an overlying series by a thin band of quartzite, which, though generally only a single bed, is remarkably persistent. It is composed of coarse angular quartz grains, which in an unweathered piece are well cemented together. Near the surface it is characterised by 1 Hatcb and Corstorphine, 1904.

the presence of small reddish clayey patches, seen in fresh specimens to be due to the weathering of felspar fragments. The weathering out of these kaolinised felspars produces a curiously pitted surface. The presence of felspar, together with angular quartz grains, suggests that this band has originated

from granite debris, or, in other words, that it is an arkose with comparatively little felspar. Lying upon softer slates, which are readily denuded from beneath it, the quartzite gives rise to many broken fragments, which produce the appearance of a much wider outcrop than is really present. The approximate position of the bed is generally indicated by the presence of such fragments, even when no outcrop can be discovered. The presence of the rusty, weathered felspar led Mr. David Draper to name it the *Speckled Bed.*

Above this thin quartzite lie the *Hospital Hill Slates*. Near their base, and often resting directly upon the Speckled Bed, there is a characteristically striped and contorted band, composed of alternating layers of brightred jaspery quartz, white quartz, specular iron and magnetite. The red, white and black stripes, which arise from the interlamination of these minerals, give it an appearance similar to that of the "Calico Rock," already described as a member of the Swaziland Series. At the present day the term "Hospital Hill Slate" is often restricted to it, but this is more appropriately applied to the whole of the slates between the Speckled Bed and the next overlying quartzite, since they all enter into the structure of the hill on which the Johannesburg Hospital stands, while the contorted or striped bed is in places somewhat inconspicuous. The slates above and below frequently show a silky lustre with more or less wavy laminae. They weather red, yellow, or brown, more rarely white. Near the contorted bed they contain much magnetite and specular iron, but, as a rule, they are not so magnetic as the Water Tower Slates. The contorted bed, however, is always very magnetic. The latter is well exposed at intervals along the northern slope of the Hospital Ridge,

Fig. 26.—Contorted Band, Hospital Hill Slate, Show Yard, Johannesburg.

as it is much more resistant than the slates above and below it. Not infrequently it is broken by faults, and its outcrop may be much twisted.

South of the Hospital Hill Slates there

is an extensive outcrop of quartzite, forming the southern slope of Hospital Hill, and at the upper end of the Bezuidenhout Valley, the conspicuous hill on which the Johannesburg Service Reservoir, the Meteorological Observatory and the Indian Monument stand. At its outcrop the quartzite is sometimes green in colour, but more often reddish or white. The green colour must be due to some material in the matrix, which, however, cannot be readily detected under the microscope. From the occasional green colour the rocks are often referred to by local geologists as the " Green Quartzites "; but since the colour is not a persistent feature, it is better to distinguish them as the *Hospital Hill Quartzites*. A better characteristic than the colour is the peculiar structure which is found on a freshly-fractured surface. The quartz grains are round and pellucid, and present an appearance resembling cooked sago. This structure is usually best developed where the rock appears compact and almost glassy at the surface. A similar structure is also noticeable to some extent in the Ripple-marked Quartzite, but it is never so typically nor so perfectly developed in the latter as in the Hospital Hill Quartzite.

Immediately south of the Hospital Hill Quartzites, the low ground, on which Johannesburg is for the most part built, consists of soft easily weathered slates, with subordinate bands of quartzite. These are the *Doornfontein Beds*. They lie between the Hospital Hill quartzites and those of the *Red Bar,* which farther south underlie the Main Reef Conglomerates.

The following table gives the thickness of the different members of the Lower Witwatersrand Beds, as shown in a section made by Mr. Luttman-Johnson at Brixton across the beds from the Main Reef to the granite:—

Red Bar..... 450 feet.
Doornfontein Beds (slates and quartzites). 5,500 „
Hospital Hill Quartzite.. 1,400 „
Hospital Hill Slate.... 620 „
Speckled Bed... 20,, 1,800 feet.
60 „ 1,400 „ 1,400 „ 12,650 feet.

In the Bezuidenhout valley, east of

Johannesburg, a portion of these beds, namely, from the Ripple-marked Quartzite to the Doornfontein Slates, is duplicated by a great reversed fault which strikes diagonally across the valley from Jeppe's Hill to near Sir George Farrar's farm on Rietfontein 1 (see Fig. 25).

Of the Lower Witwatersrand Beds the Hospital Hill Slates alone present features of interest that are worthy of detailed description. The origin of the " contorted bed" is especially difficult to explain. The fact that it is plicated and minutely faulted to a remarkable degree, while the quartzite immediately beneath and the slates above are quite normally bedded, points to the conclusion that the phenomena are due to causes inherent in the composition of the bed itself. It is improbable that any result of dynamic metamorphism should be confined to one particular bed, and not affect the slates above and below. It appears more likely that, subsequent to its deposition, some chemical change took place within the bed, resulting in an increase of its mass, so that the rock had to bend, crumple and break, in order to adjust itself to the space available for it under the pressure of the superincumbent rock.

Under the microscope the Hospital Hill slates are seen to be composed essentially of minute angular to sub-angular fragments of quartz, and to contain much iron, which is present either as magnetite, specular iron ore, or iron 1 Hatch and Corstorphine, 1904.

Red Slate

Ripple-marked Quartzite

Water Tower Slate.

Orange Grove Quartzite

pyrites. They may therefore be considered to be exceedingly fine-grained varieties of the quartzites with the addition of much iron. With regard to chemical composition, the following analyses of five samples of the Hospital Hill slates are given by Mr. H. F. Marriott:'—

The samples were taken from the cutting at the entrance to the Agricultural Show Ground, Braamfontein, Johannesburg.

No. 1 represents the composition of a fair average sample taken at intervals of 3 feet over a total distance of 225 feet across the formation.

No. 2 is a sample taken with a view to obtaining the most acid result possible; it includes some 8 inches of white quartzose bands, on the eastern face of the cutting, 60 feet north of the gate.

No. 3 is a sample selected from what appeared to promise the most basic results; it was taken over a 24-inch section on the eastern face of the cutting, 150 feet north of the gate.

No. 4 represents an average section of the typical banded and contorted portion of the series: it was taken over a section 48 inches in width, on the eastern face of the cutting, just inside the gate.

No. 5 was taken over 34 inches of bright red satiny shale on the eastern face of the cutting, 100 feet north of the gate.

It will be observed that lime and magnesia are practically not represented in these analyses, and that the alkalies, although not determined, can only vary from-06 per cent to 1 Marriott, 1904.

5 per cent, except in the ease of.sample No. 5, which differs in some respects from the other four. The analyses show further that a large proportion of oxides of iron is a characteristic feature of the beds. This iron, as already mentioned, is present both as specular iron-ore and magnetite.

It is interesting to note that these ferruginous slates, remarkable as they are both in composition and structure, are almost exactly paralleled in the Negaune Series of the Marquette Iron range—a portion of the Lake Superior district. The rocks comprising the Negaune Series, according to the description given by American writers, consist of contorted ferruginous slates in which occur alternating bands of jasper, chert, hematite and magnetite, forming a striped rock of identical appearance to the contorted bed of the Hospital Hill Slates. These Marquette rocks have been the subject of a vigorous controversy between the advocates of the theory which ascribed to them an igneous origin, and the adherents of the theory which regarded them as of sedimentary origin. To the igneous school belonged Foster, Whitney and Wadsworth: while the sedimentary party comprised Kimball, Dana, Hunt, Winchell, Credner, Newberry, Irving and Van Hise. A full account of the controversy will be found in the monograph (No. xxviii.) of the U. S. Geological Survey on *The Marquette Iron-bearing District of Michigan.* Suffice it here to say that the sedimentary theory has finally won the day. According to the theory first put forward by Irving and adopted by Van Hise, the iron was deposited originally in the form of carbonate. It was doubtless brought into solution by atmospheric agencies. probably assisted by organic acids.1 "As the iron carbonate came down into the open water it was peroxidised, and the 1 U.S. Geological Survey; monograph (No. xxviii.) on *The Marquette Iron-bearimj District oj Michigan,* p. 562. iron precipitated as hydrated oxide. When this was buried together with organic matter, the decomposition of the latter produced carbon dioxide, and the iron was reduced to peroxide by the organic matter. The two combined and reproduced iron carbonate." The other components of the series, oxides of iron, jasper, chert, etc., arose by secondary processes, partially of oxidation, partially of silicification.

The above description of the origin of the ferruginous slates of the Marquette district may supply a suggestion as to the origin of the Hospital Hill slates, which so closely resemble them. Curiously enough, like the Marquette rocks, the Hospital Hill slates have quite recently been the subject of considerable controversy, although it must be confessed that the body of local opinion has not been even approximately equally divided. The phenomena presented by the slates in the field, as well as their microscopic structure and chemical composition, have been held by Mr. George Denny1 to indicate an igneous origin. No local geologist, however, has come forward to support this view: on the contrary, the opinion is unanimous that the Hospital Hill and other slates of the

Witwatersrand Beds are true sediments. This opinion is based on the following facts":—(1) under the microscope the slates are found to be composed chiefly of fragmental quartz; (2) there is a perfect gradation to clearly recognisable quartzites; (3) slaty seams alternate with quartzitic layers in the banded varieties; (4) the chemical analyses *(vide supra)* show that these rocks have a composition incompatible with their being igneous, the chief points being the very high percentage of silica and the paucity of alkalies and alkaline earths.

1 *Journ. S. A. Assoc. Engineers,* vol. ii. (1903), pp. 18 and 125. 2 Hatch, 1903 *a,* pp. 35 and 191; I). Wilkinson, *Journ. H. A. Assoc. Engineers,* vol. ii. (1903).

Beyond a few ill-defined pebbly beds, which have been found in making excavations for foundations in Johannesburg, no conglomerates outcrop in the Lower Witwatersrand Beds of the Central Rand.

Both on the East and West Rand sections across the beds show, as might be expected, great divergence from the typical one of the Central Rand. Thus the Hospital Hill Quartzite, which at Johannesburg is not more than 1400 feet thick, increases considerably towards the west, being, according to Mr. Kuntz,1 several thousand feet on Witfontein (No. 572). In the vicinity of Roodepoort the Hospital Hill Slates contain intercalated bands of quartzite always distinctly lenticular in shape and varying from patches of a few yards in length to ridges extending for a mile or more. Again, Mr. Kuntz gives a section on the West Rand, in which he shows fourteen beds of quartzite, alternating with thirteen beds of slate. Between the Orange Grove Quartzite and the Hospital Hill Quartzite he has three belts of slate, as in the Central Rand section, but above the Hospital Hill Slates he shows a much greater alternation of slate and quartzite than is known on the Central Rand. There are also on the AVest Rand definite beds of conglomerate below the horizon of the Main Reef. Thus, about mid-way between the Hospital Hill Slate and the Main Reef (Botha's Reef), there is the North Coronation Reef, and

again, mid-way between the latter and the Main Reef, the Government Reef and Government Reef Leader.

Still farther west there is an even greater divergence from what, for convenience, may be termed the normal section of the Central Rand. Thus on Droogeheuvel (No. 716), Hartebeestfontein (No. 149), Witfontein (No. 572), and Rietfontein 1 Kuntz, *Trans. Geol. Sue. S. A.* vol. vi. p. 131. (No. 363) there are, below the horizon of the Government Reef, outcrops of numerous beds of conglomerate, locally termed the Bertha Estate and Witfontein Series, which are unknown in the central and eastern portions of the Witwatersrand. This development of conglomerate appears to increase as the Witwatersrand Beds are followed in their south-western extension, for, according to Mr. Kuntz,1 the bodies of large pebbled conglomerate characteristic of the Klerksdorp district belong mainly to the Lower Witwatersrand Beds.

On the East Rand the Rietfontein section is worthy of note. About two and a half miles north of the outcrop of the Main Reef on Driefontein there are, alternating with shales and quartzites, beds of conglomerate that have not been found to occur elsewhere. The uppermost of the conglomerate beds is known as the South Rietfontein Series. Separated from the latter by slates and quartzites measuring some 2300 feet across the outcrop, is the so-called Stable Reef, a series of grit beds about 100 feet wide, with small seams of conglomerate on the foot and hanging walls. North of the Stable Reef and separated from it by about 3000 feet of quartzites, are the small seams of conglomerate or " leaders," that have been successfully worked by the various Rietfontein companies. An extremely narrow seam of marcasite in the form of pellets of the size of buckshot is associated with the conglomerate seams. Specimens showing visible gold are frequently found, the gold being generally confined to one plane and associated with a carbonaceous mineral in small black spots (see p. 135).

East of Rietfontein the hills disap-

pear, and the beds of the Lower Witwatersrand Series are hidden from view by a deep red soil resulting from their decomposition.

1 Kuntz, *Trans. Gtol. Soc. S. A.* (1903), p. 58.

East of Van Ryn the beds pass under the Ecca Beds, but boreholes have reached them after successively traversing the Ecca Beds and the Dolomite Series. On Palmietkuil (No. 61), some 3700 feet of the Lower Witwatersrand Beds have been penetrated. These consist of quartzites and slates: the former are of varying texture, passing from grits, on the one hand, gradually into soft slaty rocks, on the other; the latter are true slates of black satiny texture, whose frequently striped and banded character is due to a rapid alternation of fine and coarse layers, doubtless the result of current bedding.

CHAPTER III THE WITWATERSRAND SYSTEM *(continued)*

Upper Division

As already mentioned, the Upper Division of the Witwatersrand System consists of conglomerates, grits and quartzites, with few slate beds. The rocks are characterised: (1) by being made up almost exclusively of quartz, originally deposited as shingle, sand and fine slime or mud; (2) by the presence of a large amount of secondary silica (in great part quartz, but occasionally of a chalcedonic character), which has cemented the loose beds of shingle, sand and fine silt into hard, compact beds of quartzite, conglomerate and slate; (3) by the presence of iron pyrites and gold in certain of the conglomerates; and (4) by the presence of sericite in lustrous silvery scales and films, especially in those portions of the beds which have been faulted, squeezed, or subjected to shearing.

Among the above-mentioned beds the quartzites largely predominate, forming the bulk of the whole series. The slate belts are, with one exception (that underlying the Kimberley Series), quite insignificant; and the conglomerates are plentiful only in certain well-defined belts, which are conveniently grouped under the following names originally given them by the gold prospectors:—

Elsburg Series.
Kimberley Series.
Bird Reef Series.
Livingstone Reef Series.
Main Reef Series.

These conglomerate beds are separated by quartzites, but between the Kimberley and Bird Reef Series a band of slate occurs. In a typical section on the Central Rand the outcrop of the beds from the Main Reef to the top of the Elsburg Conglomerates occupies a space of about four miles, the highest beds being found to the immediate north of the prominent ridge known as the Klipriversberg, where they are overlaid by a sheet of amygdaloidal diabase belonging to the Ventersdorp System. Although in most places there is every appearance of conformity between the Elsburg and the underlying beds, evidence indicating an unconformity is obtainable elsewhere. Thus on the Steyn Estate and on Doornkop on the West Rand quartzites and conglomerates occupying the position of the Elsburg Series are found dipping slightly to the north, not more than two miles to the south of an outcrop of Kimberley conglomerates, dipping south at 45. Again, in the Bezuidenhout valley there are, at Langerman's

Kopje, rocks resembling the Elsburg conglomerates which are possibly an outlier of those beds on the upturned edges of the Lower Witwatersrand.[1] If this unconformity exists, the correct grouping of the Elsburg Series would appear to be with the Ventersdorp System, which, as will be shown later, comprises not only volcanic lavas and breccias, but also boulder-beds, coarse conglomerates and quartzites not unlike the Elsburg Series in appearance. However, as the position of the Elsburg Beds cannot yet be regarded as settled, they are described in their hitherto accepted position at the top of the Witwatersrand Series.

From a section taken through the Aurora mine, west of Johannesburg, the following thicknesses for the beds on the Central Rand may be deduced:—

Another section taken through the Simmer and Jack mine and the Rand Victoria borehole (No. 2) gives the following thicknesses:—

True thickness.

From the base of the Klipriversberg Amygdaloid to

Elsburg Series: quartzites.. 1,400 feet
Elsburg Series2.... 2,800 „
Quartzite...... 1,800 „ 1 Hatch and Corstorphine, 1904.

Including everything between the highest and the lowest conglomerate bed of the series, there being, of course, much intervening quartzite.

True thickness.

Kimberley Series1.... 1,800 feet
Slates 500 „
Quartzite (in part dyke).... 800.,
Bird Reef Series1... 300 „
Quartzite to footwall of Main Reef (including Livingstone Series)..... 1,700 „
11,100 feet

The horizontal distance on this section from the Main Reef to the Klipriversberg Amygdaloid is 20,000 feet.

From the two Turf Club boreholes on the Central Rand the following average thicknesses may be deduced:—

True thickness.

Kimberley Series (incomplete). 1200 feet
Slates 900 „
Quartzite 290 „
Bird Series.... 450 „
Quartzite 470 „
Livingstone Series...-250 „
Quartzite...... 900 „
Main Reef Series. 90 „ 4550 feet

As regards the extreme East Rand, the following average section is deduced from boreholes put down on Geduld (No. 134) and Grootvlei (No. 45):—

Kimberley Series....
Slates.... 270 feet
Quartzite.... 250 „
Amygdaloidal Diabase.. 150 „
Quartzite, containing Bird, Livingstone, and Main Reef Series G50 „
True thickness. 1000 feet 1320 2320 feet 1 Including everything between the highest and the lowest conglomerate bed of the series, there being, of course,

much intervening quartzite.

A comparison of the last section with those on the Central Rand shows a most remarkable thinning out of the beds below the Kimberley Series. Thus the beds from the footwall of the latter to the footwall of the Main Reef Series, which have a thickness of 3410 feet in the Aurora section, 3350 in the Turf Club section and 3300 in the Simmer section, are in the Geduld-Grootvlei section reduced to 1320 feet. The Bird, Livingstone, and Main Reef Series are correspondingly reduced, being represented by quite small seams of conglomerate, aggregating a few feet only for each series, instead of hundreds of feet, as on the Central Rand.

From a consideration of the above sections, some conclusions may be drawn as to the total known thickness of the system. In the Central Rand, the Lower Beds have a thickness of about 10,000 feet, and the Upper Beds to the base of the Klipriversberg Amygdaloid, a thickness also of a little over 10,000 feet, making in all a total of 20,000 feet. Since, however, the entire formation cannot be seen in section, on account of the great unconformity between the Upper Beds and the overlying Klipriversberg Amygdaloid (a part of the Ventersdorp System, to be described in a succeeding chapter), it is evident that the true thickness of the series cannot be determined. Evidence, however, has been adduced to show that it varies, the series being considerably thinner in the extreme eastern, and thicker in the western, than in the central portion of the Rand.

In the following pages some details are given of the different conglomerate series, beginning with the geologically highest, and leaving to the last the Main Reef Series, which is the only one of economic importance.

The Elsburg Series

This conglomerate series derives its name from the township of Elsburg, which is situated ten miles south-east of Johannesburg. The beds are exposed along the old coachroad to Heidelberg and were opened by the early gold prospectors in numerous cuttings on

Rass' farm, in the southern portion of Turffontein. They can also be well studied in a low range of hills two and a half miles south of the Simmer and Jack mine. The conglomerates, alternating with beds of quartzite, occur in great abundance, constituting a belt about 4000 feet wide. The pebbles of which they are composed consist largely of quartz and quartzite, but occasionally irregularly shaped pieces of slate and hornstone are also found. Although small pebbles occur, the majority are large, averaging several inches in diameter and occasionally attaining to even larger dimensions. Although iron pyrites is a common constituent, gold is present in small quantity only, and the attempts of the early prospectors to develop payable mines proved a failure. As already pointed out (p. 122), an outlying patch of beds closely resembling the Elsburg Series occurs north of the Main Reef in the hills forming the south side of the Bezuidenhout valley, north of Jeppestown (see Fig. 25). Mr. Walcot Gibson first suggested that the rocks of this kopje belong to the Elsburg Series and owe their present position to faulting, either from above or below. If the beds are faulted from above, this would mean that there is a downthrow of 15,000 feet affecting a comparatively small area. If, on the other hand, the strata are faulted up from below, then, as Mr. Gibson points out, " the apparent sequence of the beds of the Rand is a false one, and the reefs which are now the highest are the oldest." 1 This, however, is not the case. If the beds belong to the Elsburg Series, the true explanation must be that the Elsburg Beds are unconformable to the Witwatersrand Series.

The Rietfontein conglomerates, which have been described with the Lower Witwatersrand Beds on p. 116, also show some sign of unconformable relations to the Lower Witwatersrand Beds, and it is possible that they also should be considered an outlying patch of unconformable Elsburg Conglomerate.

The Kimberley Series
The Kimberley Series is second only to

the Elsburg in the number and thickness of its conglomerate beds and in the size of the component pebbles. In the central portion of the Rand they outcrop over a belt of country about half a mile wide. The beds vary from the merest stringer to many feet in thickness, and in texture from grits to coarse conglomerates with pebbles as large as a hen's egg. In a borehole put down on the East Rand2 which penetrated the whole series, 108 distinct beds and stringers of conglomerate were counted, varying in size from half an inch to five feet. The pebbles, which are sometimes thickly aggregated, sometimes sparsely scattered, are rounded, sub-angular, or angular. They consist chiefly of quartz, but quartzite, striped slate and hornstone also occur, the two latter in long irregularly shaped pieces. Pyrites is abundant, but gold is present in unpayable quantities only, although richer patches attracted some attention in the early days of the goldfield. The first prospectors distinguished between the Yellow Reef, the Red Reef, the Sunday Reef, the Free State Reef and the Kimberley Reef. A characteristic feature of the series is a broad belt of underlying slates. These are of a grey to black colour and have a satiny lustre on cleaved surfaces. In places they have a banded character, due to the alternation of coarse and fine seams, the result, doubtless, of rapid variation in the conditions of sedimentation. Under the microscope they are seen to consist of minute fragments of quartz, together with chlorite, sericite and iron pyrites; rutile also occurs in aggregates of minute hair-like needles.1

Bird and Livingstone Series
The Bird and Livingstone Series consist of a variable number of beds of conglomerate, composed of pebbles smaller than those of the Kimberley Series; they lie in the quartzites separating the latter from the Main Reef Series. The pebbles consist chiefly of quartz. On the Rand west of Johannesburg (Paardekraal) and on the extreme east Rand (Modderfontein) several attempts have been made to work these reefs for gold, but only with moderate success.

The Mai n. Reef Series

On account of its valuable gold contents, the Main Reef Series has been very closely studied over a distance of 46 miles, where it has been worked in almost continuous succession by the gold-mining companies of the Witwatersrand.

The pebbles of which the Series is composed consist mainly of white or smoky quartz imbedded in a quartzitic matrix. In size they vary from a pea to a hen's egg; but 1 Hatch, 1903 *a.* there is a marked uniformity in this respect over considerable areas of any particular bed.

A comparison between sections of the Main Reef Series at points far removed one from the other shows variations both in the number of beds and in the amount of quartzite between them. This is due to the thinning out and thickening of the various beds—variations which are characteristic of conglomerate and inherent in its mode of formation. Close examination of any mine on the Rand shows that the banket beds instead of preserving a uniform thickness over large areas, are rather of a lenticular character: a particular bed will, if followed, be found to tail off until it ceases altogether, its place being perhaps taken on a slightly different horizon by another bed, which, beginning as a small seam, gradually increases to a maximum width, when it, in turn, will commence to thin. Further, some of the beds will be found to split up into several seams which may or may not reunite. In the latter eventuality lenticular patches or "horses" of quartzite are enclosed. It follows that only in a very general sense can a conglomerate bed be said to occur on the same horizon over great distances. Of the Main Reef conglomerates as a whole, however, it is true that there is, as will be shown later, a remarkable persistence over a great area.

In its most typical development, namely, between the Wolhuter and the Princess mines, the Main Reef Series consists of three, more or less payable, reefs. The lowest or most northern of these is a big body (in places as much as twelve feet thick) of low grade banket. This is termed the Main Reef, and has given its name to the whole series. Lying above and separated from the Main Reef by a varying amount of quartzite, is a much smaller body of payable banket, known as the Main Reef Leader. This ore-body

K ranges from a few inches to as much as six feet in thickness, averaging perhaps fifteen inches. It is generally split up by quartzite partings into two and sometimes even three leaders, of which the footwall or South Reef Leader is the most valuable. The quartzite separating the Main Reef Leader from the Main Reef is in places as much as six or seven feet thick, while in some mines it thins out entirely, the two reefs being then found in close juxtaposition. Occasionally the parting consists of slaty material instead of quartzite: it is often accompanied by vein-quartz, and, on its footwall. by a bed of quartzite with sparsely scattered pebbles, known

Fig. 28.—Section of Main Reef Series in the Aurora West mine. After Hatch and

Chalmers.

in some of the mines as the "Bastard Reef." In the mines east of Johannesburg this so-called "Slate-leader" becomes persistent and constitutes a useful marker for both the Main Reef and the Main Reef Leader. The distance between the South Reef and the Main Reef Leader ranges from 35 to 100 feet, this measurement being at right angles to the slope of the reefs.

Of the three reefs, two are in most cases payable, while the third (the Main Reef) has to be worked on a large scale in order to yield a profit. The tendency nowadays in Rand mining is to increase the stamping power of the mills and to work the Main Reef. Besides the conglomerates which may be considered as ore-bodies, other non-payable banket beds are frequently present. Thus in some of the mines belonging to the section under consideration there is a North Reef, lying to the north of the Main Reef, while in others there is a Middle Reef, lying between the Main Reef Leader and the South Reef (see Fig. 28).

With regard to the distinguishing features of the orebodies in this part of the Rand, the Main Reef is characterised by its great thickness, its low gold content, its interbedded seams of quartzite and the generally uniform size of its pebbles. The Main Reef Leader, on the other hand, is of small size, but comparatively rich. The pebbles consist of white and smoky quartz. Usually there is a layer of largish

Fig. 29.—Section of Main Reef Series in the Glencairn mine. After Hatch and

Chalmers.

pebbles on the footwall. Both foot and hanging walls are well defined. The South Reef in most of the mines is separable into a footwall seam (the South Reef Leader), which carries the major portion of the gold, and a larger body of banket of lower grade (the South Reef proper). In some cases there are three leaders, two of which are poor, while the third (the footwall leader) is payable. The South Reef Leader seldom exceeds eight inches in thickness, and is frequently represented by a mere layer of pebbles, or even by a thin ferruginous seam, especially in the mines between the Croesus and the Banket. It is, however, of remarkable persistence, being traceable from mine to mine throughout the West Rand. The pebbles of the South Reef are comparatively small, but larger ones occur in the leader. There is a fair proportion of smoky quartz among them. The quartzite parting between the South Leader and the upper seams of the South Reef varies from one inch to as much as. six feet, the average being about twenty inches.

On the East Rand slightly different conditions prevail (see Fig. 29). The South Reef becomes of less and less importance eastward from Johannesburg, although profitably worked as far as the Heriot: farther east it is not mined at all. Three reefs, which lie in close proximity, are worked in most of the mines in this area. They are known by various names on the different mines, attempts at correlation having been frustrated in large measure by the lenticular character of the

Fig. 30.—Section through Witwatersrand mine, showing duplication of Main Reef. beds. The East Rand mines are further complicated by reversed faulting. This may affect a single bed, or the whole series may be duplicated, as in the Witwatersrand mine (see Fig. 30) and in the East Rand Proprietary mines. A useful guide in these difficulties, however, is the Slate Leader referred to above as occurring between the Main Reef and the Main Reef Leader. On the extreme East Rand, that is to say, east of Boksburg (e.g. in the Kleinfontein, Van Ryn, Geduld and Grootvlei properties), the Main Reef Series is much thinner, and consists of a number of smaller conglomerate beds or leaders, of which the lowest rests immediately on a slate footwall. Most of the gold is usually found in this footwall leader. On the Nigel properties, the whole series is represented by a few inches of conglomerate resting on slate.

Petrographical Description of the Witwatersrand Conglomerates

The petrography of the Witwatersrand conglomerates has been somewhat neglected, Koch[1] and de Launay[2] being the chief authors who have hitherto dealt with the microscopic character of the rocks.

Macroscopically, the conglomerates consist mainly of rolled fragments of quartz; but quartzite, banded chert and slate occasionally also occur. The quartz and quartzite fragments, from their rounded character, have obviously 1;een water-borne; but the chert and slate pebbles are usually of a more angular and elongated shape. The pebbles are of all sizes, but in the Main Reef Series a small walnut probably represents the average dimensions. They lie in a matrix of quartz grains, which has been cemented to a hard and compact mass by secondarily deposited silica, partly in the form of minutely crystalline quartz, partly as opal or chalcedony. A homogeneous glassy rock resembling vein-quartz has thus been produced, in which the pebbly character is so obliterated that the rock breaks indiscriminately across pebbles and matrix. In places the secondary silica fills small fissures and cracks, forming miniature quartz-veins.

The characteristic presence of iron pyrites in the 1 See Schraeisser, 1895. - de Launay, 1896.
unoxidised "blue" conglomerate has already been noted. This pyrites occurs in grains which, even with the unaided eye, can be distinguished as round pellets, sub-angular pieces and perfect crystals, the latter showing combinations of cube, octahedron and pentagonal dodecahedron. Occasionally larger round nodules of pyrites occur, some of which have quite a pebble-like appearance. Among a considerable number of specimens of these so-called pyrites

Fig. 31.—Piece of Main Reef Conglomerate, Robinson Deep mine. Abont half scale.

"pebbles," several were found to have a radially fibrous structure, while others showed that their growth had been by concentric coats. Distinctly radiate structure was especially observable in a spherical pyrites "pebble " three-fifths of an inch in diameter, contained in a piece of quartz conglomerate from the Buffelsdoorn mine in the Klerksdorp district. Some of the pyritic "pebbles" from the Buffelsdoorn mine have a concentric structure, but none appear to show any sign of superficial weathering. A weathered coating of iron oxide has been described by Mr. G. F. Beckerl as proof 1 Becker, 1896.
that the pyrites is of secondary origin, but such a coating might be formed under the influence of ordinary percolation, even if the rest of the specimen remained fresh. In any case, its presence appears, if taken alone, to be too slight a reason for regarding the pyrites as rolled. It is a remarkable fact that almost every author who has referred to the rounded pellets of pyrites regards them as owing their shape to attrition. The bulk at any rate of the so-called "rolled" pyrites owes its shape to growth by accretion and consists of the mineral marcasite, and it is certainly questionable whether rolled pebbles of pyrites occur at all.

In the so-called "Buckshot Reef" of the Rietfontein mines the pellets of pyrites vary from 0 to f an mcn in diameter. They occur in a narrow band, associated with a thin seam of small pebble conglomerate, which is the footwall leader in these mines. Where the pellets are partially weathered, a radiate structure can be clearly discerned, and in thin sections of the fresh reef the same structure is visible even to the naked eye. An interesting feature is the so-called " Carbon Leader ": this consists of a very thin layer in which there are small black spots of carbonaceous matter,1 generally with a considerable amount of visible gold as an incrustation. It is on the hanging-wall side of the hanging-wall leader, from which it is separated by from three to eight feet of quartzite. Carbonaceous matter of a similar nature has been noticed in the Buffelsdoorn and Randfontein mines. Its bearing on the origin of the gold in the banket will be referred to later on (see p. 146).

Examination under the microscope of sections of conglomerate from various mines shows practically a constant 1 Profestor Miers of Oxford, to whom a specimen of this carbonaceous matter was sent, writes: "It appears to me to consist mainly of carbon, burns with production of C02: it is mixed with a sulphur (and arsenic) compound, probably of iron, since the ash appears to be mainly an iron residue. I do not think it contains any hydrocarbon." type of rock: the main differences in individual sections are the proportion of matrix to pebbles and the occasional occurrence of some particular mineral in greater quantity than the normal. The quartz pebbles show numerous fluid-enclosures arranged in irregular lines throughout the fragments. Between crossed nicols they generally have an undulatory extinction, in some cases being broken up into separately polarising fields, a result, no doubt, of the strain to which the rock has been subjected. As already mentioned, the pebbles lie in a quartz matrix which is mainly of a secondary origin; the latter occurs in the form of a fine mosaic of differently orientated granules. The pyrites is in all shapes, the circular prevailing: sections of cubes and pentagonal dodecahedra and octahedra are found grading into partially or wholly circular pieces. In a section of the Rietfontein "buckshot" reef one pyrites concretion was noticed which had been cracked, and re-cemented by secondary quartz, showing that the silicification of the conglomerate had to some extent been posterior to the formation of the pyrites. The matrix contains chlorite, talc, sericite and occasionally ordinary muscovite; in some sections abundant rutile is present, and zircon occurs as an accessory constituent. Magnetite is rarely seen. Corundum in pinkcoloured grains and tourmaline in needles are mentioned by Henderson.1 With the talc and chlorite chloritoid is associated in colourless prismatic sections which are occasionally bifurcated and often broken.

The occurrence of gold in certain of the Witwatersrand conglomerates has given them fame that would otherwise have been lacking. Although rarely visible in the handspecimen, the gold can be easily studied under the microscope, if specimens known to be rich in it are examined: 1 Henderson. 1898, p. 55.
it occurs in irregular angular particles, often lying on the periphery of individual pyrites grains or crystals, or in the interstices between aggregates of that mineral. In many cases perfectly round pieces of pyrites may be observed to be bounded by gold particles. *Evidence of Volcanic Activity during the Deposition of the Witwatersrand Beds*
Interbedded with the slates and quartzites of the Witwatersrand Beds are sheets of diabase, which occur at different horizons both in the Lower and in the Upper divisions. They are apparently volcanic flows, since they maintain the same horizon over great distances and often present a distinctly amygdaloidal character. Apparently the quiescent deposition of the aqueous sediments was interrupted at intervals by bursts of volcanic activity—a prelude, no doubt, to the violent volcanic outpourings which characterise a later period (see p. 148). The diabase sheets have been studied particularly in the extreme east Rand, where numerous deep borings have intersected them. One of the most persistent sheets in that district occurs immediately above the Bird Reef

Series. Its thickness averages 150 feet, but it increases from west to east, apparently indicating a flow from east to west. In the hand-specimen the rock is of a dirty greenishgrey colour and usually spotted over with small white amygdales of calcite. Though very fine-grained or aphanitic in the hand-specimen, lath-shaped crystals of felspar are distinguishable under the microscope. These are turbid through kaolinisation, and generally the rock shows much decomposition, its ferro-magnesian constituents being completely changed to secondary minerals.

In the Lower Beds several sheets of diabase have been intersected in the boreholes. These are much decomposed, the original minerals being replaced by chlorite, calcite, epidote and other secondary products, which also occur as amygdales. The presence of the remains of original porphyritic crystals of felspar can be made out under the microscope, and there are microlites of the same mineral.

Dyke rocks also occur: among other types that have been described are a quartz-diabase or norite containing enstatite and a diorite (both in the Angelo mines).[1] The usual type, however, is a uralitic diabase or epidiorite. The decomposed condition of the diabase sheets and dykes enables them to be readily distinguished from the much later Karroo dolerite dykes which, in great number, are found cutting the Witwatersrand Beds. The latter are characterised by a remarkable degree of freshness, the plagioclase felspar and augite being quite unaltered and the olivine only partially so.

Distribution of the Witwatersrand Beds
The Witwatersrand Beds, together with the Basement Granite, are exposed on the Rand in the axial portion of a great anticline formed by the Pretoria Beds and the Dolomite Series. East of Springs and west of Krugersdorp the Dolomite covering remains intact; but for a distance of sixty miles the Witwatersrand Beds have been exposed by the removal of the superincumbent strata. In the Potchefstroom district also the Dolomite has been removed, exposing

the Lower Witwatersrand Beds together with the Basement Granite between Fredrikstad and Ventersdorp. Beyond Klerksdorp the Lower Beds can be traced in a southwesterly direction for a distance of over sixty miles. That they also have been affected by the anticlinal flexure, is 1 Henderson, 1898, . 54; see also Koch in *Schmeisser,* 1895, p. 57. evidenced by the fact that they can be seen dipping away from the Ventersdorp granite mass, both on its northern and on its southern boundary.

Following on the anticlinal fold there is to the south a syncline, the axis of which runs in a south-westerly direction from Springs through Potchefstroom into the Orange River Colony, crossing the Vaal River near the confluence of the Mooi River. The Witwatersrand Beds, forming the southern limb of the syncline, are partially covered by the Ecca Beds of the Karroo System and by the Dolomite and Pretoria Series; but they outcrop in the Heidelberg district and on the Vaal River near Parys and Venterskroon. A section drawn from a point five miles north-west of Boksburg to a point some seven miles south-east of the Nigel mine, a distance of thirty-five miles, shows this syncline fairly completely. The northern limb is composed of the following beds, with south-easterly dip, in ascending order:—

Quartzites and Ferruginous Slates.. Lower Witwatersrand Beds.

Main Reef Series "1
Bird and Livingstone (Modderfontein) Series
Diabase Sheet
Kimberley Slates
Elsburg Series

Upper Witwatersrand Beds.

Klipriversberg Amygdaloid.. Ventersdorp System.

In the continuation of this section the same beds are recrossed in the reverse order with a dip to the northwest, the Lower Witwatersrand Beds resting on granite, as is the case with the northern limb of the syncline. The Main Reef horizon has been identified in the Nigel Reef. A series of bore-holes put down on the farm Palmietkuil (No. 61), east of Springs, has proved the connection be-

tween the Nigel and the Van Ryn Reef (the latter being the name by which the Main Reef is known on the extreme eastern Rand) under the Dolomite and Ecca Beds. The Lower Witwatersrand Beds probably extend under the Dolomite for several miles to the east, the westerly dip being at an extremely low angle; but still farther to the east boreholes have intersected granite.[1]

Since the granite is the basement rock on which the Witwatersrand Beds were laid down, it must at one time have been uniformly covered by these beds over a large area in the southern Transvaal. Subsequent earth-movements caused the formation of a series of anticlinal and synclinal folds in the Witwatersrand Beds, the former of which naturally fell an easy prey to denudation, thus bringing the granite to the light of day in these places. Consequently, if it were possible to remove all later deposits, we should see shallow synclines of the Witwatersrand Beds separated by the granite floor of the former anticlines. Immediately surrounding the granite we should find the Lower Witwatersrand Beds and, succeeding the latter in natural sequence, the Upper Witwatersrand Beds: always provided that the 1 Hatch, 1904 *h.* denudation had not been sufficiently severe or prolonged to have removed them, before the deposition of the later formations (Dolomite and Karroo Beds) could cover them up and preserve them.

It is possible, or even probable, that still farther east such synclinal areas of the Witwatersrand Beds exist under the Ecca Beds and the Dolomite Series. Whether these areas, if found, would consist of only the Lower Witwatersrand Beds, or whether the Upper might also be found, depends on the amount of denudation that supervened before the deposition of the younger series.

Along the border of Swaziland and Natal the Witwatersrand Series reappears from under the Karroo Beds. It is well exposed in the vicinity of Amsterdam southward to Paul Pietersburg, Amsterdam standing just on the boundary between the Dwyka Conglomerate and the older rocks. West of Amsterdam, on the farm Kliprug (No. 1071), the lowest Witwatersrand Quartzites are seen resting on granite, which is again well exposed on Paardekop (No. 73) and Edelgesteente (No. 92), being doubtless the basement rock throughout the whole district. The strike of the Witwatersrand Beds is in general north and south, but considerable local variations occur. The outcrop on Kliprug shows that there is probably a narrow syncline with a north and south axis. The section east and west through Merrie Kloof (No. 259), Amsterdam Townlands and Sterkfontein (No. 112) shows a distinct syncline with the bottom of the basin covered by Dwyka Conglomerate and Ecca Sandstones. The rocks exposed comprise typical contorted and striped slates, well seen on Redcliff (No. 62) and Cascade (No. 68); the quartzites and conglomerates of the series are especially well developed on Kranskop (No. 53) and on Sterkfontein (No. 112). Throughout the series there are many basic intrusions, occurring either as dykes or as small bosses.

The Origin of the Gold in the Conglomerate

The origin of the gold in the Witwatersrand conglomerate has been the subject of much discussion, and there is still a considerable diversity of opinion as to the correct explanation.

The inherent difficulty of accepting any one hypothesis lies in the fact that some of the peculiarities of the conglomerate can be explained by more than one view of the mode of deposition of the gold. The facts appear, however, to lend themselves most satisfactorily to the theory that the gold is an impregnation subsequent to the sedimentation of the conglomerate, but some discussion of the several hypotheses which have been advanced will not be out of place.

Three main theories have been put forward to explain the presence of the gold; they are:— 1. The gold was mechanically deposited with the pebbles of the conglomerate as the result of the denudation of some pre-existing auriferous rocks. That is to say, the conglomerates represent ancient alluvial or placer deposits.

2. The gold was present in solution in the waters by which the conglomerate was laid down, and while the pebbles were accumulating as a result of mechanical action, the gold itself was being chemically precipitated. 3. The gold, with the other minerals (quartz, chalcedony, pyrites, etc.) which now form the bulk of the matrix, was introduced by percolating waters into the interstices of the partially solidified conglomerates.

Briefly, the question is whether the gold was formed before, during, or after the deposition of the conglomerates.

1. *The Placer Theory.*—To view the Rand conglomerates merely as ancient placer deposits in which the gold is as much a product of denudation as the pebbles that accompany it, is, perhaps because of its simplicity, the first explanation that presents itself to one's mind. This view was suggested by several of the earlier writers, who found support for it in a superficial resemblance to certain Californian alluvial deposits, but the chief argument seems to be based on the occurrence of the rounded grains or pellets of pyrites in the cementing matrix, which are assumed to have acquired their shape by trituration or rolling.

An interesting variation has been presented by Mr. G. F. Becker,[1] who regards the conglomerates as ancient marine placer deposits, of which the original pyrites has been partially, and the gold entirely, dissolved and redeposited. Like the supporters of the simple placer theory, Becker lays stress upon the rounded form of the pyrites, which he considers to be the original condition of the pyrites in the rock, and due to an early attrition, the presence of complete or partial crystals being attributed to recrystallisation. He also dwells on the fact that the round pebbles or pellets of pyrites are in some cases superficially converted into a brownish-black mineral which is probably hematite. The free gold in the matrix is, on Becker's view, also present in two different conditions. He accepts both Koch's description of the metal as occurring in minute crystals or in irregular, hackly

aggregates, and Pelikan's statement that the gold is in irregular particles, grains and scales, corresponding to alluvial occurrences, concluding, on his own part, that the angular outlines of some of the gold particles are due to their having been moulded by pressure against the accompanying minerals.

With regard to this theory, there is little in the character of the conglomerates that supports such an 1 Becker, 1897. explanation: whether we regard the conglomerates as simple or modified placer deposits, the invariably fine state of subdivision of the gold and the regularity of its distribution remain a difficulty. The gold in placer deposits occurs either in nuggets, or is characterised by a coarseness which is quite foreign to the Rand conglomerates. Again, though the average gold content or grade of the conglomerates is not a high one, it is higher than that of the general placer deposit. There is also the fact, to which reference has already been made, that the gold particles appear to aggregate around pieces of pyrites. It is difficult to explain this on the placer theory, since it is obvious that the gold particles would have become detached from the pyrites during the attrition which gave the quartz pebbles their rounded form. Even Becker's hypothesis that the banket is a placer in which the gold has been partially dissolved and redeposited does not simplify matters, since it involves both the assumption of a free percolation of waters capable of dissolving the pyrites and the gold, and an almost simultaneous precipitation of these minerals. 2. *The Precipitation Theory.* — The second theory, namely, that the gold and pyrites are chemical precipitates from the waters in which the conglomerate pebbles were laid down, was formulated by W. H. Penning[1] in 1888, and elaborated by de Launay[2] in 1896. Penning put forward this view because he considered that it best explained the occurrence of the gold in hackly aggregates and rude crystal shapes. It is, however, open to many objections. It presupposes waters rich in dissolved gold, and the occurrence of some chemical change at a time when the waters were disturbed by movements capable of causing the formation of fairly coarse conglomerates. 1 Penning, 1888. 2 de Launay, 1896. 3. *The Infiltration Theory.*—The infiltration theory satisfactorily accounts for most of the phenomena, without postulating any especially abnormal conditions. The fact that the cementing material of the conglomerates is so largely composed of secondary minerals shows that the beds must have been subject to much percolation by mineralising solutions before final consolidation. The slow and repeated passage of such solutions, even if carrying only a minute quantity of gold, would gradually enrich the matrix.

The most striking feature of the gold contents of the Rand conglomerates is the limitation of the gold practically to the zone known as the Main Reef Series. That only certain beds should be the main gold carriers, seems to speak strongly for the theory of subsequent infiltration, for it is difficult to believe, as required by the placer theory, that only one serias of conglomerate beds should be derived from pre-existing gold-bearers. The assumption necessary on the infiltration theory, that the entire series of conglomerates and quartzites was permeated by the auriferous waters, presents no serious difficulty. The limitation of the gold deposition to definite zones was probably governed by certain chemical conditions, such as, for instance, the presence of a reducing agent in these and not in the other beds. In this way alone does it seem possible to explain the existence of the gold in beds near the centre of a conformable series. At the same time, the theory of a general percolation of auriferous waters accounts for the occasional presence of payable gold in conglomerates above and below the Main Reef horizon, as well as for the existence of richer chutes or patches in the main gold-bearing series: for, wherever the necessary conditions prevailed, precipitation took place. What this reducing agent was it is difficult to say. The frequent association of the gold with pyrites suggests that the latter *h* had something to do with precipitation. On the other hand, in some rich conglomerate reefs, carbonaceous matter is plentifully present: possibly this substance may have played a part in the precipitation.

Summarising, it may be said that the theory of subsequent infiltration is preferable to the others for the following reasons:— 1. The gold is practically confined to the matrix of the conglomerate, occurring there in association with other minerals of secondary origin: the rare cases in which gold occurs in the pebbles are obviously instances of infiltration along cracks, a fact which in itself lends support to the theory. 2. It occurs in crystalline particles often surrounding or lying in close association with pyrites crystals or marcasite concretions, which are of secondary origin. 3. It is uniformly distributed to a remarkable degree. 4. It is restricted to certain definite beds. *Yield of Gold from the Witivatersrand Banket*

The gold is present in the Witwatersrand Banket in finely divided particles, and, as above explained, is to a great extent mechanically associated with pyrites. Only in rare cases are the particles of sufficient size to be visible to the naked eye, unless the ore has been previously crushed and the bulk of the sand removed by careful washing or "panning." The average gold-contents of the ore crushed in the Rand mills has diminished year by year since the start of the gold-fields, *pan passu* with the increase of the total yield. The reason for this is evident: at first only the richest portions of the reefs were mined; but, as the appliances for the recovery of the gold were improved, lower-grade ores were found capable of profitable treatment. Thus, while in 1890, the first year in which a complete record was kept, 702,828 tons were treated, yielding 408,569 ounces of fine gold, or 11 "63 dwts. of fine gold per ton, during last year (1904) 8,058,295 tons were milled, yielding 3,658,241 ounces of fine gold, or 9-08 dwts. to the ton. Previous to 1890 only a few hundred thousand tons per annum had been treated, the yield per ton being correspondingly higher: that for 1889 has been estimated at 16 dwts. of fine gold to the ton.

This table shows the gradual decline in the yield of the ore per ton, as it became possible to treat lower and lower grade ores at a profit. The rise in yield per ton during the years 1899-1901 inclusive, is due to the fact that during the war the Boers worked only the mines of highest grade.

CHAPTER IV THE VENTEKSDORP SYSTEM Overlying the Witwatersrand Beds, and separated from them by a great unconformity, is a series of acid and basic lavas, tuffs, breccias and conglomerates, which, being typically developed at Ventersdorp in the western Transvaal, may be conveniently grouped together as the Ventersdorp System.1 The basic lavas are well represented by the rocks of the Klip River Hills south of the Rand, where they have an aggregate thickness of some 5000 feet. The rock there exposed is a fine-grained amygdaloidal and porphyritic diabase, long known as the Klipriversberg Amygdaloid. The amygdales consist chiefly of silica (as quartz, agate and opal), calcite and chlorite. Under the microscope, the rock is seen to consist of a felt-like aggregate of felspar microlites and augite granules, with small porphyritic crystals of augite and larger phenocysts of plagioclase felspar. Occasionally the felspar occurs in quite large crystals and crystal aggregates, so as to impart a distinctly porphyritic character to the rock, even in the hand-specimen.

Acid lavas are of less frequent occurrence. They have been observed, however, in the Makwassie Hills in the Wolmaranstad district,2 where a series of fine quartzporphyries were noticed by Hübner and Cohen, and have 1 Hatch, 1904. Since the publication of this paper Molengraaff has suggested the name Vaal River System (Molengraaff, 1904 *b*, p. 29).

2 Dahms, 1891. been included by Molengraaff in the System.1 Similar rocks occur at Platberg, twelve miles north of Klerksdorp.2

The fragmental rocks have until quite recently received but little attention. This is to be attributed partly to their poor development near the Rand, and partly to the fact that although breccias and conglomerates had been noticed, their position in the geological succession was not understood. The proper position of the beds and their connection with the Klipriversberg Amygdaloid has been only recently recognised.3

At Ventersdorp, in the Potchefstroom district, their association with basic lava-flows similar to the Klipriversberg Amygdaloid and their unconformable relation to the underlying Witwatersrand Beds and to the overlying Black' Reef and Dolomite Series are clearly shown. Clastic rocks of two distinct types are found there: (1) volcanic breccias, consisting of angular fragments of various rocks both igneous and sedimentary, imbedded in a clastic matrix which is itself either of sedimentary or of igneous origin; these pass, by a gradual diminution in the size of the fragments, into fine tuffs; (2) boulder and pebble beds, consisting of boulders and large rounded pebbles of quartzite and conglomerate, which are unmistakably derived from the Witwatersrand Beds, imbedded in an arenaceous matrix. These are very variable as regards the aggregation of the boulders and pebbles, passing by rapid gradation from densely pebbled conglomerates into sandstones in which pebbles are only sparsely scattered. The conglomerate boulders are sometimes auriferous: in some cases this has led to prospecting operations being undertaken under the mistaken idea that the boulders represented the outcrop of a permanent banket reef. Both breccias and 1 Molengraaff, 1904 b, p. 19. 2 Hatch, 1898, p. 94.

Molengraaff, 1903 a; Hatch, 1903 c; Corstorphine, 1904. boulder beds have occasionally a markedly schistose character, due to the development of talcose and chloritic minerals along secondary divisional or foliation planes, a result to be attributed, no doubt, to shearing.

The fact that the boulder beds are, to a large extent, made up of the debris of the Witwatersrand Series points to a considerable denudation of the latter after their elevation above sea-level and before the deposition of the Ventersdorp System. The existence of a great unconformity between the two series is indeed clearly shown by their stratigraphical relation; on the farm Ratzekaai's Kraal, west of Ventersdorp,

Fig. 33.—Section showing the unconformity between the Ventersdorp Series and the Witwatersrand Beds on Ratzekaai's Kraal near Ventersdorp.

for instance, the boulder beds can be seen with a dip of 5 to the west, lying on Lower Witwatersrand quartzites having a dip of 30 to the south (see Fig. 33). That the period to which the Ventersdorp System belongs was marked by great volcanic activity is evidenced in the enormous accumulations of lava, volcanic ash and breccia. But this activity must have been to some extent localised, so that while lava and fragmental rocks were being ejected in one place, sand and gravel were simultaneously accumulating elsewhere: only in some such way can the great diversity of the beds grouped together as the Ventersdorp System be explained. *Distribution of the Ventersdorp Beds*

The Klipriversberg Amygdaloid attains an enormous development in the Heidelberg district, forming the upper portion of the hills known as the Suikerboschrand, and extending to the Vaal River, the latter taking its course through it for a distance of twenty-five miles. South of the river it passes under the Ecca Series of the Karroo System. Near Vereeniging the river wash contains numerous agates which represent the residuum of the disintegration of the amygdaloid.

Fig. 34.—Diabase-breccia belonging to the Ventersdorp Series, Bezuidenhout valley.

East of Heidelberg the central portion of the HeidelbergGreylingstad syncline is to a great extent covered by masses of diabase of the amygdaloidal type. Volcanic breccias are associated with the flows, especially in the valley of the Suikerboschrand River,1 while Van Kolders Kop shows cherts in association with coarse brecciaB.

In the Bezuidenhout valley, near Johannesburg, and for some distance east of the Johannesburg-Pretoria railway, 1 Corstorphine, 1904.

both the diabase (there with large por-phyritic felspars) and the volcanic breccia occur. The outcrop of the latter rock is marked by a peculiar structure somewhat suggestive of sharks' teeth (see Fig. 34); this may be due to weathering along original bedding, flow, or shearing planes. The included fragments, as well as the cement, are chiefly of basic igneous material, but partially rounded pieces of quartzite are also occasionally found. The boulder beds are represented by a small outcrop near the Bezuidenhout homestead.

Perhaps the greatest superficial development of the Ventersdorp System is to be found in the Lichtenburg, Klerksdorp, Wolmaranstad and Bloemhof districts, the greater part of this area being covered by diabase and breccia. Molengraaff1 has especially referred to the occurrence of banded cherts and conglomerates on the farm Hartebeestfontein, to the west of Klerksdorp, and to beds containing boulders of auriferous conglomerate at Zendlingsfontein in the same district. He considers the so-called Vaal River Amygdaloid to be a part of this formation. The recent progress of the shaft-sinking at the Kimberley diamond mines has shown the presence of boulder beds beneath the quartzites and associated quartz-porphyries that underlie the amygdaloidal diabase. There can therefore be no doubt that all these beds belong, with the Vaal River amygdaloids, to the Ventersdorp System. At Kromdraai, north of Krugersdorp, Dbrffel2 has described as belonging to the Ventersdorp System a slaty conglomerate which must be at least 500 feet thick. The boulders of quartzite and conglomerate are derived from the Witwatersrand Series. The conglomerate underlies the Black Reef Series, and can be followed along its base across Tweefontein to Rietfontein, gradually changing to a 1 Molengraaff, 1903, p. 68.-Dorffel, 1904 «.

slaty rock without boulders. In the Marico district1 the Ventersdorp Beds (there also consisting of lavas, breccias and conglomerates) may be traced from Mafeking northward to a double-peaked hill lying north of the Dwarsberg and known to the natives as Zuni-Zuni.

Other occurrences of

Fig. 35.—Black Reef resting unconfonnably on Ventersdorp Series; Rietfontein (286), Kast of Johannesburg. The hammer-heads lie in the direction of the dip.

the Ventersdorp Beds which have been described are: on Rietfontein (No. 286),2 north of the East Rand, where the unconformity with the overlying Black Reef Series is well exposed (see Fig. 35); in the Venterskroon-Parys district (amygdaloidal type); at Hoopstad,3 in the Orange River 1 Hatch, 1904 a. 2 Corstorphine, 1904. 3 Molcngraaff.

Colony (conglomerate type); and at Stinkhoutboom, near Reitzburg, in the Orange River Colony, where, under the Black Reef Series, 500 feet of boulder beds are found lying on basic amygdaloidul lavas.1 The exposures at Ventersdorp have been described on p. 149. 1 Hatch. CHAPTER V THE POTCHEFSTROOM SYSTEM

Under the name Potchefstroom System it is proposed to group the Black Reef, the Dolomite and the Pretoria Series, as all three members are typically represented in the district whence the name is derived (see Fig. 36).

Recent observations have shown that the Black Reef quartzites and conglomerates are simply the basement beds of the Dolomite: that there is, in fact, a transition from a sandstone to a limestone facies. The beds of the overlying Pretoria Series are also quite conformable to the Dolomite. At the base of the Pretoria Series slate predominates, and in some localities it is of a banded character, not unlike that of the Hospital Hill Series.

The Black Reef Series

The Black Reef has also been named the Boschrand Series, from a small bush-clad range in the Klerksdorp district. It has, moreover, been called the Kromdraai Series, the Kantoor Sandstone and the Drakensberg or Berg Sandstone.

The series is usually quite insignificant, being often only a few feet in thickness; occasionally, however, it is more extensively developed, attaining in the Lydenburg district, according to

Molengraaff, an average thickness of 1000 feet.1 1 Molengraaff, 1904 b. It consists of dense hard quartzites, usually of a dark colour, often with a conglomerate or an arkose at the base. In some places the upward passage from the quartzite to the dolomite is marked by beds of slate: thus Dorffel1 has described slates 100 feet thick occupying this position on the farm Kromdraai, north of Krugersdorp, to which he gave the name Kromdraai or Tweefontein Slates.

The conglomerate seams at or near the bottom of the quartzite are generally rich in iron pyrites and sometimes carry gold. The pebbles composing them are usually quite small, and consist chiefly of quartz, but jaspery or cherty pebbles also occur. The matrix is darkcoloured, owing to its pyritic constituent, and hence the name "Black Reef." Nodules of pyrites also occur. The gold content is extremely erratic: it is true that patches have been found sufficiently rich to repay working; but on the whole the Black Reef has had an unfortunate mining history, and has consequently acquired an undesirable reputation.

Owing to its unconformity to all the known older formations, the Black Reef Series rests on the most diverse rocks: the Granite, the Witwatersrand Series and the Ventersdorp Beds being all found directly beneath it in different localities.

1 Dorffel, 1904 a.

The Dolomite Series

The Dolomite Series has been designated by some authors the Malmani Dolomite and by others the Lydenburg Series. It corresponds to the Ngami Beds of Beehuanaland and probably to the Cango Beds of the Cape Colony.

Phoio Nicol Brown.

Fig. 37.—Chert Bands in the Dolomite on the Blyde River, near Grootfontein Spruit, Pilgrim's Rest.

The magnesian limestone which constitutes the bulk of this series is a rock of characteristic appearance. When fresh it is of a bluish colour-but on weathering it acquires a whitish-brown crust. Its curiously wrinkled or corrugated surface (see Fig. 39), resembling

an elephant's skin. has earned for it among the Dutch the name of Olifantsklip (elephant rock). The irregularities of the surface are caused by differential weathering: the softer calcareous portions having been removed by solution, the harder, more siliceous or cherty nodules and ribs are thereby brought into prominence. The colour of the crust is due to the presence of a hydrated oxide of manganese (wad), which is produced by the oxidation of the carbonate of manganese in the limestone.

Chert layers are common (see Fig. 37): they appear at the outcrop as smooth, hard, white masses resembling compact quartzites; and sometimes boulders of this material are the only indication of the presence of the formation. The chert layers occur most frequently in the upper beds of the series; but a brecciated chert is often found at its base.

Under the microscope the rock is seen to consist of minute calcite or dolomite crystals in close aggregation. Chemically the rock is a magnesian limestone. According to an analysis made by Mr. G. T. Prior of the Mineralogical Department of the British Museum,1 a typical specimen had the following composition:—

CaO..... 29-61
MgO..... 19-71
FeO..... 1-35
MnO..... 118
Si02..... 0-94
C02 and H20.... 46 69 99-48
Sp. gr. 2-88.

From the above analysis the following percentage proportion of carbonates is obtained:— 1 Hatch, 1898, p. 89.

CaC03..... 52-87
MgC03..... 41-39
FeC03..217
MnC03...1-99

From dolomite of the above composition, practically every gradation to a purely siliceous chert can be found. A

Fig. 38.—Dolomite with Chert, Grootfontein Spruit, Pilgrim's Rest.

siliceous specimen analysed by Dahms gave the following result1:—

Si02..... 62-16
CaO..... 9-07

MgO..... 301 84-24

Various silicates of lime and manganese also occur. For instance,[2] tremolite is a common constituent in radial [1] Dahms, 1891, p. 118. Jorissen, 1904, p. 34; Hatch, 1898. aggregates of needles, especially where the dolomite has been altered by dyke intrusion. The hydrated oxide of manganese known as wad is often abundantly produced in the weathering of the rock.

Economically the Dolomite is of the utmost importance as the great water-carrier of the country. Owing to the comparatively soluble character of the rock, channels and caverns are formed which in many places serve as reservoirs of underground water and, where connected, as routes for the passage of subterranean rivers. Surface springs are often produced where dykes of syenite dam up this underground water. From the overflow of the hidden reservoirs nearly all the perennial streams of the Transvaal have their origin. The Mooi, the Klip, the Malmani, the Marico, the Molopo, the Notwani, the Harts, Crocodile, Aapies and Pienaars Rivers, and the Schoon Spruit may be quoted as examples.

Some of the caverns have been made accessible, and are remarkable for beautiful aragonite stalactites and stalagmites, which have been formed by a redeposition of the dissolved carbonate of lime: as examples, Wonderfontein north-east of Frederikstad, Sterkfontein north of Krugersdorp, and Godwaan River on the Delagoa line may be quoted.[1] Unfortunately these occurrences of pure carbonate, having been largely exploited for the manufacture of a high-grade lime, no longer present the wonderful sight they did when first opened. The calcareous sinter which forms the floor of the caves often contains fossil bones, and would, on systematicexploration, no doubt yield interesting results.

The so-called "wonder-holes" (Wondergats) may be mentioned in this connection. They owe their origin to the subsidence of the roof of an underground cavern.

[1] The historical caves at Makanans Gat, where the Makapan Kaffirs after a long resistance were finally exterminated by the Boers in 1854, are also in the Dolomite. and are comparable to the "swallow-holes" that occur in the Carboniferous Limestone of England. According to Mr. David Draper,[1] the "Baviaan Gat," near Ottoshoop in the Malmani district, has at the surface a diameter of 100 yards, narrowing to 60 yards at a depth of 120 feet. At this depth there is a pool of water which has been plumbed to 105 feet. A similar *Wondergat* occurs near Donkerpoort in the northern Transvaal. Another described by Mr. A. L. Hall[2] on the farm Rietvlei south of Pretoria consists of a nearly circular opening with perpendicular walls, the diameter being about 40 feet and the depth about 30 feet. Mr. Hall has no doubt, from the disturbed character of the rocks at the opening, that this hole was formed by the falling in of the roof of a cave.

It is a remarkable fact that the Dolomite, which, from its enormous development and considerable thickness (1500 to 5000 feet), was most probably a marine deposit, has yielded no organic remains—in striking contrast to the rich fauna of the Silurian, Carboniferous and Triassic limestones of Europe. The siliceous chert layers are also devoid of fossil remains, notwithstanding the fact that these most probably originated from the accumulation of the siliceous skeletons (spicules, frustules, etc.) of such organisms as sponges or diatoms. Re-crystallisation has, however, destroyed every trace of organic structure.

The only reference to fossils is a statement by Cohen[2] that he found traces of crinoids and brachiopoda *(Orthis* and *Chonetes)*; but the fact has never been confirmed by subsequent observation.

[1] Draper, 1894, p. 563. [1] Hall, 1904, p. 41. [3] Dahms, 1891, p. 118. *Igneous Hocks in the Dolomite Series*

Besides the dolerite dykes of Karroo age which of course traverse the Dolomite in places, dykes of a syenitic rock are common. A series of parallel dykes striking north and south cuts

through the belt of Dolomite which runs parallel to, and south of, the Witwatersrand. The best known of these is a syenite-porphyry on the farm Wonderfontein (No. 40) in the Potchefstroom district. This rock consists of porphyritic crystals of orthoclase, plagioclase and augite imbedded in a granophyric ground-mass of quartz and felspar; in addition, nepheline has been recently discovered by Molengraaff.[1] It is quarried for use as a building-stone.

Recent boring operations on the extreme east Rand" have disclosed the existence of numerous intrusive sheets of red and grey syenite. They are remarkably persistent, being found at practically the same horizon in boreholes many miles apart. Varying in thickness from 10 to 125 feet, the several sheets aggregate from 100 to 180 feet. Under the microscope they are seen to consist of a holocrystalline aggregate mainly of felspar, in short prismatic crystals that have become slightly reddish and turbid through kaolinisation. A considerable proportion of the felspar crystals shows lamellar twinning, and these consequently belong to the plagioclase group; but orthoclase is on the whole predominant. Quartz is subordinate and interstitial, having been the last mineral to crystallise from the original magma. Occasionally there is a tendency towards the formation of micro-pegmatite. Ferro-magnesian constituents are represented by white and greenish-brown micas, green hornblende, and patches of a green mineral (chlorite) which has no doubt been formed as an alteration product from hornblende or augite. The large amount of plagioclase felspar present in this rock brings it near to the diorite family; but the fact that orthoclase is on the whole preponderant justifies its classification among the syenites.

Near the junction with the dolomite, the syenite is more finely crystalline, the felspar crystals becoming microlitic, until at the actual junction the rock has a crypto-crystalline character, and in one instance (borehole on the farm Modderfontein, No. 46) is distinctly spherulitic, apparently having consolidated as a glass, which subsequently became partially devitrified. At both upper and lower contacts the dolomite is "marmorised," that is, the more compact, dark-coloured dolomite is converted into a white marble.

Distribution and Thickness of the Black Reef and

Dolomite Series

In the Witwatersrand district the Black Reef and Dolomite Series are exposed on both limbs of the great anticline, the denudation of which has exposed the Granite and the Witwatersrand Beds. Consequently a section taken, say from Vereeniging, through Johannesburg to Pretoria, shows the Dolomite with its basement Black Reef Series outcropping along the valley of the Klip River to the abandoned Black Reef mines south of the Klipriversberg, with westerly, south-westerly and southerly dips; while north of the granite the series appears at Brakfontein, and extends thence to just south of Pretoria, with a northerly dip, this northern outcrop constituting, west of Pretoria, the Kalkheuvel range.

The northern and southern belts of Dolomite circle round the *massif* of older rocks, uniting on the west about halfway between Krugersdorp and Frederikstad, at winch point the anticlinal arch is intact. Farther to the west an outcrop of the older beds separates the series again into two belts— a northern extending to Ventersdorp and thence through Lichtenburg and Ottoshoop into Bechuanaland, and a southern passing Frederikstad, leaving Potchefstroom on

Fig. 39.—Dolomite Outcrop at Klip River at Vereeniging.

the east and crossing the Vaal River just east of Klerksdorp. Along this line of country the Black Reef Series appears as a bush-clad ridge, locally known as the Boschrand.

Frequently the quartzites of the Black Reef Series rest as an outlying cap on the older beds. This is especially evident on the Avest Rand, where outliers occur on both Lower and Upper Witwatersrand Beds. In such places the Dolomite has been removed by denuda-

tion, the basement quartzites alone remaining by reason of their superior resistance to the disintegrating and dissolving influences of the weather.

On the east side of the JohannesburgPretoria *massif* of older rocks, the Dolomite outcrops do not unite, being separated by a narrow neck of the former between Springs and Withoek. Eastward, the northern belt passes under the Ecca Series of the Karroo System, a few miles east of Springs; while the southern belt also passes under the same series at Vereeniging. The Parys-Venterskroon *massif* is surrounded by Dolomite, which is no doubt connected under the overlviny Pretoria Beds with the main outcrop of the formation on the north.

In the Marico district the Dolomite and Black Reef Series, together with the overlying Pretoria Beds and the underlying Ventersdorp System, constitute a great syncline, having a breadth of eighty to ninety miles and stretching from a line between Ventersdorp and Ottoshoop to north of the Dwarsberg range near the Bechuanaland border (see Fig. 40). The Black Reef quartzites are exposed south of Ventersdorp, and are again seen immediatelv south of the Zuni-Zuni range, north of the Dwarsberg, where they form a low range of bush-clad hills, resembling the Boschrand of the Klerksdorp district. The Dolomite is well developed south of Zeerust, forming the country-rock of the Malmani quartz veins. North of the syncline it occurs between the Dwarsberg on the south and the Zuni-Zuni range on the north, in a tract of country known, from its rough and stony character, as the Klipveld. This part of the country is rather flat, with the exception of occasional peaks like Apjaterskop, which rises to over 1000 feet above the plain. The Dolomite of the Klipveld trends east and west, dipping to the south under the Pretoria Beds of the Dwarsberg. Eastward it follows the course of the Witfontein Range, extending towards the Waterberg. Westward it crosses the Notwani River and passes into Bechuanaland. It then turns southwest, extending across the CapeBul-

awayo Railway. Near Lobatsi station it re-crosses the railway, and enters the Transvaal on Moilo's Location, whence it runs south-east to the Malmani goldfield. Mr. Holmes,1 who has recently examined the country to the west of Vryburg, states that the Dolomite and Black Reef Series cover a large area, extending southward from Vryburg to Taungs and Kuruman.

The Dolomite of the Campbell Rand and the Kaap Plateau is a continuation south-westward of the same series. Underlying the Campbell Rand Dolomite conformably is a series of quartzites which Stow termed the Keis Series, and which therefore must be taken as correlative with the Black Reef Series of the Transvaal.

In the north-eastern Transvaal there is a great development of the Black Reef and Dolomite Series. They extend from Pietpotgietersrust in a half circle through Pilgrim's Rest and Lydenburg to a point half-way between Barberton and Carolina, where they are covered by the Karroo System. Under this covering the Dolomite no doubt unites with the northern belt of the same formation, which is last seen a 1 Holmes, 1905.

few miles east of Springs, where it becomes hidden by the Karroo Beds. The linear extension of the series in this part of the country must therefore be upwards of two hundred miles. The abrupt escarpment of the Black Reef quartzites lying unconformably on the older beds develops in many places into prominent hill ranges, for example, in the Makapan Hills, the Chunie range and the Drakensberg.

At Lydenburg the whole succession from the Black Reef to the Pretoria Series can be studied. Mr. Nicol Brown' has published a section compiled from information obtained at Pilgrim's Rest and in the gorges of the Blyde River. According to this author the Black Reef Series (" Lower or Berg Sandstone") has a thickness of 110 feet: it is succeeded by 2400 feet of Dolomite, the latter being overlaid by 1700 feet of the Pretoria Series ("Upper Sandstone and Shales "). The State Geologist in his Report for the year 1897"' gives another section of the same beds, extending from Belfast through the Duivel's Kantoor (Kaapsche Hoop) to the Godwaan River. In this he estimates the Black Reef Series (Kantoor Sandstone) at 90 feet, the Dolomite Series at 900 feet, and the overlying Pretoria Beds at 4000 feet. The escarpment of the Duivel's Kantoor is formed by Black Reef resting on the granite and associated igneous rocks of the De Kaap valley. The summit of the Kantoor at Kaapsche Hoop shows the Black Reef quartzites lying almost horizontally and weathered into the most fantastic shapes. Throughout the entire district the gently undulating outlines of the dolomite hills afford a sharp contrast with the abrupt escarpments made by the underlying Black Reef and overlying Pretoria quartzites.

According to Schenck,3 Dolomite of identical character, 1 Brown, 1896.

J Molengraaff, 1898.

3 Schenck,1888. and presumably of the same age as that of the Transvaal, occurs in the Harib and on the Hanami Plateau in Great Namaqualand. *Ore Deposits in the Dolomite and Black Reef Series*

Reference has already been made to the auriferous character of the thin bed of conglomerate which occurs at the base of the Black Reef Series: in places its gold-content has been such as to raise hopes of profitable mining operations; it has, however, been of too irregular and patchy a character to permit of continuous profitable development, although in some cases *(e.g.* Orion, Minerva, Midas, Eastleigh) profits have been made and even dividends paid, while the rich " patch" held out.

At Kromdraai, ten miles north of Krugersdorp, an auriferous quartz vein is interbedded with the quartzites of the Black Reef Series. It has been described in detail by DdrffeL1 According to this author, the vein was formed by the filling of a fissure along a thin band of slates, intercalated between two beds of quartzite overlying the basal conglomerate. The vein-filling consists partly of a blue laminated quartz with stringers of iron and arsenical pyrites, partly of a milky-white compact quartz with irreg-

ular bunches of the same minerals. The gold is associated with the pyrites. In some places galena occurs, and then the silver-content is higher than the gold. Associated minerals are barytes and siderite.

Quartz veins are of frequent occurrence in the Dolomite, and many are gold-bearing. The best known are the bedded veins of the Lydenburg district (Theta and Sherwell's Reef) and the vertical fissure veins of Malmani in the Marico district. The auriferous quartz veins of Malmani strike roughly parallel to the bedding, namely, from north-northwest to south-south-east, and have a vertical dip. They can be traced from Malmani northward into Ikalafyn's Location. The vein-filling is either quartz or brecciated dolomite cemented by quartz, or again brecciated quartz cemented by carbonate of lime. Besides gold, a great variety of minerals is found in the veins, including the sulphides, carbonates and silicates of zinc, lead and copper, together with the hydrated oxides of manganese. Several of the veins have been worked at Malmani for gold and not always without success; but the difficulties caused by the great volume of water found below the 150-foot level brought the struggling gold-field to an early end.

Small deposits (pockets) of galena, in some cases argentiferous, are frequent in the Dolomite. Oxides of manganese (wad, pyrolusite, etc.) are often found in considerable abundance near the outcrops. The latter are no doubt derived from the carbonate of manganese, which, as mentioned above, is associated with the carbonates of lime and magnesia of the country-rock.

The disintegrated and decomposed lower beds of the Dolomite have been worked for gold at Barrett's Berlin, near Kaapsche Hoop. According to the State Geologist's Report, "a dark brown tufaceous earth, rich in iron, with decomposed pyrites, is mined in big open quarries," and treated for gold by the direct cyanide process.1 1 Report of the State Geologist, *Trans. Geol. Soc. of HoiUh Africa,* vol. iv. (1898), p. 135.

CHAPTER VI

Potchefstroom System *(continued)*
The Pretoria Series

As already pointed out (p. 155), the Pretoria Beds succeed the Dolomite conformably. This series, known also as Magaliesberg and Gatsrand Beds, consists of quartzites, flagstones and shales, with many dykes and sheets of basic igneous rock. The various members of the series can be well studied in the two parallel belts of country that constitute the crests of the opposing limbs of the great Witwatersrand anticline, to which reference has already been made. Of these the northern comprises, near Pretoria, three parallel ranges, namely, the Magaliesberg, the Witwatersberg or Daspoort range and the Timeball range — all composed of beds dipping to the north; while the southern belt is distinguished by only one range of importance, namely, the Gatsrand, with beds dipping to the south. The outcrop of the northern belt has a minimum width of seven miles, the dip varying from 5 to 20; while in the southern belt the beds occupy some 15 miles of country before the Dolomite is re-encountered (in the Venterskroon district), the average dip being much less. A large portion of the latter area is occupied by outcrops of basic igneous rock.

On the hill ranges a gentle slope marks the dip, while an abrupt escarpment faces the axis of the anticline. The escarpments, or "kranzes," as they are termed locally, are generally formed by thick beds of hard quartzite, with a steep talus slope below: this is especially characteristic of the Magaliesberg range, whose bold mural crest forms a prominent feature of the landscape from Pretoria to Rustenburg, a distance of 70 miles. In the valleys separating the hills, soft shales and intercalated basic igneous sheets are found. Thus the distribution of hill and valley depends, as is often the case in the South African landscape, on differences in the power of resistance to the forces of denudation: topographical features being governed by geological conditions.

The quartzites of the Pretoria Series consist of grains of quartz cemented by secondary silica. Although they sometimes appear as a hard, glassy, compact rock, the quartzites are usually of a looser texture than in the Witwatersrand Beds. Some outcrops contain much magnetite and haematite, the percentage of iron often being as high as sixty.

Intermediate between the quartzites and the shales there are rocks which split easily into slabs, and may therefore be termed flagstones. These are of a dark grey to blue colour, and are largely quarried for paving material.

Molengraaff has estimated the thickness of the series near Pretoria to be as follows:—
Valley north of the Magaliesberg.. 330 feet
Magaliesberg..... 1300 „
Magaliesberg valley.... 2600 „
Daspoort range..... 800 „
Valley west of Pretoria.... 2100 „
Timeball range..... 1300 „ 8430 feet
In the original the measurements are in metres.

The following section, given by Mr. A. L. Hall (Geological

Survey Report, 1904, p. 39), is from the neighbourhood of the farms Zwavelpoort and Donkerpoort, 10 miles south-east of Pretoria:—
Upper Quartzite (Magalieslierg Quartzite), with intrusive dialiase sheets; 1 oOO feet.
Shale and Slates, in jected by numerous dialiase sheets; 530 feet.
Middle Quartzite (Dasloort Quartzite).
Diabase (a thick sheet underlying the Middle Quartzite).
Shales and Slates, injected by subordinate dialiase sheets; 320 feet.
Lower Quartzite (Timeball Quartzite).
Shales (a thin development of soft shales).

The total thickness is estimated at not less than 10,000 feet.

Igneous Rocks associated with the Pretoria Beds

As already pointed out, the shales and quartzites of the Pretoria Series are intimately associated with interbedded *J* igneous rocks, which are chiefly of a basic character, and consist of various types of diabase or dolerite. Some are

fine-grained and are seen under the microscope to consist of a plexus of felspar microlites with interstitial augite granules —in fact approximating to a basalt type; while coarser varieties are found to have the ophitic structure characteristic of the dolerites. Intrusive rocks, occurring in sheets and dykes, are common. Mr. Kynaston 1 says "they vary from thin sills of about twenty feet in thickness up to extensive sheets with a thickness of several hundred feet." In places these basic rocks are replaced by rocks of a more acid character (felsites), into which they appear to pass gradually. Thus surrounding the Premier diamond mine there occurs a pinkish rock consisting of plagioclase felspar, augite, with micropegmatitic intergrowth of quartz and felspar. This rock has much resemblance to, and is perhaps genetically 1 Kynaston, 1904, p. 5. connected with, the "red granite," which will be described presently.

The metamorphism of the Pretoria Beds at their contact with these intrusions has been studied at several places. At Waterval Boven, Molengraaff1 observed that the shales are baked and otherwise metamorphosed at both contacts. The quartzite does not show as much alteration as the shale, but at Meintjeskop,2 near Pretoria, the former, in contact with a diabase intrusion, has been hardened and charged with small crystals of epidote and actinolite; and Mr. Mellor3 describes a case on Onverwacht (No. 534), where the quartzite, in addition to being bleached and hardened, has developed a marked columnar structure.

Syenite dykes, similar in petrographical character to the sheets which have been described as occurring in the dolomite, are found cutting through the Pretoria Beds. Such a dyke forms a prominent feature of the landscape in the valley of the Magalies River, 40 miles west of Pretoria: it strikes north and south and appears to be connected with the well-known dykes of porphyritic syenite which occur on the farms Wonderfontein (No. 653) and Wonderfontein (No. 685), half-way between Krugersdorp and Frederikstad.

In some cases the dykes are full of fragments derived from the rocks traversed by them. An example of this occurs at Deerde Poort, five miles northeast of Pretoria:4 in this rock the fragments are so numerous as to impart the appearance of a true breccia, in which the igneous material plays the role of a cement. Another example is mentioned by Mr. Mellor 5 on Onverwacht (No. 534), where the igneous 1 Molengraaff, 1898 *a*. 2 Molengraaff, 1901, p. 46.
3 Mellor, 1904 *b*, p. 10. 4 Molengraaff, 1901, p. 57. 5 Mellor, 1904 , p. 10. rock over a considerable area is full of brecciated fragments of the quartzite, ranging from half an inch to six inches in diameter. *Distribution of the Pretoria Series*

East of Pretoria, the beds of the series spread out until their outcrop extends over a distance of nearly 25 miles, this increase iD the width of the outcrop being accounted for partly by a diminution of dip and partly by a series of step faults which cause a repetition of the beds. East of Van der Merwe station on the Delagoa Bay Railway, the series begins to be covered up on its northern margin by the unconformably overlying Waterberg Sandstone. Near Balmoral station the eastward extension is lost to view under the Karroo System. The last place where the most southern outcrop is exposed is on Moabsvelden, 23 miles east of Springs. West of Pretoria the series extends uninterruptedly as far as Zeerust, which lies 140 miles from the capital. At Zeerust it has already acquired a northerly trend, running more or less parallel to the Bechuanaland Railway for a distance of about 40 miles. South of Ramutsa the outcrop turns eastward again, constituting then the east and west range of the D wars berg. There the dip is southerly, so that with the northerly dip of the Zeerust Hills a true syncline is formed. The Zeerust Hills consist of a series of parallel step-like ranges, each with an abrupt escarpment to the south, and to the north a gentle slope corresponding to the dip, which is there about 10. The beds of the Dwarsberg range dip south at about 20. The total width of the syncline as far as the Pretoria Beds are concerned is about 60 miles. Its central portion is occupied by intrusive igneous rocks of ultra-basic character (peridotites, pyroxenites, etc.), belonging to the Plutonic Series of the Bush veld, which will be dealt with later. From the Dwarsberg the Pretoria Series, trending north-eastward, follows the Witfontein range, where the beds are repeated by step-faulting (see Fig. 41). Farther east, and south of the Zand River, a large patch of Pretoria Quartzites forms the Elandsberg and Boshof Mountains. These quartzites can be traced eastward to the foot of the Rooiberg, and southward to the Aapies River.1

South of the Rand the Pretoria Beds attain a considerable development in the Gatsrand, which extends

Fig. 41.—Sections through the Witfonteinberg in the Eustenburg district, showing the repetition of the Pretoria Beds and the Dolomite by step-faulting. Section AB represents a distance of 14 miles; Section CD represents a distance of 9 miles. After G. G. Holmes.

in an east and west direction from near Potchefstroom to a point near Klip River station on the old Johannesburg Yereeniging Railway. At this point the hills are bent sharply to the south, striking towards Vereeniging, near which town the Pretoria Beds finally pass under the coal-measures of the Karroo System. At the western extremity of the Gatsrand, the outcrop of the beds turns to the south-west: passing Potchefstroom, which lies on them, it crosses the Vaal River, finally disappearing under the coalmeasures at the Wilge River colliery. The range of hills which forms the outermost wall of the Venterskroon sold 1 Communicated by Mr. Holmes. field constitutes the southern limit of this outcrop of Pretoria Beds.

In the north-eastern Transvaal the Pretoria Series forms the highest beds of the Drakensberg range in the Lydenburg district, which are known there as the "Upper Sandstones": in the section of the Blyde valley given by Mr. Nicol Brown, 1700 feet of these beds are noted. Molengraaff, in a section taken

along the Delagoa Bay line, east of Belfast, describes the Pretoria Beds as consisting of frequent alternations of quartzite, shale, slates and diabase, the shale and slate being altered at the contact with the diabase into hornfels and silicified slate. The beds are well exposed in the upper portion of the Elands valley; and their sequence has been found by Molengraaff to be identical with that of the Pretoria section. He puts the total thickness of the Pretoria Beds in this section at 4200 feet.

On p. 166 reference was made to the dolomite of the Campbell Rand and Kaap Plateau. These beds are overlaid conformably by a series of quartzites, slates and jasper rocks, to which the term Griqua Town Series has been applied. The position of the latter shows them to be correlative with the Pretoria Series of the Transvaal.

Ore Deposits in the Pretoria Series

In the Pretoria Beds there is a variety of ore deposits: these consist of (1) interbedded deposits of iron-ores and (2) true veins carrying, either alone or in association, ores of gold, silver, lead, copper and cobalt.

As an example of the bedded iron-ore deposits, a sandstone heavily charged with magnetite, which occurs on the northern slope of the Timeball range, south of Pretoria, may be quoted. Molengraaff1 has described a similar occurrence in the Elands valley, near Waterval Boven, at about the same horizon. Thin seams of haematite are found in ferruginous shales belonging to the Series on Ikalafyn's Location, some 12 miles west of Zeerust; and Mr. Holmes2 has observed beds of haematite several feet thick in the lowest shales of the Witfontein range, in the Rustenburg district.

Auriferous quartz veins in the Pretoria Series have been prospected in many localities, unfortunately without much permanent success. Some of the earliest work was done on farms lying to the west of Krugersdorp, *e.g.* Koesterfontein (No. 108) and Blaauwbank (No. 104). More recent prospecting has been carried out on veins traversing the Magaliesberg and the adjoining Moet val-

ley, 25 miles west of Pretoria, on Scheerpoort, Remhoogte, Broederstroom and other farms. Both strike and cross veins are found; in all cases, however, the dip is steep. The vein material is a white quartz, filling fissures of an irregular character: here pinching to small stringers, there swelling out to big bodies. The gold-contents are very variable, being limited to patches.

Vein deposits containing lead and copper ores occur in many localities in the Pretoria, Rustenburg and Marico districts. In the Pretoria district silver-lead veins have been opened up and exploited to some extent; but at the present moment the mines are dormant. The veins worked in the Willows Silver mine, near Hatherley, and the Transvaal Silver mine are best known: both strike east and west in the slates that lie between the quartzites of the Magaliesberg range and those composing the Daspoort range. The ore of the Willows mine consists of copper pyrites, pyrites, tetrahedrite and copper carbonates in a 1 Molengraaff, 1898 *a*. Personally communicated.

N gangue of carbonate of iron (siderite), the vein being associated with a dyke of diabase. In the Transvaal Silver mine there is, in addition to the above-mentioned minerals, a notable proportion of galena: the silver occurs as a constituent partly of tetrahedrite, partly of galena.

At Edendale, 4 miles north of Hatherley, a vein is worked in which galena occurs in conjunction with blende, cerussite, pyromorphite and calamine, the three last named being decomposition products. The gangue material is mainly quartz and calcite. The cobalt lodes of Eenzaamheid (No. 421), near Balmoral station, on the Middelburg line, are, according to Dorffel,1 in Magaliesberg Quartzites, which have been invaded by gabbro intrusions. The veins are irregular in width, varying from two or three inches to thirty inches or more. The gangue consists of felspar, hornblende and chalcedony, the first-named mineral forming the centre of the vein, with hornblende on one side and chalcedony on the other. The main lode has a north-east and south-west strike; while secondary veins which cross it have an east and west strike. The cobalt occurs as smaltite, irregularly dispersed through the gangue or in small bunches. Nickel is associated with the cobalt in the proportion of one part of nickel to eight or ten of cobalt. Molybdenite is present as an incrustation; and in the more decomposed parts of the lode erythrite (cobalt bloom) is found.

1 Dorffel, 1904, p. 93. CHAPTER VII THE WATERBERG SYSTEM

The Waterberg System consists of a great thickness of sandstones and grits, with occasional conglomerates, separated from the Pretoria Series by a marked unconformity. Cohen1 appears to have been the first to draw attention to this formation, although he did not determine its position in the stratigraphical succession. He described it as a red sandstone, resembling the "Buntsandstein" of Germany, and mentioned its occurrence at Noord Drift and Buiskop. He also noted the presence of conglomerates containing flat quartz pebbles. Attention was again drawn to the formation by Mr. Harger2 in 1897, who described the occurrence of a "red sandstone," hitherto undescribed, in the Pretoria district. Its widespread occurrence in the Waterberg district (Palala plateau) was described by Molengraaff, who gave it the appropriate name of "Waterberg Sandstone." Its geological relations have been recently studied in some detail by E. T. Mellor,3 E. Jorissen4 and G. G. Holmes.5

The sandstones are of a brownish-red to purple colour. They often have a remarkable degree of false-bedding, and show distinct ripple-marks. Conglomerate beds occur at several horizons. These are often very coarse, being made up 1 Gotz, 1886. 2 Harger, 1897, p. 107. 3 Mellor, 1904 *a*. 4 Jorissen, 1904. 5 Holmes, 1904. of boulders of over a foot in diameter. In many places the base of the series is formed by conglomerates and breccias, knit to a hard rock by a ferruginous cementing material.

Pretoria Shales Waterberg Conglomerates & Sandstones

S. 27W. DIP 20 S.67W. (TRUE BEAKING

DIP 10 N. 27E. N-27E.

Sola of Peci

0 jo i 4Q. fro, 8p t lyo

Fig. 42.—Section on left bank of Wilge River. 1. Alluvium. 2. Hard greenish and purple black shales (Pretoria Series). 3. Conglomerate, 5 feet. 4. Brown sandstone, 8 inches. 5. Conglomerate, 3 feet. 6. Purple sandstone. 7. Conglomerate. 3, 4, 5, 6, 7, Waterberg Series. After E. T. Mellor.

The pebbles and boulders consist largely of cmartzite, shale and diabase derived from the Pretoria Series; but rocks coming from other formations also occur, as, for example, older conglomerates, banded ferruginous slate, jasper and felsites.

Fig. 43.—Section across kopje J mile S.W. of Balmoral station. 1. Quartzite of Pretoria Series dipping away from observer at 23 N. 21 E. 2. Breccia of angular fragments of quartzite in brown sandy matrix. 3. Coarse soft sandstone. 4. Hard brown quartzite with black bands rich in magnetite (dip 10-12 due E.). After E. T. Mellor.

Scattered pebbles are found in the sandstones separating the conglomerate zones. Shales occur, but only in thin bands. Beds of impure iron-ore, chiefly magnetite, are occasionally found, especially near the Crocodile River.

With regard to the relation of the Waterberg System to the underlying Potchefstroom System, Mr. Mellor has described two sections at Wilge River and at Balmoral (see Figs. 42, 43, 44) which clearly demonstrate an unconformity. In the Wilge River section the line of junction between the two systems is well exposed, and Waterberg sandstone and conglomerate are seen dipping at 10 in a direction north 27 east, and resting on an eroded surface formed by the upturned Pretoria Beds, dipping at an angle of 22' in a direction south 67 west. In the Balmoral section the flat-lying Waterberg Sandstone is seen resting on Pretoria Quartzites, dipping at an angle of 20 to 25" in a direction north 24 east. The immediate base of the systems in these localities is a breccia consisting of fragments of hard white quartzite in a brown sandy matrix. The quartzitic

fragments are identical in character with, and doubtless have been derived from, the Pretoria quartzites on which the breccia lies. Other evidence of the unconformity is not wanting: Mr. Holmes1 has pointed out that in the northern Transvaal the Waterberg System is found resting directly on the old granite and schists; again, the 1 Holmes, 1904, p. 56.

Zoutpansberg consists of Waterberg Sandstone which, on the northern as well as on the southern slope, lies directly on the old granite.

The occurrence of coarse breccias and conglomerates at the base of the Waterberg System indicates, as pointed out by Mr. Mellor,1 torrential origin and deposition close to the shore-line of the Waterberg sea. The general character of the formation points to rapid sedimentation in waters affected by strong but variable currents. To this must be ascribed the constant occurrence of false-bedding.

Igneous Intrusions in the Waterberg System

Dykes of igneous rock (diabase and felsite) are of frequent occurrence in the Waterberg Sandstone of the Palala plateau, being especially common in the Waterberg range itself, where, according to Mr. Holmes, dykes are so frequent "that it is impossible to travel more than a mile or so in any direction without encountering igneous rock."

Distribution and Thickness of the Waterberg System

The Waterberg Sandstone is found covering an enormous extent of country in the northern Transvaal. In the Waterberg district, from the Zwagershoek Mountains on the west and Warm Baths on the east, to the Blaauwberg, a distance of over 100 miles, it extends in uninterrupted continuity over the Palala plateau. This plateau, which is traversed by the Palala River, has a mean elevation of 4800 feet; but it rises in places to peaks of greater altitude, for example at Hanglip and Geelhout. Both on the north and south it is bounded by escarpments, known in the south 1 Mellor, 1904 *b*, p. 17.

as the Zand River Hills, and in the north

as the Blaauwberg and Macabene Hills.

Besides this main occurrence there are several large outliers: for instance, the area that extends on the north side of the Delagoa Bay Railway, from the Elands River to near Middelburg, a distance of over 40 miles, the breadth being about 15 miles; the area formed by the Zoutpansberg; and again a broad belt which lies on the Limpopo River east and west of Rhodes Drift, and probably extends for some considerable distance into Rhodesia.

The Matsap Series of quartzites and conglomerates which Stow described in Griqualand West as lying unconformably on the Griqua Town Series (Pretoria Series), must represent a southern development of the Waterberg System of the Transvaal; and, as will be shown later, there is good reason for regarding the Table Mountain Series of southern Cape Colony and Natal as being on the same geological horizon.

CHAPTER VIII THE IGNEOUS COMPLEX OF THE BUSHVELD

A Great and varied complex of igneous rocks has now to be described. They have on the whole a plutonic character, but in places are associated with rocks of undoubted volcanic origin. So far no locality has been discovered which can be definitely assigned as their centre of eruption, unless the crater-like depression known as the "Salt-pan," on the farm Zoutpan (No. 467), 25 miles north of Pretoria, can be considered as such. Cohen, who first described the geological character of the pan, pointed out its resemblance to the explosive craters or "Maaren" of the Eifel, although the volcanic ejectmenta which are usually found in the neighbourhood of the latter are completely absent in this case. The depression is almost perfectly circular; the bounding ridge, which consists of granite, sinks steeply to the flat bottom, the vertical distance being about 260 feet. The bottom is generally covered by water, which on evaporation yields a deposit consisting of chloride and carbonate of soda. Since Cohen's visit a borehole has been put down in the middle of the pan,[1] and the results obtained have proved the existence of a consider-able deposit of natron below the present surface. A section of the beds intersected is as follows:— 1 Under the supervision of one of the Authors.

Thickness.

Brine (sp. gr. 1-25, and containing 21-28 % of chloride

The presence of this deposit of carbonate and chloride of sodium to a depth of 200 feet, which is nearly 500 feet when reckoned from the top of the hollow, appears to strengthen the view that the pan is a result of volcanic action.

The igneous complex of the Bushveld extends from some 15 miles west of the Marico River eastward to a point 25 miles west of Lydenburg, a distance of over 250 miles; it has a mean width of, say, GO miles, and therefore covers an area of at least 15,000 square miles. It is probably much larger, however, since it can be seen outcropping between the Magalakwin River and the sources of the Matlabas, whence it extends northward to a point on the Palala River some 20 miles south of the northern boundary of the Transvaal.[1] It includes the Pilandsberg, the Zwartkoppie range, the Pyramids, Makapansberg, Bothasberg and numerous other 1 Holmes, 1904.

small kopjes and ridges lying north of the Magaliesberg and south of the Dwarsberg and Chunie ranges.

Comprised in it there is a great variety of roek-types, varying in chemical composition from acid to ultra-basic. They are apparently genetically related, being probably derived by a process of segregation from one original magma. At the extreme western end of the complex, in the Marico district, felspar-free ultra-basic rocks occur as peridotites and pyroxenites. Eastward, zones of gradually increasing acidity are traversed: first norites and gabbros, then nephelinesyenites, and finally "red granite," in which quartz is usually an abundant constituent. The " red granite," which derives its name from the prevalent red colour imparted to it by its felspathic constituent, extends over a large area in the eastern portion of the complex. It was first mentioned by Hi-ibner,[1] who, in 1872, traversed its outcrops near the Pilandsberg on his route from Rustenburg to Mashonaland: specimens collected by him were, many years later, described by Henderson." Molengraaff, who has suggested the name "Plutonic Series of the Bushveld" for the whole complex, regards it as a laccolitic, or rather batholitic, intrusion, between the Pretoria Series and the Waterberg Sandstone. Quite recently Mr. Mellor[3] has advanced evidence to show that the red granite invades the Waterberg Sandstone: in all probability, therefore, the main period of intrusion was posterior to the deposition of the latter; but since boulders and pebbles of a red felsite are of frequent occurrence in the basal conglomerates of the Waterberg System,[4] it is possible that there was more than one period of eruption.

A few of the main types of the rocks of the complex are selected here for detailed description.

Rocks of Acid Type

The " red granite " occurs frequently as a coarsely crystalline rock; but fine-grained and felsitic varieties are also found over large areas. In petrographic character it is clearly distinguishable from the Archaean granite: that it belongs to a later period of intrusion was noted by Hubner[1] as early as 1872, from the fact that he found, included in it, fragments of slate and of the older granite. The felspathic constituent is invariably kaolinised, appearing under the microscope as a reddish impellucid mass. Its optical determination is therefore difficult; it appears, however, to be orthoclase, with microperthite intergrowths of a plagioclase felspar (andesine). In some porphyritic varieties there are large reddish phenocrysts, usually twinned on the Carlsbad type. Henderson suggests that the felspar is an anorthoclase. In a specimen from the neighbourhood of the old powder factory—on the farm Leeuwfontein (No. 320), not Hatherley as he has it—Henderson succeeded in isolating and analysing this felspar, and found that it had the following composition:— 1 A. Hiibner, 1872. Molengraalf was therefore scarcely correct in stating, in the

State Geologist's Report for 1898, that in none of the early descriptions of the Transvaal is there " any distinction made as regards age between this red granite and the granite occurring so abundantly elsewhere in this State, such as, for instance, between Pretoria and Johannesburg and in the Low Country."

Under the microscope it showed polysynthetic twinning, and an extinction angle of 9 to 12, which is somewhat higher than previously observed in anorthoclase. There can be little doubt that the rock in which this felspar occurs, though poor in quartz, is only a variation from the normal type of the red granite. On account of its poverty in quartz, Henderson1 regarded it as an amphibole-pyroxenesyenite and named it hatherlite; but Lacroix terms it a monzonite.

Quartz occurs in micro-pegmatitic intergrowth with the felspar, and every gradation between this and true spherulitic structure appears to exist. The amount of quartz is always most variable: it may predominate to the almost complete exclusion of the felspathic element, producing a granular quartz-mica rock (greisen),2 which by itself would scarcely be recognised as of igneous origin; on the other hand, many occurrences have been observed in which the quartz becomes quite subordinate to the felspar The ferro-magnesian constituents, which are as a rule subordinate, consist of biotite and green, strongly pleochroic hornblende. Muscovite as an essential constituent is absent, but Jorissen3 mentions its occurrence in the form of inclusions in the quartz. Accessory minerals are iron ores, apatite and epidote.

The main mass of the red granite, which includes true felsites, in part probably of volcanic origin, outcrops over a large part of the Bushveld, north of the railway from Pretoria to Middelburg, and extends north for about 100 miles. Smaller outcrops occur at Balmoral, at Pietpotgietersrust and north of the Palala plateau, between the Palala and Magalakwin Rivers.

1 Henderson, 1898, p. 47. 2 Hovwood, 1904, p. 113. 3 Jorissen, 1905, p. 158.

Rocks of Intermediate Type

Nepheline-syenites occur in the central, southern and south-eastern portions of the Pilandsberg. The first and most detailed description of specimens of these rocks, collected by Cohen from the Zwartkoppie range "between Rensburg and Rustenburg," was made by Wulfing. It is a typical porphyritic sodalite-bearing nepheline-syenite—a variety of foyaite—the constituent minerals being orthoclase, plagioclase, augite, nepheline and sodalite, and in smaller quantities hornblende, mica, sphene and opaque iron-ores. Zeolites occur as alteration products. The phenocrysts consist of a felspar with 5'04 per cent of soda; from its optical properties, however, Wulfing thinks it is more likely a normal orthoclase than an anorthoclase. The felspar of the groundmass is partly orthoclase, partly plagioclase. The pyroxene is in two varieties, the larger crystals being of a dark olive-green colour, with strong pleochroism and an extinction angle of 33 to 36: this is an ordinary augite. The smaller crystals are also green with strong pleochroism, but have an extinction angle of only 3 to 6; chemical analysis shows the presence of soda, and the absence of lime and magnesia: this is consequently a variety of acmite. The nepheline and sodalite occur in considerable quantity, the latter being distinguishable from the former by a slightly dusty appearance and bluish tint.

Nepheline-syenite occurs in several places in the Bushveld: it is found on the farms Zeekoegat (No. 287) and Leeuwfontein (No. 320), both situated north of that portion of the Magaliesberg which lies between Deerde Poort and Franspoort; also near Bothasberg, north of Middelburg. At Leeuwfontein, Molengraaff found a great variation in structure—coarse-grained varieties with unusually large felspars passing into quite fine-grained varieties. Differentiations into basic types in which the dark-coloured constituents prevail (so-called "raelanocrates") are found as dykes of monchiquite and camptonite. Differentiations into acid types (so-called "leucocrates") in which the felspathic element prevails are found as bostonite, and there are varieties composed almost entirely of nepheline.1 *Rocks of Basic Type*

The rocks of this type occur on the southern and eastern flank of the Pilandsberg, and in a range which runs on the northern side of the Magaliesberg, from the Pilandsberg north of Rustenburg to a few miles north of Pretoria, comprising the Zwartkoppies and the Pyramids. They consist of gabbros and norites, being characterised by a holocrystalline granular structure. Under the microscope they are seen to be aggregates of plagioclase (bytownite or anorthite) and pyroxene (diallage and salite in the gabbros, hypersthene in the norites).2

Associated with these basic rocks on the southern side of the Zwartkoppie range are deposits of magnetic iron-ore, and chrome iron-ore, which no doubt must be regarded as magmatic segregations.3 The magnetite occurs as a coarsely granular mass of pure iron-ore of strongly magnetic character. A similar ore occurs in the valley of the Blood River at the foot of the Bothasberg in the Middelburg district. Jvlr. Holmes has also observed large deposits of magnetic iron-ore associated with basic intrusions at several points in the Bier 1 Molengraaff, 1904 a.

2 See Henderson, 1898; Dahms, 1891; Hatch, 1898 and 1904 a.

3 Molengraatf, 1898 a.

spruit valley, west of the Crocodile River, in the Rustenburg district.

Rocks of Ultra-Basic Type

Felspar-free rocks (pyroxenites and peridotites) occur in the Marico and Rustenburg districts, west of the Pilandsberg. The pyroxenite, which is predominant, consists exclusively of a granular aggregate of a green-coloured rhombic pyroxene (enstatite). A chemical analysis of this rock given by Henderson 1 is as follows:—

This rock covers an immense area, having been found in the Marico district on the farms Brakfontein, Strydfontein, Alewijnspoort and Cyfergat; also in the Rustenburg district south of Jan's Kop on the western side of the Pilandsberg.

Only one occurrence of peridotite has hitherto been described, namely, on Rooikopjesfontein in the Marico district, not far from the above-mentioned farms. This rock is a granular aggregate of olivine, partially altered to serpentine. Under the microscope, pieces of unaltered olivine are found enclosed in a fibrous mesh of the serpentine, and the original boundaries of the olivine grains can still be discerned.2 1 Henderson, 1898. "Hatch, 1904 a.

Ore Deposits Associated With The Bushveld Igneotjs

Rocks *Iron.*—The magnetic iron-ore deposits associated with the gabbros and norites, and probably derived from them by a process of magmatic segregation, have already been referred to. As an instance of this class of ore, the magnetite of Onderstepoort, about 9 miles north of Pretoria, may be mentioned. This ore, which occurs in norite, contains from 60 to 68 per cent of magnetite, equivalent to 45 to 48 per cent of iron, and a small percentage of titanic acid, as is shown by the following four analyses taken from the Report of the Geological Survey for 1904 1:— 12 3 4

Fe304 62-25 63-8 63 8 67-5 per cent

Tib,.. 2-04 3-92 6-25 8 9 *Copper and Silver.*—Lodes or mineralised zones of these metals are fairly frequent in the red granite country. The best known of them is the copper-silver lode which has been worked in the Albert mine on the farm Roodepoortje, 20 miles north-east of Bronkhorst Spruit station on the Middelburg line. This lode is a replacement deposit along an east and west line of Assuring in a porphyritic type of the red granite. A diabase intrusion along the fissure forms a portion of the lode matter, being in places impregnated with the silver and copper ores. The Albert mine has been developed in a lenticular portion of the lode, where it is enlarged to a considerable thickness. The veinfilling consists mainly of haematite, with which is associated various sulphides of silver and copper—bornite, chalcopyrite and tetrahedrite *(fahlerz)*. Quartz is subordinate.

1 Hall, 1904, p. 32. *Tin.* — On Enkeldoorn (No. 373) there is a mineralised zone in the red granite in which tin occurs. It consists of a number of small veins or stringers of quartz, occurring in an irregular manner over a width of 8 to 10 feet. The general strike is north and south. The tin occurs as small grains or crystals of cassiterite, mainly in the quartz, but also in the granite. Some miles farther east, on Vlaklaagte (No. 39), a small outcrop richly impregnated with cassiterite has recently been found in the red granite, which is there traversed by veins of greisen. A similar occurrence has also been discovered on Roodepoortje (No. 149). *Cobalt.*—The cobalt lodes of Balmoral (farm Eenzaamheid, No. 421) have already been referred to in the section dealing with the ore-deposits in the Pretoria Series (p. 17G). Mr. Horwood, in a recent paper on these lodes,1 states that he considers them as pegmatite veins associated genetically with the red granite, and owing their cobalt and nickel contents to subsequent pneumatolytic action. 1 Horwood, 190J. PART II THE KARROO ROCKS CHAPTER I THE KARROO SYSTEM The term Karroo System is here used to include all the strata from the base of the Dwyka Conglomerate to the uppermost beds of the Stormberg Series on the summits of the Drakensbergen—a thickness not far short of 20,000 feet. Bain1 named these rocks " The Karroo or Reptiliferous Series,'' and the appropriateness of the first part of the name has left no room for subsequent alteration. There has been much difference of opinion, however, as to the best subdivision and grouping of the beds within the system. Bain himself used a distinctive geographical name, " Fort Beaufort Grit," for the middle division only. Wyley 2 gave a grouping which is chiefly interesting as showing that he was aware of the shales beneath the Dwyka (his Trap Conglomerate), and their resemblance to the underlving Witteberg Series:—

Upper. Stormberg Beds, upper beds of the

Sneenwberg, Xienwveld, and Roggeveld, etc.

Coal Measures. Middle Proper reptilian or dicyuodon beds, etc.

Lower Brown sandstone and shales with plants, etc.

1 Bain, 1856 a. Wyley, 1859, Table at end of Report.

Dunn in 1873 1 and 1875 " classified the Karroo System thus *i* Stormberg Beds. Triassic-j Upper Karroo Beds.

I Lower Karroo Beds.

The " Lower Karroo" is shown on his map as a band along the west and south of the Karroo, roughly coincident with the Ecca outcrops, while the "Upper Karroo" covers the rest of the country to the north, no outcrop of lower beds being indicated there. The Stormberg Beds are shown as occurring in the Stormberg and Drakensberg areas, as well as over a large portion of the Orange River Colony, the Transvaal and Natal, where, however, Lower Karroo Beds alone are present. On his 1887 map the same author gave an extended classification of the system, which he then knew to be conformable from top to bottom 3:—

On this map the Dwyka is shown as a part of the sedimentary series—a view which Dunn first presented in a report to the Cape Parliament in 1878:4 the classifica tion as a whole was given in several of his parliamentary reports previous to 1887. It has been followed by most subsequent writers with but little variation. Rupert. Jones1 and Green,2 however, both considered that the shales outcropping at Kimberley were a distinct subdivision, unconformable on the Ecca Beds; while Moulle,8 Cohen,4 and Feistmantel5 made a threefold division of the system into Lower, Middle, and Upper—their Lower being fairly equivalent to that of Dunn, their Middle to his Upper Karroo, and their Upper group to his Stormberg Series. Schenck in 1888 also adopted a threefold division: *(a)* Dwyka Conglomerate and Ecca Beds, *(b)* Beaufort Beds, (c) Stormberg Beds.

In the work of the Cape Survey the Dwyka and Ecca have been mapped and described as separate scries. In 1902, Mr. A. W. Rogers6—then Acting Geologist, now Director, of the Survey—gave the following classification, which is based on the work of the Survey itself, on the palaaontological work of Seeley, and on Dunn's grouping of the Stormberg Series:—

Volcanic Beds.
,.. 0. Cave Sandstone.
Stormberg Series-. _,
Red Beds.
Molteno Beds.
Karroo System-(
Beaufort Series
Ecca Series
Dwyka Series.
(Zone of specialised *ThirimhmU Dicynodon* Beds.
I *I'areiasaurni* Beds.
(Shales and thin sandstones.
-j Laingsburg Beds.
I Shales.
(Upper Shales.
Conglomerate.
I Low er Shales.
1 Rupert Jones, in Tate, 1867. 2 Green, 1888. 3 Moulle, 1880. 4 Cohen, 18S7. 5 Feistmantel, 1889. 6 *Rep. Geol. Commission Cape Town.* 1902.

In the following pages the older three-fold arrangement is reverted to, the Dwyka Conglomerate being regarded as part of the Ecca Series. The reason for this lies in the fact that in the Orange River Colony, the Transvaal and Natal, and to some extent in the Cape Colony, the Dwyka is simply a band of conglomerate, or of breccia, occurring at or near the base of the Ecca Series. This has led Anderson,1 in the last report of the Natal Survey, not only to include the conglomerate with the Ecca, but even to abandon the name "Dwyka." This name, introduced by Dunn in 1878, is, however, here retained, since it has secured a firm position in the literature, and is known throughout the world. The older term Ecca Conglomerate may, however, also be used as an appropriate synonym. The Kimberley Beds, which are simply a northern outcrop of the Ecca, and the Koonap Beds, which include a part both of the Ecca and of the Beaufort Beds, disappear as separate subdivisions. The entire Karroo System is grouped as a conformable sequence thus:— , (Volcanic Beds.

Upper Karroo or Cave Sandstone.
Stormberg Series I Red Beds.

jlolteno Beds. J
T. *(Zone of the specialised Theriodonts.*
Middle Karroo or Samlstone8 and sl,ales wiUt Wc;/n0i/on.
Beaulort henes (Sandstones and shales witn *Pareiasaurus. r ir I* Upper Sandstones and Shales.) ,, ,,,
Lower Karroo or J Dyka Conglomerate'
Ecca Seiies (.Lower Sandstones and Shales.I iesosaur
Karroo System ,-Zone of the *Zanclnd.onts.*

The Ecca Series

The name Ecca Series was practically introduced by Bain,'2 in a reference to the shales and sandstones which

'Anderson, *Second Jicp. Natal Survey,* p. 12.
2 Bain, 1856, p. 54.

outcrop at the Ecca Heights near Grahamstown. Wyley named them "Ecca Beds," and since his time the name *has* been commonly used, with varying significance, to indicate the basal portion of the Karroo System. Neither Bain nor Wyley, however, gave any precise specification of the strata which they grouped under the term. E. J. Dunn, who used the name in his report on "The Camdeboo and Nieuwveldt Coal," and on his map of 1887, included under it the Dwyka Conglomerate. In the reports of the Cape Survey the basal portion of the Karroo System is grouped as the Dwyka Series. It comprises the shales beneath the conglomerate proper (which in the south rest conformably on the Witteberg Quartzites), the conglomerate itself, and the shales above it, up to and inclusive of a so-called "White Band," consisting of black shales with calcareous nodules and iron pyrites, the decomposition of which produces gypsum and iron oxides and leaves the carbonaceous shales white. Above the Dwyka Series, thus defined, follows the Ecca, which includes the beds between the White Band and the lowest bed of the Beaufort Series—that is, the first bed containing *Pareiasaurus* remains.

While the series occurs mainly in the Karroo, there are also outcrops south of the Langebergen, in the Breede River

valley, west and east of Worcester, south of the fault to which reference was made in describing the Cape System (p. 71). This outcrop of Lower Karroo rocks, consisting of sandstones, shales and glacial conglomerate, is faulted down to the same level as the Malmesbury slates—a displacement of over 10,000 feet. This indicates a former much more extended distribution of the Ecca Series beyond the Karroo area. The upper sandstones in the Breede River valley are reddish brown in colour and quite felspathic, but the Dwyka outcrops are not to be distinguished petrographically from those of the Karroo.

Outliers of the Ecca Series may be found on any of the older formations in northern South Africa. There are many in the northern Transvaal and in Rhodesia—as, for instance, on the northern slope and in some of the valleys of the Zoutpansberg, on the Brak River, on the Limpopo, near Francis Town, on the Rhodesia railway, and near Avankie. In most cases the beds consist of conglomerate, sandstone and shale; while coal of varying quality is very commonly present.

Lower Sandstones and Shales, and the Dwyka Conglomerate

In the south of Cape Colony the Dwyka Conglomerate has a greater thickness than anywhere in the north: the series, as defined by the Cape Survey, including the overlying shales, has a thickness of over 2000 feet, while the Ecca is not less than 2500 feet. In all other parts of South Africa the actual thickness of conglomerate is much less. Evei along the southern margin of the Karroo the shales below and between the conglomerate beds do not differ from those above, and the same types of plant-remains occur throughout. There is, therefore, neither a stratigraphical nor a palaeontological reason for their separation.

The Ecca Series first outcrops as a narrow band at the mouth of the Gualana River, south of East London, where the older rocks pass into the sea, and continues along the margin of the Karroo north of the Zwartebergen.

Turning northward on the western boundary of the Karroo, the beds pass through Bushmanland, and thence trend eastward into the basin of the Orange River, with a continuously increasing width of outcrop. The western and central portions of the Orange River Colony are covered by the Series; and it spreads over the southern and eastern Transvaal into Natal, whence, as a narrowing band, it passes southward to the coast of Pondoland. On the rim of this extensive area there are outcrops of the basal Dwyka Conglomerate, and boreholes, put down in

Fig. 45.—Outcrop of Dwyka Conglomerate near Prieaka, Cape Colony.

the Orange River Colony and in the Transvaal, show that the conglomerate is invariably represented by one or more bands beneath, or interbedded with, the sandstones and shales: it may therefore be considered certain that the entire Karroo area is underlaid by the conglomerate.

The shales below the conglomerate on the south side of the Karroo lie conformably on the Witteberg Series. In the north-west and north of Cape Colony, however, there is always a marked unconformity between the base of the Karroo System and the underlying rocks; and the same relation prevails throughout the Orange River Colony, the Transvaal and Natal, in all of which regions beds of conglomerate or of breccia occur at the base.

The shales beneath the conglomerate are well seen on the southern margin of the Karroo, where the Buffels, the Dwyka and the Gamka Rivers have cut through them deep into the Cape System. At Laingsburg the Lower Karroo Beds stand almost vertical, and have been intersected by the Buffels and Witteberg Rivers. The conglomerate there is much sheared, but the true bedding is revealed by the presence of a boulder-bed. The underlying shales rest directly on the Witteberg Quartzites, and contain indeterminate plant stems. They show in their upper beds an occasional angular fragment of foreign rock,, thus passing gradually into the conglomerate, which in this neighbourhood, and

for a considerable distance westward and eastward, is not less than 1000 feet thick. It consists mainly of a dark compact matrix with interspersed fragments, angular and sub-angular, but also' rounded, of all sizes up to masses of several tons weight. Under the microscope even the matrix is seen to be fragmental, consisting largely of quartz and felspar frag-1 ments,—the latter often perfectly fresh,—and small pieces of rock of the same kind as those composing the boulders. The latter consist of quartzite, granite, gneiss, diabase and diabase-porphyrite, amygdaloidal diabase, dolomite, jasper rock, vein-quartz, and felspar fragments. Most of the boulders show the result of the shearing to which the rock as a whole has been subjected, breaking readily along a number of superinduced cleavage-planes. Not infrequently the dolomite boulders which occur at the surface have been partially dissolved, and, being thus reduced in size, lie loose in the matrix. The largest boulder so far recorded from the conglomerate is one of granite in the vertical bed at Witteberg River, with a diameter of ten feet. The jasper boulders in the conglomerate along the south of the Karroo resemble, according to Dunn, the rocks of the Doornberg in the north, and there can be no doubt of the correctness of this observation. The many varieties of granite which occur are also typical of northern exposures; and the same may be said of the amygdaloids.

The outcrops on the Dwyka River — whence Dunn derived the name—resemble those of the Buffels River in consisting of alternating shale and conglomerate beds. The conglomerate shows no sign of any regular arrangement of the pebbles and boulders. The bedding planes are often widely separated, or obscured by intense shearing. The same description applies practically to the entire outcrop along the northern Hank of the Zwartebergen to the sea south of East London. Everywhere along this line the conglomerate has shared in the intense movements which produced the Zwartebergen. For many miles from north of Willowmore to Gra-

hamstown, it is included in the folds of the mountain chain, the outcrop being duplicated. The conglomerate is well seen in the neighbourhood of Grahamstown, where, on the Queen's Road or Ecca Pass, the whole Ecca Series is exposed, as Bain and Green have described. Along the entire outcrop boulders may be found showing well-marked glacial striatums and facets, which, in specimens recently removed from the matrix, are as sharp and distinct as those on stones from existing glaciers. At Matjesfontein and Prince Albert, Dunn found such boulders in 1885, and his observations may be easily confirmed there and elsewhere along the southern outcrop.

On the western side of the Karroo the Dwyka outcrop turns northward with the course of the Dwequa River, passing through the Ceres and Calvinia districts into Bushmanland. The Witteberg Beds at Karroo Poort and in the Wittebergen, pass conformably under the conglomerate, and this relation prevails northward to some point as yet undefined, but, according to Messrs. Rogers and Schwarz,1 probably between the Tanqua and Brak Rivers, tributaries of the South Doom River in the

Fig. 46.—Scratched Boulder of Amygdaloidal Diabase, from the Dwyka Conglomerate,

Vereeniging. (J scale.)

Calvinia district. North of this point the Witteberg Series thins out, the conglomerate lying first on the Bokkeveld, then on the Table Mountain, then on the Ibiquas Series, and finally on the granite of Namaqualand and Bushmanland. After resting on Bokkeveld Beds from the Bosch River northward, the conglomerate is seen, in the valley of the Oorlog's Kloof River, lying directly on Table Mountain Sandstones, and then, north of Stinkfontein Poort, on Ibiquas Beds and granite. In the valley of the North Doom River, from Bokkefontein to Avelbedacht Gerustheid, there is a steep escarpment formed of Ibiquas Beds, with a thin covering of Table Mountain Sandstone; above the latter there is a hundred feet or so of Dwyka covered by a thick sheet of dolerite, at the contact with which the conglomerate shows a columnar structure, the columns being hexagonal and about 18 feet long.

1 Rogers and Schwarz, 1901 *h.*

From Welbedacht Gerustheid the conglomerate rests on Ibiquas Beds; and it covers the surface of the northern extension of the Bokkeveld Mountain plateau to its termination near the Kromme River. In the valley of this river the Dwyka rests on the granite; the Langchers; shows the same relation, but with dolerite and shale above the conglomerate.

Throughout the northern part of this western outcrop the conglomerate is less indurated than on the south side of the Karroo. North of Karroo Poort it resembles a hardened boulder-clay, and has the more metamorphosed appearance of the southern outcrops only in the neighbourhood of dolerite intrusions. The same variety of boulders occurs as in the southern outcrops, but there is a more localised distribution of particular boulders: thus in one locality quartzite may predominate, with granite and other igneous rocks in subordination; while in another, the opposite distribution may hold good. Near Leeuwen Riet, on the Oorlog's Kloof River, Messrs. Rogers and Schwarz found conglomerates with pebbles of jasper, of the same type as are found in the Ezelberg near Prieska. This locality also shows peculiar calcareous concretions in the conglomerate. These consist largely of matrix, but include many small pebbles and angular fragments which tend to project from the concretionary surface. They are sometimes quite spherical, with a diameter of from three inches to two feet or more.1 1 *Loc. rit.*

The extreme north-western outcrop of the conglomerate in Bushmanland is, according to Dunn,1 20 to 40 miles wide. From Kromme River it continues eastward to the junction of the Orange and Vaal Rivers, finally following the valley of the latter to Vereeniging. Dunn described the northern con *Phola A. Rogers.*

Fig. 47.—Glaciated Surface showing Grooving and Striatum, Jackal's Water, near Prieska, Cape Colony.

glomerate first in 1873,'-and again in 1886,3 by which time he had learnt its true stratigraphical position, and its continuity with the southern outcrops. Wyley, in 1859, knew of the northern outcrops below Hope Town, which he mentioned as a "peculiar trap (?) conglomerate"4 apparently interbedded with the schists. It was in the conglomerate at Pniel that Stow found the striated pebbles which led him to 1 Dunn, 1873. 2 Dunn, 1873. 3 Dunn, 1886. 'Wyley, 1859. the idea that there had been a South African glacial period contemporaneous with the Great Ice Age of the northern hemisphere.1

Dunn's description of the northern outcrops in the Hope Town and Prieska districts was confirmed by the Cape Survey in 1899." Throughout the area the rock resembles the outcrops of the western rather than of the southern Karroo. The matrix may be sandy, clayey, or occasionally calcareous. In some places boulders are scarce, and shale or sandstone patches may occur in the conglomerate. The conglomerate is well exposed near Prieska (see Fig. 45), where it rests on the Griqua Town jasper rocks; at the junction of the Brak and Orange Rivers there are also extensive outcrops. Near Hope Town it is largely concealed by surface material.

The particular interest of these outcrops is the fact. recorded first by Stow, that the rocks underlying the conglomerate show distinct glacial striae and *roches moutonnees.* On the farm Jackal's Water, Prieska, and southward to Bosjeman's Berg, such surfaces were noted by the Cape Survey (see Fig. 47). There the underlying rocks are Keis Quartzites, with striations trending S. 10 W. — in some cases with very distinct *Stoss-seiten* and *Lee-seiten.* Sixty miles farther east, on Vilet's Kuil, near Hope Town, the direction of the striae is east of south. There the striated rock is a hard amygdaloidal felsite.

At the junction of the Harts River with the Vaal, and on the latter near Riverton, similar phenomena are seen. The underlying rock is an amygdaloidal diabase belonging to the Ventersdorp System; it shows perfectly preserved

strial and *roches moutonnees.* Stow, in 1880, gave a description, as yet unpublished, of the phenomena in this locality, 1 Stow, 1871. 9 Rogers and Schwarz, 1900 *d. e.* the accuracy of which was confirmed by Molengraaff in 1903. 1

In all cases the striae are only distinct in the neighbourhood of the conglomerate outcrop. When exposed to the influence of the weather they disappear, and are consequently not seen on the older outcrops.

In the southern Transvaal and in the northern portion of the Orange River Colony near Vereeniging, a considerable outcrop of Dwyka Conglomerate rests on the Dolomite Series. But in this vicinity, owing to the horizontality of W. E.

1. *Red Granite* 2. *Glacial Congtomerate* 3. *Shale and Mudstone* 4. *Coarse Grit and Sandstones*

Sole-Horizontai t B Ve'tical *f.* V V 'M

Fig. 48.—Section on right bank of Elands River (Slagboom). After E. T. Mellor.

the entire formation, the coals and sandstones above the conglomerate generally cover the Dwyka, which is exposed only towards the margin. Numerous boreholes show, however, that the conglomerate is invariably present. The same is true of the eastern part of the Witwatersrand, where the conglomerate is concealed by the overlying coals and sandstones.

E. T. Mellor,'2 of the Transvaal Geological Survey, found outliers of Dwyka Conglomerate with underlying striated surfaces in the neighbourhood of the Elands River, and near the Douglas colliery north of Balmoral (see Figs. 48 to 50). The striated rock is Waterberg Sandstone. The direction of the striae at both localities is almost north 1 Molengraaff, 1904.

-Mellor, 1904. and south magnetic, the flow of the ice having been from the north.

In the eastern Transvaal, on the Natal border, there are many good exposures. Molengraaff in 1898 described

Fig. 49.—Plan showing outliers of Dwyka Conglomerate, near Balmoral,

Transvaal. After E. T. Mellor.

some of these in the Vryheid district, where he saw the evidence which induced him to abandon the igneous in favour of the glacial mode of origin. In several localities the old rocks (the Swaziland Series) are grooved and scratched where they appear from under the Dwyka—as, for instance. on Doornpan (No. 177) and Naauwpoort (No. 536). On the farm Basan (No. 882) there is a small kopje showing Dwyka boulders in the former. The conglomerate is also well exposed in the valley of the Black Umfolosi River.

In Zululand the glacial conglomerate frequently appears as an outlier on the " Palaeozoic Sandstones" or on the Archajan Schists, covering considerable areas to the north and northwest of Eshowe, in the neighbourhood of Melrnoth and Ulundi, and north of Mahlabatini towards the Vrvheid and Swaziland borders. At several places Anderson noted sandy deposits with the conglomerate: one is to be seen in the face of the Umgeni Quarry, Durban; others near Ulundi in Zululand. The best glacial pavement which the Natal Government Geologist has seen so far, occurs near Ulundi in the bed of the Umfolosi River, at the north-east end of a sharp bend north-west of Mabehlane Hill. It consists of well-striated quartzite, with still undenuded remnants of the glacial conglomerate resting on it. 1

In the Orange River Colony, in the Transvaal, and in the Utrecht and Vryheid districts of Natal the conglomerate differs petrographically from the hard compact rock of the southern Karroo, and from that found in the neighbourhood of Maritzburg and Durban. In the former localities the matrix is sandy, or slightly clayey, the rock tending to be incoherent. Above the conglomerate there are frequent beds of sandstone with interspersed boulders, so that it is often difficult to say where it really ends. In the north of the Orange River Colony and in the southern Transvaal the glacial beds are frequently represented by breccias consisting of angular fragments, mainly of quartzite and

chert.

1 Anderson, 190J. *Upper Sandstones and Shales*

On the south side of the Karroo the Upper Ecca Shales are generally dark grey, or almost black in colour, frequently fairly carbonaceous in composition, with thin coaly laminae and lenticules an inch or less in thickness. They weather

Fig. 51.—Ecca Shales aml Sandstone, Botha's Kraal, near Prince Albert.

into splintery fragments. The sandstones arc generally of a light bluish grey, extremely hard and tough, their outcrops often projecting from the shales like dykes. They tend to weather by concentric coats into spheroidal pieces (see Fig. 51), which externally can scarcely be distinguished from igneous rock.

The dip on the northern slope of the Zwartebergen is a high one, the entire Ecca Series from Buffel's Poort to east of Prince Albert having shared in the over-tilting. The greater portion of the southern Karroo consists of the Upper Sandstones and Shales from the slope of the Zwartebergen northward to the line where the Middle Karroo or Beaufort Series comes in. On the north the series outcrops again; and the shales at Kimberley and Stow's Olive Shales of Griqualand West belong to it, overlying in each case the glacial conglomerate. The junction between the Beaufort and the Ecca Series has, however, not yet been carefully defined.

In the Orange River Colony the upper beds of the Ecca consist mainly of sandstones; but they are often clayey and thin-bedded, passing into true shales. The western, central and northern portions of the Orange River Colony are composed of the series, but in the east the Beanfort and Stormberg overlie it. To the east of Blcemfontein. in some old quarries, the sandstones contain boulders which are striated and partially facetted like those belonging to the Dwyka. Good sections have been obtained in boreholes at Bloemfontein, Kroonstad, on the farm Ankom near Wolvehoek station and near Viljoen's

Drift. The thickness of the beds in these localities ranges from 450 to over 100O feet.

The upper portion of the Ecca Series throughout the Transvaal is much the same petrographically as in the Orange River Colony—coarse sandstones, passing into finer varieties and finally into shales. The coal seams east of Springs are often overlaid by bands of breccia, quite indistinguishable from the underlying breccia; and the upper sandstones, as at Benoni, are frequently crowded vvith boulders of varying size, all the result of glacial activity.

The following section of a borehole on Modderfontein (No. 46) gives a typical succession of the coal-bearing eds of the Ecca Series in the Springs district1:— 1 Hatch, 1904 *b*, p. 61.

In the eastern Transvaal and in Utrecht and Vryheid, the upper sandstones are well developed, attaining a thickness of 600 to 700 feet. According to Molengraaff,1 these sandstones probably belong to the Beaufort Series, but the recent work of the Natal Government Geologist confirms the view expressed by one of the present writers2 that they are of Ecca age. Both stratigraphical and palEeontological evidence points to this conclusion, from which it follows that the upper divisions of the Karroo System are confined in the east to the Drakensbergen and Stormbergen.

Economic Products of the Ecca Series

The great economic interest of the Ecca Series in the Orange River Colony, the Transvaal and Natal is the presence of coal. The whole of central South Africa is practically one enormous coal-field. Coal-mining is at present principally carried on at Viljoen's Drift and Vereeniging, at Brakpan and Springs on the East Rand, in the Middelburg-Belfast district and at Newcastle and Dundee in Natal; but mines are being opened in the 1 Molengraaff, *Trans. Gcol. Soc., S.A.* vi. 1903, 1. 45. 2 Corstorphine, 1903., "South Rand" coal-field south-east of Heidelberg and in the Ermelo and Carolina districts in the eastern Transvaal, and as the need arises many more localities will be exploited.

In most cases the coal seams are at the base of the series— some of them, as at Viljoen's Drift and on the East Rand, being actually interbedded with the glacial conglomerate. The seams vary considerably in thickness, but although some of them attain to 20 feet and over, generally only a portion of their thickness is of sufficiently good quality to be saleable. There is also a rapid variation in the nature of the coal within any given area, so that large portions of a coal-field may contain coal of too poor a quality to be marketable. Though much inferior to the product of English collieries, the Ecca coal is generally superior to that found in the Stormberg Series.

The following are analyses of some of the Transvaal coals:—

The Ecca Series also provides a large amount of buildingstone in the Orange River and Transvaal Colonies. Quarries have been opened at Molensteenpan, Vereeniging, Benoni and Boksburg for supplying stone on a fairly large scale; while numerous smaller quarries minister to local needs. The stone is of a felspathic character; in places it approximates to a freestone, but is often much laminated. The laminae are carbonaceous, and the blocks have a tendency to split along them after exposure.

Fig. 52.—Plant remains from the Ecca Series. After A. C. Seward. *a, Bothrodendron leslii; b, Olossopteru browniana,* var. *indica; c, Noeggerathiopsis hislopi; d, Psygmophyllum kidstoui; e, Gangamopteris cyclopteroidei; /, Neuropteridium validum. (a,* nat. size; *b-f,* about J nat. size.) *Fossils of the Ecca Series*

The plant fossils from the Ecca Series include *Glossopteris hrowniana* var. *indica* (Fig. 52 *b*) and *angustifolia, Gangamopteris cyclopteroides* (Fig. 52 *e*), and *Nenropteridium validvm* (Fig. 52 *f*) umong the ferns; *Bothrodendron leslii* (Fig. 52 *a*), *Psygmophyllum kidstoni* (Fig. 52 *d*) and *Noeggerathiopsis hislopi* (Fig. 52 *c*) represent the Lycopods, and *Sigillaria brardi* is of frequent occurrence in the quarries at Vereeniging.

1

The greatest variety of forms has been found at Vereeniging, in the sandstone above the coal, by Mr. T. N. Leslie and described by Mr. A. C. Seward. Throughout the Transvaal and Orange River Colony plant impressions are by no means uncommon, and in the latter colony especially silicified stems are frequently found. In the Cape Colony the Ecca outcrop on the Karroo contains many localities— as, for instance, at Botha's Kraal, between Prince Albert and Prince Albert Road — where leaf and stem fragments are abundantly present in the dark shales. The faulted outcrop at Worcester yields plant remains which, though obscure, are referred by Seward to the Ecca flora. As in the Orange River Colony, so in the Cape, fossil wood is of frequent occurrence.

The reptilian remains hitherto found consist of specimens of *Mesosaurus tenuidens* (see Fig. 53) from the neighbourhood of Kimberley and from Nieuwoudtsville near Calvinia.

1 For the fossil flora see Tate, 1867; Feistmantel, 1889; Seward, 1897, 1898, and 1903; Zeiller, 1896. CHAPTER II

The Karroo System *(continued)*

The Beaufort Series

The term Beaufort Series is a modification of Bain's " Fort Beaufort Grits" of the Eastern Province, with which the beds at Beaufort West, in the Karroo, were correlated later.

The Beaufort Series includes all the beds from the lowest *Pareiasaurus* zone to the plant-bearing shales of the Molteno Beds at the base of the Stormberg Series. Although the change from the steeply dipping Ecca Beds on the south of the Karroo to the practically horizontal Middle Karroo Beds gave rise at one time to the view that the two series were unconformable, later investigations show that the passage from the Ecca is conformable. Green gives a section from a locality two hours north of Aberdeen, showing the Beaufort Beds unconformable on the Ecca; but this may simply be an instance of contemporaneous erosion such as is to be seen elsewhere.

The Beaufort Series, as here understood, is equivalent to the "Upper Kar-

roo" of Dunn and to the "Karroo Beds" of Green. In the Orange River Colony and Natal it occupies a portion of the area which was formerly regarded as being composed of the Stormberg Beds. It includes Seeley's *Pareiasaurus, Dicynodont,* and "highly specialised *Theriodont*" zones.[1]

The Beaufort Series occupies the central portion of the Karroo; but its actual boundary has not yet been traced, and the lines shown on the map (Frontispiece) must be taken in a general sense. The series outcrops as a comparatively narrow strip on the eastern side of the Orange River Colony, and comes to the surface again in Natal on the slopes of the Drakensbergen.

In the Beaufort Series, as in the Ecca, sandstones, mudstones and shales are the prevailing rocks, with, however, a much greater preponderance, so far as the Cape outcrops are concerned, of basic igneous rocks, which are almost exclusively doleritic. The sandstones differ from those of the Ecca in showing no spheroidal weathering, and fall into two main types: the one coarse, hard and resistant, occurring in thick beds and forming conspicuous escarpments or kranzes on the hill-sides or on the summits of typical flattopped kopjes; the other soft and shaly, in thin beds, weathering with the associated shales to gentle slopes. Schwarz[2] has suggested the names "defining sandstones" for the former, and " intermediate sandstones" for the latter. The sandstones have a clayey cement, which is occasionally slightly calcareous. The mudstones and shales resemble those of the upper portion of the Ecca Series, but are more frequently purplish or brownish red in colour. They weather into innumerable fragments, which lie on the talus slopes as a loose, dry rubble, the dryness of the climate and the prevailing winds preventing the accumulation of fine material. There is generally a good deal of carbonate of lime in the shales, and the laminae glisten with minute scales of mica. Bot h sandstones and shales show numerous ripple 1 Seeley, 1892c. J Schwarz, 1897.

markings and, in places, sun-cracks,

while false-bedding is conspicuous throughout. Evidence of contemporaneous erosion is obtainable in various localities, as in the valley of the Dwyka River near the junction of the Steenkamp, where sandstone lies in hollows eroded in shales and mudstones. Many sandstone beds contain small pieces of clay or shale, more or less irregular and angular in shape, forming in places what Schwarz has termed a "clay-pellet conglomerate." There is little doubt that the presence of such a conglomerate, considered in conjunction with the ripple-marks and sun-cracks, affords evidence of shallow water deposition: the pellets being formed by portions of the clayey surface of preceding deposits becoming hard and dry, and then included in the sands subsequently laid down. Limestone occurs as nodules or as thin beds among the sandstones and shales, sometimes containing infiltrated chalcedony which may also replace plant stems or reptilian bones.

The Beaufort Series is well seen in numerous sections on the escarpment of the Nieuwveld Mountains, where the bands of both "defining" and "intermediate" sandstone can be seen thickening and thinning out within very varying distances. It is doubtful whether the series occurs in the Transvaal, but in Natal it outcrops on the lower slopes of the Drakensberg, and covers a considerable area eastward. North of Pietermaritzburg *Dicynodont* fossils are found in Beaufort Shales. Seward concludes, from his determination of the fossils from Umhlali, on the north-east coast of Natal (some of which, however, are doubtful), that the beds there are of Beaufort age.[1] Owing, however, to the small number of species which it was possible to determine, he expresses this opinion with considerable reserve.

[1] Seward, 1904. *Fossils of the Beaufort Series*

The Reptilian fossils from the Beaufort Series have long been known. The lowest beds yield *Pareiasaurus* and *Tapinocephalus,* the former especially being of very widespread occurrence. The *Pareiasaurus bainii,* now in the British Museum, was obtained by H. G.

Seeley at Tamboersfontein. In the course of the survey of the Cape in 1902, Messrs. Rogers and Schwarz found a very perfect skeleton of *P. serridens* on the farm Hoogeveld, near Van der Byl's Kraal in the Gouph.[1] *Tapinocephalus* has been found in the Prince Albert gold-field. In the Dicynodont zone there are many species of *Dicynodon* and *Oudenodon*, e.g. *D. lacerticeps, D. leoniceps, D. bainii, D. tigriceps, Oudenodon magnus, O. brevirostri, O. bainii,* etc. Of the Theriodonts in the next zone, *Lycosaurus* occurs in the Sneeuwberg and at Fort Beaufort, *Cynodraco* at Fort Beaufort, and *Cynosuchus* and *Galesaurus* in the Sneeuwberg.

A Ganoid fish, *PalcBoniscus bainii,* is recorded from Stylkrantz in the Sneeuwberg, and from Spitzkop north of Beaufort West.

Plant fossils belonging to a few genera are also widely spread, and, in some localities, abundant. *Glossopteris* passes from the Ecca into the lower zones, and is found with *Pareiasaurus.* Stems of *Phyllotheca,* CalaFig. M. — *oiossomites* and *Schizoneura* are also known. The *pteris browniana.* Species Gf *Glossopteris* hitherto found include

After Tate..

G. browniana (see Fig. 54), *G. angustt'folia, G. tatei, G. communis, G. striata, G. retifera, G. dainudica* var. *stenoneura.* 1 Rogers and Schwarz, 1903. CHAPTER III

The Karroo System *(continued)*

The Stormberg Series

The name Stormberg Series was introduced by Wyley; following an independent suggestion of Huxley, Rupert Jones adopted it in his synopsis of the Karroo Strata which accompanies Tate's paper. It was Dunn,[1] however, who made the four-fold division of the series:—

The three upper names were introduced by Dunn, but "Molteno Beds" was suggested by Green'[2] as less liable to misconception than "Coal Measures," by which the former author had designated the basal division. Anderson[3] has recently employed "Stormberg Series" as equivalent to "Molteno Beds."

Bain, on his map, showed the beds as present over north-eastern Cape Colony, the Orange River Colony, Natal and a portion of the Transvaal. Dunn, on his last map, showed the series as covering a much wider area than is now known to be correct: in this he was guided by the coal occurrences of the Transvaal and Natal, which he assumed to be of the same age as those of the Molteno district in Cape Colony.

At present the exact distribution of the series is not known, but it appears to be confined to the Stormberg district, the eastern portion of the Orange River Colony, Basutoland and the western portions of the Transkei and

Natal, forming in the three last-named the higher levels of the Drakensbergen. The junction between the Beaufort Beds and the lowest of the Molteno Beds is a conformable one, but little detailed work has been done in tracing it. The base of the Molteno Beds is distinguished by the appearance of a new facies of fossil plants, of which *Thinnfeldia* is typical, and up to the present day none of the Stormberg Series has been found to contain *Glossapteris.*

As in the Beaufort Series, the beds of the Stormberg lie almost horizontal, producing a table landscape (see Fig. 55).

The Molteno Beds.

The Molteno Beds have received a great deal of attention in Cape Colony, as in them occurs the only workable coal so far discovered in that country. As developed in the neighbourhood of Stormberg Junction, Molteno and Cyphergat, they consist of sandstones, often fine-grained, like some of those in the Beaufort Series, but generally coarse and gritty, with large grains, or crystals, of glittering quartz, and also with pebbles of vein-quartz. Associated with the sandstones there are often coarse conglomerates with boulders as large as a man's head. The finer varieties of sandstone have a dull greenish colour; they show numerous thin coaly laminae and are in many places marked by the presence of concretions. In composition they are felspathic.

In the neighbourhood of Molteno and

Cyphergat the upper beds are well exposed: they consist of sandstones and shales, the latter showing many plant remains, among which Seeley found a stem with rootlets *in situ* beneath the coal (Fig. 56). The coal is for the most part interbedded with the shales and is very impure. Green 1 gives the following as the mean result of the analysis of two samples from the Molteno mine:—

Fig. 56.—Stem with Rootlets in Molteno Beds. After Seeley.

Another sample from Van Wyk's farm, 10 miles south of Burghersdorp, gave the following as the mean of two analyses:—

At Indwe the beds attain the same thickness as at Molteno, namely, 1000 feet. Of the several seams of coal which occur, only one, lying about 200 feet above the base of the beds, is worked. The coal is interbedded with shaleand a thickness of 6 to 7 feet is worked, of which about 4 feet is coal. Galloway1 gives the following section of the seam:—

He states that the quality of the coal varies in different localities, but normally contains about 30 per cent of volatile constituents and 20 to 30 per cent of ash, with a specific gravity of 1-4 to 1"5. An analysis by Professor P. D. Hahn, of Cape Town, given by North,1 is as follows:—

Carbon
Hydrogen
Nitrogen.
Sulphur.
Oxygen
Ash
Coke 61 021
3-208
2190
0431
2-178
30320
75-260

The road from Indwe to Cala affords a good section of the Molteno Beds; in the vicinity of the latter village seams of coal outcrop at the base of the steep kranz near the junction of the Cala and Tsomo Rivers. An analysis of this coal by Mr. J. G. Rose,-of Cape Town, gave the following:—

The Molteno Beds outcrop at Maclear and Ugie, where a yellowish sandstone is conspicuous, shale and coal being associated with it at the former locality.

The Red Beds

The Red Beds consist of a varying thickness of purplish or reddish-brown sandstones, shales and mudstones, with occasional conglomerate beds. According to Dunn,1 they attain a thickness of 600 feet in the Stormberg area; while farther east, in Elliott, du Toit found them 1400 feet thick ; and Schwarz assigned them a thickness of 200 feet at Matatiele.3 In the Ladybrand district, and northward along the eastern border of the Orange River Colony, they are well seen underlying the Cave Sandstone, having there a thickness of 100 to 300 feet. Near Harrismith they are about 100 feet thick, and contain a bed of bone-breccia made up chiefly of reptilian remains.4 On the face of the Drakensbergen the Red Beds are also represented beneath the Cave Sandstone, but are not so clearly separated from the latter as is elsewhere the case.

7Jhe Cave Sandstone

The Cave Sandstone is the most prominent of the Stormberg sedimentary beds (see Fig. 57). Although often only 100 to 200 feet thick, it forms a conspicuous capping to many of the flat plateaus of the Stormberg district and of the eastern portion of the Orange River Colony. It is a massively bedded sandstone with little lamination, generallv fine-grained, but occasionally coarse and of a yellowish-cream colour.

The outcrops of the Cave Sandstone often weather into most fantastic shapes: huge monoliths are produced in places, and generally the lower portion of the beds ia hollowed out, sometimes into proper caves, but more usually as an undercut cliff.

The Volcanic Beds

The Volcanic Beds form the summits of the Stormbergen and Drakensbergen, attaining a thickness in the latter of 4500 feet. A large portion of the upper part of the Maluti

Flo. 57.—Outcrop of Cave Sandstone, Hoogfontein, Ladybrand.

range in Basutoland is composed of these beds. They consist chiefly of true lava-flows, amygdaloidal melaphyres and diabases, ordinary diabases and melaphyres. The amygdaloids are of the ordinary type; but in many places throughout the Drakensbergren and in the Malutibergen a "pipe" amygdaloid is found. In this the amygdales are often three or four inches long, branching and coral-like. They are about three-eighths of an inch in diameter, and are vertical in the lower sheets. Cohen found that the infilling material was heulandite, and du Toit has determined thomsonite, stilbite, scoleeite in addition, while calcite and calcedony also occur. *Fossils of the Stormberg Series*

The chief fossils hitherto found in the Stormberg Series are:—Reptilia: *Euskelesaurus browni, Tritylodon longavus, Phulo E. II. MdviU.*

Fig. 58.—Slab of Cave Sandstone with *Scmionotus capcnsis*, Ficksburg, Orange River Colony. (About £ nat. size.) *Dicynodon testudiceps, Rytidosteus capensis.* Pisces: *Ceratodus capensis, C. kannemeyeri, Semionotus capensis* (see Fig. 58), *Cleithrolepis extoni.* Plants: Cycads, *Baiera schencki, B. stormbergensis*; Equisetae, Stem fragments; Ferns: *Thinnfeldia odontopteroides* (Fig. 59 a), *T. rhomboidalis* (Fig. 59 b), *Stenopteris elongata, Taeniopteris carruthersi, Cladophlebis, Phamicopsis elongata. Economic Products of the Beaufort and Stormberg Series*

Apart from the coal of the Molteno Beds, the Beaufort and Stormberg Series have so far yielded little of economic value. There are a few abnormal coal occurrences in the Beaufort Series; such as that at Leeuw River Poort. The sandstones of the Beaufort Series are used for building, and quarries are opened at Beaufort West, near Graaff Reinet, at Dordrecht, and at Queenstown, the latter supplying a good quality of stone.

Fig. 59 *a.* — *Thinnfeldia odontoptcrmdes.* Fig. 59 *b.*— *Thinnfeldia rhomboidalis.*

The sandstones of the Molteno Beds are much used locally for building purposes, but suffer in quality from the presence of coaly laminae. Throughout the areas where they occur they furnish pillars for fencing purposes.

The Cave Sandstone gives a high quality of building-stone, only in many cases it is not well situated for quarrying. At Lady brand, however, where it forms the summit of the Platberg, it can be easily reached, and quarries have been opened in it.

Igneous Rocks Of The Karroo System

After the deposition of the beds of the Karroo System there was a period of great igneous activity, resulting in the intrusion of typical dolerites as sills or dykes, the latter often passing into the former. The southern Karroo shows little or no evidence of this activity: but in the west, the centre, and the north of the Karroo; in the Stormberg and the districts south of it, in Cape Colony; in the Orange River Colony, and throughout the southern and eastern Transvaal and Natal, there are numerous intrusions. The Ecca Beds of the southern Karroo have scarcely, if at all, been invaded by the dolerite, which may be merely because the volcanic influence did not extend so far south, or may have some connection with the intense folding to which the area was subjected.

The intrusions probably all belong to the same period: boulders of the typical dolerite were found by Messrs. Rogers and Schwarz in the Umtamvuna rocks on the Pondoland coast;1 consequently the invasion of the strata was anterior to the deposition of the Upper Cretaceous Beds. So far no such boulders have been found in the Uitenhage Series, but it is not safe to conclude that the invasion of the Karroo sediments occurred between the deposition of the Lower Cretaceous (Uitenhage) Series and the Upper Cretaceous (Umtamvuna) Series. At present all that can be said is that the intrusions were later than the deposition of the Stormberg and earlier than that of the Umtamvuna Beds.

The Nieuwveld Mountains and the country which surrounds them present typical examples of the intrusions, and over a wide belt of country north of Beaufort West (see Fig. 60), and again over a great area stretching from the Stormberg district southward and eastward, there are numerous outcrops of the dolerites, forming promineit surface features. In the Orange River Colony and southern Transvaal the outcrops are less conspicuous, being for jthe 1 Rogers and Schwarz, 1902 a. most part intruded in rocks which do not weather so easily as the shales and shaly sandstones of Cape Colony. In the eastern Transvaal, however, the dolerites form distinct ridges and hills, and the same feature is noticeable throughout Natal.

In the Cape Colony the sheets are for the most part ordinary dolerite, but olivine dolerite often appears. The edges of the dykes are frequently quite glassy, becoming s.w. NE*Stoliz Hoek Wiiimm Kraal*

Fie. 60.—Section west of Beaufort West, showing intrusive diabase in the Beaufort Series. After E. H. L. Schwarz. The diabase is shown by the black line. tachylitic. The texture of the rocks varies from glassy to quite coarse-grained, the latter nearly always showing ophitic structure; some are almost black in colour, others light grey. The shales in immediate contact with the igneous rock are often converted into Lydian-stone, and the sandstones become spotted and micaceous: but no extensive metamorphism has been noted.

Cohen1 gives the following analyses of some of these rocks:— 1 Cohen. table I. Olivine diabase 1 from Oudedrift, near Beaufort West. II. „ from Nels Poort. III. „ from Colesberg. IV. „ Lobbea Farm, between the Orange and Riet Rivers, Orange River Colony. V. „ between Kiinberley Mine and Dutoitspan. VI. „ Pietermaritzburg, Natal. VII. Diabase from Richmond. VIII. Quartz-diabase from the powder magazine, Colesberg. IX. Dialiase-porphyrite from Botha's Drift, between Philippolie and Colesberg. X. Diabase-porphyrite, near Philippolis. XI. Olivine-diabase-porphyrite, Colesberg. XII. Olivine-diabase-porphyrite from Pfandstall, near Colesberg. I. to IX. occur as sills, X. to XII. as dykes.

In the Transvaal numerous sheets and dykes of dolerite have been intersected in the boreholes which have been put down in the district east of Springs to cut the Main Reef. That they all belong to one period of intrusion, which was later than that in which the Ecca Beds were deposited, is made almost certain by an identity of composition and structure, and by the remarkable freshness of the constituent minerals, whether they are found in the Witwatersrand Beds, in the Dolomite Series, or in the Ecca Beds. In this feature they are quite distinct from the dykes and interbedded diabases of the Witwatersrand Beds, which are characterised by their advanced state of decomposition.

When examined in thin sections under the microscope, the dolerites are found to consist of an aggregate of lath-shaped plagioclase felspar and a brown augite, the two minerals being in ophitic intergrowth and of remarkable freshness. In addition, ilmenite is present as an accessory constituent, together with its characteristic alteration product, leucoxene. In some cases olivine is not present; 1 Cohen names these rocks "diabase" in accordance with German practice—they being of Pre-Tcrtiary age. but when it occurs this mineral is usually, but not always, serpentinised. In the latter case fragments of the original substance remain unaltered; in the Palmietkuil-Grootvlei Joint Borehole a dyke of felspar microlites, with porphyritic crystals of olivine completely altered to serpentine, but retaining the original crystal outlines of that mineral; and in a borehole on Modderfontein (No. 46), a dyke cutting the Dolomite consists of a mesh of lath-shaped crystals of plagioclase felspar, with granular augite and olivine crystals, partially altered to serpentine along cleavage cracks.

The characteristic passage from a fine-grained or even tachylitic margin to a coarsely crystalline centre is well illustrated in the dykes and sheets intersected in these boreholes. Thus, in

Palmietkuil Borehole No. 4, a dyke cut in the Dolomite, which in the central portion is a typical dolerite with ophitic structure, consists, at its contact, of a crypto-crystalline ground-mass containing slender porphyritic crystals of felspar. This ground-mass, which probably consolidated as a glass, has become partially devitrified. The contact metamorphism of the rocks into which the dykes are intruded is most strikingly illustrated in the Dolomite, although the slates of the Lower Witwatersand Beds also show signs of " baking," being hard and splintery within the contact zone. In the Palmietkuil-Grootvlei Joint Borehole already referred to, a big dyke which extends to the hanging wall of the Van Ryn Reef has caused considerable alteration in the slates immediately underlying the reef, the original quartz fragments lying in a matrix, which is partially re-crystallised and so rendered doubly refractive. It is also thickly strewn with slender needles of rutile. In Palmietkuil Borehole No. 4 the Dolomite near the contact with the dyke is converted to a highly variegated green serpentine.

PART III POST-KAROO ROCKS

CHAPTER I

THE COASTAL SYSTEM—UITENHAGE AND UMTAMVUNA SERIES

The term Coastal System is here introduced to embrace the various rocks of Cretaceous age that occur in the Cape Colony and Natal. The palaeontological evidence shows them to belong to two divisions—the Uitenhage Series of Lower, and the Umtamvuna Series of Upper, Cretaceous age. The former is confined to the Cape Colony proper, the latter to Pondoland and Natal. The youngest beds observed beneath the Coastal System are of Ecca age, so that its relation to the upper portion of the Karroo System is fixed by the palaeontological evidence only.

The name Uitenhage Series has been applied to a considerable thickness of conglomerates, sandstones and shales lying unconformably on older formations. They occur in the Breede River valley, from Worcester to Ashton; in the districts of Swellendam, Riversdale,

Mossel Bay and Knysna; in the Olifant's River valley, south of the Zwartebergen; on the shores of St. Francis and Algoa Bays; and inland from the latter, especially in the Sunday's and Zwartkop River valleys.

Opinion has varied as to whether these beds are of Lower Cretaceous or of Jurassic age. The earlier writers, Plausmann and Krauss, regarded them as Cretaceous. Recently this view has been confirmed by Seward, who, as a result of his determination of the fossil plants collected by the Cape

Fig. 61.—Enon Sandstones overlaid by recent Limestone, Mossel Bay.

Survey and sent to him for description, considers that "the Uitenhage plants include types in part characteristic of Wealden, and in part indicative of Jurassic lloras." He adds that he has " little hesitation in stating that the flora exhibits more well-defined points of contact with plants of Wealden age than with the older floras." The Uitenhasre flora, which is represented by a few species only, "marks a phase of Mesozoic vegetation on the boundary of the Jurassic and Wealden periods."

On the coast of Pondoland, Natal and Zululand, as well as farther north beyond the confines of South Africa, other deposits containing an abundant Cretaceous fauna have been known since 1824. These were first described by Garden as occurring "near the Umtafuna." Some years later, Sutherland also described their position as south of the Umtamvoona, although he gave their correct locality, *Photo A. D. Lewis.*

Fig. 62.—View west of Cape St. Blaize—the point on the left shows horizontal Enon Beds lying on the Table Mountain Series.

namely, on the Umzumbe (Umzamba) River. Dunn on his 1887 map names them the "Umtamvoona Beds," and Schenck, in 1888, used the name "Umtamfuna." On the latest official map of Cape Colony the name of the river is printed " Umtamvuna." Though the beds do not actually occur in this river basin, the name has found a place in the literature, and it is perhaps better to retain it, even at the expense of geograph-

ical accuracy, rather than to introduce a new one.

Etheridge, in describing the fauna collected by the Natal Government Geologist at Umkwelane Hill, quotes the view adopted by Kossmat and gives a comparison, derived partly from that writer and partly from Bullen Newton, which is included in the following table:—

It, thus appears that the Uitenhage Series may be accepted as the equivalent of the Neocomian or Wealden, and the Umtamvuna Series as representing the Upper Cretaceous from the Gault to the Upper Chalk.

Thk Uitenhage Series

Our knowledge of this series dates back to 1837, when Hausmann described some of the fossils sent to him 1 Griesbach's lettering is retained here; his " *a* " denotes the old rocks unconformable beneath the Cretaceous Beds. from Enon and Uitenhage. The first geological account of the series, however, was given by Bain in his paper of 1845; while in his second paper he gave more details regarding the occurrence of the beds. He made two subdivisions of the series, naming the lower one "coarse conglomerate," the upper "the Lias(?). " Bain stated that the series occupied small indentations of the coast about the estuaries of the largest rivers; he also noticed the existence of forests of calcified trees of large size in the vicinity of the Sunday's and Bushman's Rivers. He noted that ferns and Zamias occur with fragments of gypsum, reptilian bones, Trigonia and Ammonites. The upper part of the series was sub-divided by Atherstone in 1857, and his classification has formed the basis for all subsequent work. In 1867, Tate, in describing a large suite of the fossils, introduced the name " Uitenhage Series."

The series in the neighbourhood of Algoa Bay shows the following sub-divisions, numbered from below upwards:— 4. Sunday's aud Bushman's River Beds—yellow and green sandstones and limestones, marls and clays, with abundant marine fossils.

3. The Wood Bed—grey, brown, or greenish sandstones and shales, some-

times saliferous; calcareous sandstones and limestones; with numerous plant fossils. 2. Zwartkop Sandstone—a series of white and red variegated sandstone beds. 1. Enon Conglomerate—a coarse, sandy conglomerate consisting of quartzite boulders, often with intercalated lenticular sandstone beds, resting unconformably on the older formations.

There can be no doubt that the series is subject to considerable variation, since in places—for instance west of Uitenhage and south-east of Blue Cliff Station—the basal conglomerate does not appear to be present, while elsewhere the Wood Bed and the Zwartkop Sandstone are not sharply separated. The above succession may vary: for example, at Heidelberg and Riversdale, Messrs. Rogers and Schwarz1 found beds of conglomerate overlying a set of plant-bearing beds. The foregoing table, therefore, can only be regarded as presenting the typical complete succession: in individual outcrops the series may show considerable variation from it.

The Enon Conglomerate was so named by Atherstone

Fig. 63.—Hills of Enon Conglomerate near Herbertsdale.

from its occurrence near the Moravian village of Enon, on the Witte River, a small tributary of the Sunday's River. The conglomerate there forms cliffs of over 200 feet. It comprises quartzite boulders and pebbles of varying dimensions, imbedded in a reddish, partly sandy, partly clayey matrix. In places the matrix is quite subordinate, the cliff face then resembling a dry rubble wall. Where 1 Rogers and Schwarz, 1900 a. the matrix is clayey it weathers, and irregular holes are left in the cliff where the boulders fall out.

At the source of the Zwartkop's River Atherstone1 found narrow precipitous kloofs with conglomerate walls rising to a height of over 400 feet; and it was in this locality that he first noted the presence of the beds to which he gave the name Zwartkop Sandstone. These, where typically deAreloped, are well bedded, white and red, and rather fine-grained. Interspersed pebbles generally occur in the lower beds, and there is

thus a gradual passage from the Enon. Above the Zwartkop Sandstones there occur in places soft, clayey, calcareous and sandy rocks, varying in colour, to which the term "variegated marls" has been applied.

West of the main area there is an immense development of Zwartkop Sandstone and Enon Conglomerate in the Gamtoos River valley, hills of Enon rising near Hankey to a height of over 700 feet.

The name Wood Bed was first applied by Atherstone to outcrops in the valley of the Bushman's River which consist of glauconitic sandstone, alternating with beds of brown sandstone and small pebble conglomerates, and containing innumerable calcified trunks and stumps of trees, many of which show *Teredo* borings. From the presence of the glauconitic sandstone Atherstone suggested that the formation might be Lower Greensand. He found that the Wood Bed was largely developed throughout the valley, and that many of the fossil trunks were covered with a layer of 1£ to 2 inches of lignite. The drift timber was traced down the Bushman's River past Dassies Klip and Bakkers, and up the Sunday's River for some *30* or 40 miles.

The Wood Bed appears in a small valley between the Elands and Zwartkops Rivers lying against the Table 1 Atherstone, 1857.

R

Mountain Series, and dipping a few degrees to the northeast. In the valley of the Bezuidenhout River, which flows eastward into the Sunday's River, it is well exposed, attaining a thickness of from 500 to 1000 feet: it includes sandstones, limestones, soft sands and clays, all dipping to the south. On the north lies the Enon Conglomerate; to the south, the marine Sunday's River Beds. A greenish

Fig. 64.—Cave in the Enon Conglomerate south of Oudtshoorn.

sandstone, tough when fresh, but crumbling at the surface to loose sand, and containing numerous casts of tree trunks, appears on the river banks, above the railway bridge. The dip there

is 30 to the east-south-east. Sandy marls and two more green sandstone beds lie below these and pass down into the variegated marls, which are red and light green in colour. Below the railway there are many good exposures in the river valley, where large numbers of petrified trunks are exposed; one of these, noticed by Messrs. Rogers and Schwarz,1 measured 2a feet in length, and many were 3 feet in diameter. On the farm Paltjes Kraal beds of sandstone and nodular limestone occur with *Zamites (Palceozamia) recta, rubidge* and other species, *Cladophlebis* and *Cycadolepis,* all well preserved. Stems, often upright and with their bark converted into lignite, are found in great abundance. Similar exposures continue to the confluence of the Bezuidenhout River with the Sunday's River. A little below this point is the junction of the Witte River, *Photo E. H. V. MdvUl.*

Fig. 65.—*Oleostcphanus bainii* from Sunday's River Beds.

where, on Geelhoutboom, Atherstone found numerous tree trunks and other plant remains in the upper portion of the Wood Bed.

The Sunday's and Zwartkop's River Beds consist of shales, clays, calcareous sandstones and limestones. The clays are poor in fossils, but the limestone and calcareous sandstone bands are generally crowded with many varieties of lamellibranchs. Good exposures occur on the banks of the Sunday's River, from the junction of the Witte River to the mouth. Some of the upper beds show imprints of ferns and other plant remains, while the lower beds contain fossil wood with many marine invertebrates.

1 Rogers and Schwarz, 1901 *a.*

The exposures on the Zwartkop's River were first described by Krauss, who visited the locality in 1839. On the left bank of the river, about five miles below Uitenhage, he found a section of green sandstone, 20-24 feet thick, on the top of which lay 6 to 7 feet of variegated sandstone boulders. He described the section as follows:— 10. Boulders of variegated sandstone cemented by carbonate of lime to a loose conglomerate.

... 6-30' 9. Loam and weathered rock... ..12' 8. Green sandstone—hard, ferruginous, rich in fossils, especially *Astarte herzoyii, Exogym imhricata, Anoplomya lutruria, Lyrodon ventricosus...* .. 1' 7. Green sandstone, hard, without fossils 1j' 6. Weathered green sandstone. 15' 5. Green sandstone, coloured by iron oxide, fossiliferous lj' 4. Green sandstone, alternating hard and weathered beds 6' 3. Weathered green sandstone....10' 2. Hard green sandstone, coloured by iron, lowest bed fossiliferous....... 60' 1. Bed containing worn and imperfect specimens of two species of *Lyrodon* ...... 4'

The rock of the lower fossiliferous beds is a fairly hard, greyish, or greenish sandstone, rich in shell fragments: *Lyrodon herzogii, L. conocardiiformis, L. ventricosus, Mytilus, Pinna,* two species of *Ostrea* and other indeterminable smaller bivalves occur in it. The rock of the upper fossiliferous beds is hard, coloured reddish grey by iron oxide, and contains abundant shell fragments.

The marine beds are also seen in the bed of the Coega between the Zwartkop's and Sunday's Rivers, and in the Bushman River Valley.

On the south coast the Uitenhage Series outcrops at Plettenberg Bay, in the basins of the Bitou and Pisang Rivers and at Knysna Harbour, where cliff's of Enon Conglomerate, with interbedded sandstone, rise to a height of over 400 feet. The cliff on the east bank of the Knysna

River gives a good exposure of the conglomerate: the lenticular shape of the sandstones, as well as the coarse boulder beds are very conspicuous. The Enon, in this locality, lies unconformably on the Cape System, chiefly as a capping on the Table Mountain Series, as, for example, to the west of Seal Point. At the latter place the conglomerate reaches sea-level; and there the sandstone beds become almost quartzitic, a result of secondary silicification. To the east of Seal Point Schwarz found *Trigonia, Gervillia* and *Ammonites* in the sandstones, which may therefore be considered equivalent to

the marine lx;ds' of the Sunday's and Zwartkop's Rivers.

At Mossel Bay the Uitenhage Series lies horizontally on southward-dipping Table Mountain beds. The unconformity is well seen at Cape St. Blaize and on the cliffs to the west of it (see Fig. 62). The rocks are conglomerates, sandstones and quartzites, the basal bed being a breccia with numerous fragments of Table Mountain Quartzite. The conglomerates are, as usual, very coarse, the boulders consisting almost exclusively of quartzite. In the sandstones an occasional boulder appears, and some beds show many casts of plant stems, while patches of lignite are not infrequent. North-west of Mossel Bay, around Herbertsdale, are numerous fine shales, which are often full of plant remains inter 1 Schwaiz, 1900 c.
bedded with the conglomerate. South of Herbertsdale the series consists chiefly of conglomerate, in many places over 500 feet thick (see Fig. 63). West of the Mossel Bay outlier a considerable area south of the Langebergen is covered by Uitenhage Beds. They extend to Swellendam, and thence up the Breede River valley to beyond Worcester. It is not easy in these localities to find the exact boundaries of the series, as there is generally a considerable covering of superficial deposits, which often consist of boulders weathered out of the Enon conglomerate and re-cemented by calc-sinter.

Another considerable outlier extends from the east of Riversdale to the west of Heidelberg, over an area twenty miles long by five wide. As at Herbertsdale, it comprises shales and fine sandstones with plant remains. These are well seen in the bed of a small stream north-west of Heidelberg, where some of the strata contain a great many *Estheria* valves, described by Rupert Jones as a new species, *Estheria anomala.*[1] Associated with the *Estheria* Schwarz found in one case a coleopterous wing-cover.

On a hill on the farm Spiegel River, about six miles east of Heidelberg, the Enon Conglomerate is broken through by a small boss of melilite basalt. The

rock is dark in colour, and quite fresh and tough even at the surface. It contains much magnetite: in thin section that mineral together with augite, olivine, melilite and perofskite are seen lying in a palebrown glassy matrix. Both the melilite and the olivine are quite fresh. The rock has been analysed by Mr. J. Lewis,[5] of the Government Laboratory in Cape Town, with the following result:— 1 Rupert Jones, 1901. Given in Rogers and du Toit, 1904.
A little sulphide, which would slightly increase the figure for ferrous iron, is inclnded. The sulphur present as sulphide is included in the SO₃.

At Ash ton, and westward to Worcester, the Uitenhage Series occurs as coarse conglomerate beds. It forms hills from one to two hundred feet above the general surface. In this area its boundaries are obscured by much recent conglomerate, formed by the weathering out and recementing of Enon boulders. Around Worcester the Enon Conglomerate rests on the Ecca as well as on the older formations.

In the Olifant's River valley, between the Langebergen and the Zwartebergen, the Uitenhage Series has a considerable outcrop, resting sometimes on Bokkeveld, sometimes on Cango beds. It is well seen at the southern ends of the main river gorges coming from the north, namely, in Coetzee's, Potgieter's and Schoeman's Poorts. Throughout the district it form a series of low hills, which are red in colour, and often carved into irregular shapes by the weathering out of the sandstone layers. On the south bank of the Olifant's River many small caves are formed by such weathering (see Fig. 64). The beds consist mainly of conglomerate and coarse sandstone; as a rule they are horizontal, and are of an extremely lenticular character. At Vlakte Plaats, south-east of Meirine's Poort, the conglomerate contains a deposit of lignite, which is used locally as fuel.

In all these western outcrops there is not the same definite sequence of beds as in the east. The marine beds seem to be quite absent in the outcrops west of Plettenberg Bay; but though conglomerate is the chief rock present, it is not likely that it represents the Enon of the Eastern Province only, but also some, if not all, of the higher divisions.

Fossils of the Uitenhage. Semes

The fossil plants of the Uitenhage Series have recently been described by Seward, who has revised the nomenclature assigned to many of them by Tate in 1867. Though numerous specimens occur throughout the Wood Bed, the number of species represented is comparatively small. Seward found the following forms among the specimens sent him by the Director of the Cape Survey:— Ferns: *Onychiopsis mantelli* (Fig. 67 c), *Cladophlebis browniana* (Fig. 67 a) = *Asplenites lobata,1 C. denticulata = Pecopteris Atherstonei* and *P. rubidgei* forma *Atherstonei* (Fig. 67 b), *Sphenopteris Jittoni, TcBniopteris*. Cycads: *Zamites recta* (Fig. 67 e and f) _ — *PalcBozamia (Otozamites) recta, Z. morrisii* (Fig. 67 d) = *Palreozamia Podozamites) morrisii, Z. africana -Palceozamia (PterophyUum) africana Z. rubidgei* = P. rubidgei, *Nilssonia tatei, Ci/cadolepisjenkinsiana = Ci/clopteris jenkinsiana*. Conifers: *Araucarites rogersi, Taxites, Brachyphyllum, Conites*.

The fossils from the Zwartkop's and Sunday's Rivers Series 1 The names in square brackets are those given by Tate in 1867.

are chiefly Mollusca. Reptilian remains have however been found: in 1900 Schwarz discovered the almost complete *Fin. 68.—Cephalopoda from tbe Uitenhage Series.—a, Ammonites (Olcostephanus) atherstonei*, 4 nat. size (after Shariie); *b, Ammonites (Olcostephanus) bainii* (after Sharpe); c. *Ammonitei subanceps* (after Tate); *d, Belemnites africanns* (after Tate). skeleton of a plesiosaurian, which has not yet been determined nor described. The cephalopods are represented by *Nautilus, Ammonites (Olcostephanus) atherstonei* (Fig. 68 a and Fig. 65), *A. (Olcostephanus) bainii* (Fig. 68 b), *A. subanceps (Crioceras spinosissimum)* (Fig. 68 c), *Hamites africanus*, and *Belemnites africanus* (Fig. 68 d). The Kig. 70. — 1-amelliljranclis from the

Uitenhage Series *(continued).—a, Lyrodon conocardiiform.is* (after Krauss); *b, Pectm prqjeelus* (after Tate); *c, Pholadomya dominicalis* (after Sharpe); *d, Pinna sharpei* (after Tate); *e, Psammobia atherstonei* (after Sharpe); /, *Trii/onla eaisiope = (T. Tatci)* (after Neumayr). gastropods are *Actceonina atherstonei, A. morrisiana, A. jenkinsiana, A. sharpeana, Alaria coronata, Chemnitzia africana, Natica atherstonei, Patella caperata, Trochus bainii, Turbo atherstonei, T. bainii, T. stoivianus, Turitella rubidgeana*. The lamellibranchs are represented by *Anoplomya lutraria* (Fig. 69 a), *Area jonesii* (Fig. 69 b), *Astarte bronnii (Seebachia bronnii)* (Fig. 69 c); *A. herzogii* (Fig. 69 d), *Avicula bainii, Crassatella complicata, Cucutrea atherstonei, C. hraussi* (Fig. 69 /'), *Cypricardia niveniana, Oyprina borcherdsi* (Fig. 69 e), *C. rugulosa, Gervillia dentata* (Fig. 69 g), *Lima obliquissima, L. neglecta, Lyrodon conocardiiformis* (Fig. 70 a), *Mytilus jonesii, Mytilus (Modiola) atherstonei, Ostrea imbricata, Exogyra jonesiana, Pecten projectus* (Fig. 70 b), *Perna atherstonei, Pholadomya dominicalis* (Fig. 70 c), *Pinna atherstonei, P. sharpei* (Fig. 70 d), *Placunopsis imbricata, Pfeuromya bainii, P. lutraria, Psammobia atherstonei* (Fig. 70 e), *Trigonia conocardiiformis, T. cassiope (T. tatei)* (Fig. 70 f), *T. goldfussi, T. herzogii, T. van, T. ventricosa. Cidaris pustulifera* and *Isastrcea richardsoni* represent the echinoderms.

The Umtamvuna Series

The Umtamvuna or Upper Cretaceous Series outcrops in patches along the coast from near the eastern boundary of the Cape Colony to St. Lucia Bay in Zululand; and Bullen Newton's determination of a fossil, found by Draper at Sofala, as *Alectryonia ungulata*, shows that it is exposed on the East African coast also.1 Recent observations by Anderson2 in Natal and Zululand prove that the series covers a much greater area than the actual outcrops indicate; for the occurrence on the beach of boulders with fossils, and the results of certain boreholes, show that it underlies much of the recent sandstone and

limestone of the coastal zone, and must in places form the sea-floor not far below the tide limit.

1 Bullen Newton, 189ti. '-Anderson, Report, 1904.

The beds are unconformable to the older formations; and there is no evidence that the Uitenhage Series anywhere underlies them. It appears, therefore, as if the coast of Natal and Pondoland had only been submerged towards the close of the Cretaceous, at a time when the coast around Algoa Bay was above sea-level, ite submergence having occurred during an earlier part of the period.

The most southerly outcrops of undoubted Umtamvuna Beds occur along the coast for a distance of about ten miles, between the mouths of the Umtentu and the Umtentwana, south of the Umtamvuna River. The beds rest on a coarse quartzitic sandstone belonging to the Table Mountain Series, and are bedded horizontally, or with a low easterly dip. They form a rough platform, with a width of 100 yards at low water during spring tides, and attain a maximum elevation of from 60 to 100 feet above sea-level. Shoreward the formation usually disappears beneath the sand-dunes. Garden, Sutherland and Griesbach described, at the Umzamba mouth, a good outcrop, consisting of a line of low caves, or rather undercut cliffs, caused by the weathering out of the softer beds from beneath an upper hard limestone. Since the visits of the earlier writers there appears to have been a considerable change, for when Messrs. Rogers and Schwarz visited the locality in 1900 they found that some of the former exposures were covered by sand. The line of caves, which Garden described as extending ""for about 800 yards," was found in 1900 to occur along a mile of outcrop, and north-east of the larger caves, outcrops of Griesbach's bed " b" were found, which are not mentioned bv the earlier writers. The beds are seen for about 300 yards up the Umzamba River.

Griesbach1 considered that the fossils occurred in five 1 Griesbach, 1871. zones coincident with the five-fold petrographical subdivision of the series in this locality: he gave the succession from above downward, as:— (/) Hard limestone, which forms the roof of the caves. (e) Softer sandstone and grit, containing many fossils, mostly bivalves and gastropods. *(d)* Sandstones and grits, containing ammonites. (c) A bed of softer brown sandstone, with great abundance of *Trigonia*; this led is more exposed near the Umzambane (Umzamba) River. (6) A hard calcareous stratum, very much worn by the sea; large trees and branches are included in it; much traversed by *Teredo* borings. *(a)* Karroo shales and sandstones.

The Cape Geological Survey in 1900 found the underlying rocks to be Table Mountain Series instead of Karroo Beds: an examination of the entire section, some 20 feet in all, showed that the fossils that Griesbach considered typical of the higher zones occur also in subdivision *"b,"* which is a coarse shelly sandstone, with occasional boulders of grit and slate. In this lower zone, in addition to the *Teredo*-bored wood, there were found chelonian bones and sharks' teeth; *Nautilus, Ammonites soutoni, A. stangeri, A. umbulazi, A. (Puzosia) gardeni* and *Baculites*; *Fasciolaria* and *Chemnitzia* among the gastropods; lamellibranchs were represented by *Pecten, Inoeeramus, Protocardium, Trigonia, Pectunculus, Area,* and *Cardium*. To the south-west of the Umzamba a similar bed occurs below the high-water line for a distance of eight miles along the coast.

The upper beds are well seen at the caves nearest the mouth of the Umzamba River, where some 13 feet of shelly limestone, sandy clays, shales and conglomerates pass up under the surface sand and soil. The limestones contain many water-worn fragments of *Trigonia, Area,* and *Pectuncuius*. The sandy clays contain foraminifera. *Inoceramus* occurs in considerable quantity. Messrs. Rogers and Schwarz state that the same fossils are found in this Umzamba section throughout its entire thickness, the difference in the distribution being, according to them, simply due to the fact that in the coarser beds the stronger

shells alone are preserved. The total thickness of the series exposed in this locality does not exceed 30 feet.1

Chapman found six species and varieties of ostracoda, in material from the lower bed; two of these were new. The ostracod valves were not abundant; but Chapman concludes, from the species represented, that they are intermediate between the Upper and the Lower Cretaceous, with a stronger affinity to the Upper forms. The foraminifera are more abundant, especially *Xodusaria, Yaginulina, Globigerina, Pulvinulina*: the species are all such as would be found in quite shallow water.2

Farther south, at the Embotyi River, coarse green sandstones and conglomerates containing boulders of Karroo dolerite occur. They lie sometimes nearly horizontal, sometimes with a dip of 20" to the north-east. It is probable that these also belong to the Umtamvuna Series, forming a basal conglomerate similar to the Enon of the Uitenhage Series.

Across the Natal boundary Umtamvuna Beds are found at the mouth of the Impenyati River. Recent borings show that they occur under the bluff sandstone at Durban, and Anderson considers that beneath the Pleistocene and recent alluvials they form the entire littoral from Port Durnford northward to beyond Delagoa Bay, extending westward as far as the foot-hills of the interior. They also outcrop on the south of the Umfolosi River, and between the Lebombo 1 Rogers and Schwarz, 1902 a. 2 Chapman, 1904.

range and the coast in Amatongaland. The beds are of the same type as those occurring in Pondoland, namely, conglomerate, calcareous sandstone, limestone, chalk and chalk marl with numerous fossils. At the mouth of the Umhlatuzi River they probably rest on the coal formation; then, as far as the Umsinene River, on the basaltic rocks that overlie the beds of the St. Lucia coalfield; while farther north they lie on the rhyolitic lava of the Lebombo range.1

At Umkwelane Hill, between the Lower Umfolosi River and Lake Isitesa, the fossiliferous bed is, according to

Anderson, an impure limestone of bluish-grey and greyishbrown colour; lithologically it is a shell-agglomerate with a hard matrix full of fossils. Above it lies a greenish-yellow calcareous sandstone. The fossils from this locality have recently been described by R. Etheridge.2

On the north-western side of False Bay and at the St. Lucia Lakes the beds consist of gritty felspathic sandstone, more or less calcareous, interbedded with clays and marls: gastropods and corals are the chief fossils.

In the bed of a stream, about two miles east of Crossly's Store, Bombeni, near the southern end, and at the foot, of the eastern slope of the Lebombo range, there are exposures of a coarse conglomerate of quartzite and basalt boulders imbedded in a light-yellow calcareous matrix. No pebbles of the Lebombo rhyolite were found in it. It is-evidently a beach deposit with fragmental and worn gastropod shells, a few lamellibranchs and an occasional cephalopod. The outcrop is much obscured by recent sands.

On the Umsinene River, some miles to the west of the north end of False Bay, a portion of St. Lucia Lake, there outcrops a fine-grained calcareous sandstone of greenishyellow colour resembling the upper beds of Umkwelane 1 Anderson, 1904. 2 Etheridge, 1904.

S

Hill. It contains ammonites and Terec/obored wood, one of the former being over a foot in diameter; bivalves are common; but gastropods rare. The beds are only locally fossiliferous, and the individual fossils are not very abundant. Anderson identifies this locality as being probably the one in Zululand mentioned by Griesbach.

On the coast south of Cape Vidal, and farther north, at Uquobeletini Lake, south of Sordwana Point, the Umtamvuna Beds are represented by calcareous sandstones and grits, quartzitic in places; locally they become conglomeratic, with pebbles of transparent quartz, slate and other metamorphic rocks.

Fossils of the Umtamvuna Series

Of the fossils collected from these beds

by the Cape Survey only the foraminifera and ostracoda have so far been described; but many specimens of the chief types formerly determined by Baily and Griesbach were obtained. The leading species of the fauna are given in the following list, some being identical with those described from Umkwelane Hill by Etheridge, whose nomenclature is also given:—Cephalopods— *Ammonites soutoni* (Fig. 71 *b), A. stangeri, A. (Pvzosia) gardeni, A. umbulazi* (Fig. 71 *a), A. rembda, A. kayei, Anisoceras rugatum, Bacidites sulcatus.* Gastropods—*Solarium pulchellum, S. wiebeli. Turritella bonei* (= *T. multistriata* of Griesbach), *Cerithium defectum, C. kaffrarium* (Fig. 71 *c), T. meadii* (Fig. 71 *e)* (= *C. undosa* of Griesbach), *T. renavxiana* (= *Euchrysalis gigantea* of Griesbach), *Scalaria ornata* (= *S. turbinata* of Griesbach), *Chemnitzia sutherlandii* (Fig. 71 *d)* (= *C. undosa* of Griesbach), *Voluta rigida* (Fig. 71 */), Natica multistriata, Dentalium.* Lamellibranchs—*Cardium denticulatum, Area* (= *Trigonarca,* Eth.) *umzambaniensis* (Fig.

Fig. 71.—Fossils from the Umtamvuna Series (Pondoland). — Cephalopoda: a, *Ammonites umbulaxi* (after Baily); b, *Ammonites souloni* (after Baily) (about h nat. size). Gastropods: c, *Cerithium kaffrarium* (after Griesbach); d, *Chcmnitzia sutherlandii* (after Baily); e, *Turritclla meadii;* «', 3 times nat. size (after Baily); /, *Voluta rigida* (after Baily). 72 *a), A.* (= *Latiarca* (?), Eth.) *natalensis* (Fig. 72 *c), A. capensis, Trigonia elegans, T. shepstonei* (Fig. 72 *b), Inoceramus expansxis, PectuncuJus africanus, Pecten quinquecostatus, Ostrcea.* Echinoderms— *Hemiaster forbesii* (Fig. 72 *d).*
Fig. 72.—Fossils from the Umtamvuna Series (Pondoland), *continual.* — Lamcllibranohs: «, *Area umzambaniensis* (after Baily); b, *Trigonia s/upstonei* (after Griesbach); c. *Area natalensis* (after Baily). Eehinoderm: *d, Hemiaster forbesii* (after Baily).

In the exposures at Umkwelane Hill vertebrates are represented by fragments of chelonian skeletons and the teeth of *Lamna;* the cephalopods by

Placenticeras kaffrarium, P. umhwelanensis, Creniceras (?), *Hamites, Baculites.* The gastropods are—*Fulguraria, Zaria bond* (Fig. 73 *b)* (= *Turritella bonei,* Baily = *Turritella multistriata,* Gries bach), *Pyropsis* (?), *Oylichna griesbachi, C. fusuliniformis, Aetceonina atherstonei* var. *umkwelanensis* (Fig. 73 *c),*

Flo. 73.—Fossils from the Umtamvuna Series (Umkwelane Hill, Zululand). —Gastropods: a, *Alalia bailyi,* x2; b, *Zaria bnnei,* x3; e, *AcUronina atherstonei* var. *uinkwelanensis;* rf, *Protocardium hillanum* var. *umkwelanensis;* e, *Latiarca witalensis; f, Mactra zulu,* x 2. (All after Etheridge.) *Alarm bailyi* (Fig. 73 a), *Cliemnitzia, Solarium.* The lamellibranchs are — *Ostrea, Exogyra, Neithea, Melina (zndersoni, Gervillia, Pinna, Mytilus, Trigonia umkwelanensis, Trigonarca umzambaniensis* (= *Area umzambaniensis* of Baily), *Latiarca* (?) *natalensis* (= *Area natalensis* of Baily) (Fig. 73 e), *Cardium bvilen-newtoni, Protocardium hillanum* var. *umkwelanensis* (Fig. 73 *d), Eriphyla* (?) *mpert-jonesi, Cytherea* (?) *kaffraria, Cicatrca, Tapes, Donax andersoni, Mactra(?) zidu* (Fig. 73/), *Corbida.* CHAPTER II SUPERFICIAL DEPOSITS

A Considerable variety of superficial deposits is found throughout South Africa. While some are quite recent, others must date back at least to Tertiary times; but in the absence of fossil evidence it is impossible at present to classify all of these deposits according to age. In this chapter, therefore, the beds are provisionally grouped according to their chemical characteristics, namely, as calcareous, ferruginous, and siliceous deposits.

Calcareous Deposits

The calcareous deposits are of three main types: (a) sandy limestones formed near the coast from old dune accumulations; *(b)* deposits of calc-tufa occurring over a considerable area of the Karroo and in the Orange River Colony, the Transvaal and Bechuanaland; (c) stalactitic and stalagmitic deposits in the dolomite caves.

On the coast there are considerable dune deposits (see Fig. 74), and the un-

derlying rocks have been much abraded by the wind-blown sand. For instance, at Camps Bay, near Cape Town, the granite is scored and polished where the sand has passed freely over it (see Fig. 75), and pitted on those portions that stand broadside to the direction of the wind (see Fig. 76). The moving dunes have covered much of the country immediately adjoining the coast, but the Forestry Department of the Cape Colony has for some time past taken steps to minimise the destruction by planting grasses suitable for arresting the movement of the sand.

Many of the dunes have been in part or entirely cemented to a fairly compact rock by the deposition of carbonate of lime derived from the solution of shell fragments. These old dune-deposits are very extensive round the coast, and in some places, as for instance on the north of False Bay and at Struys Point (See Fig. 77), have been carved by the sea into cliffs of considerable height. At Saldanha Bay the dune limestone is quarried and actually used as a buildingstone for important public buildings in Cape Town—a purpose for which, by the way, it is totally unsuitable. On the south coast near Bredasdorp the dunes have yielded skulls and other bones of rhinoceros, elephant and various species of antelope. The Bluff at Durban consists in its upper portion of a sandy dune limestone.

Large areas in the central and northern portions of South Africa are covered by a typical calc-tufa the origin of which is difficult to explain. The Karroo sedimentary rocks contain a good deal of carbonate of lime, and lime is present in the felspar and augite of the dolerites: possibly the

Fig. 75.—Wind-denuded Granite, Camps Bay, near Cape Town.

material of the tufas has been derived from the weathering of these different rocks. In many places the tufa attains a thickness of twelve feet, while the average is certainly not less than four. It affords good material for ordinary limemaking. In the beds of the Karroo rivers and elsewhere the tufa often contains numerous boulders or pebbles, which in places impart to it the form of a conglomerate with a calcareous cement.

Reference has already been made to the calcareous deposits in the caves in the Dolomite (see Fig. 6 and pp. 56 and 160).

Ferruginous Deposits

The ferruginous deposits consist mainly of laterite. This substance is known in the Transvaal as "oudeklip," and is

Fig. 76.—Portion of wind-denuded Granite showing pittings, Camps Bay.

almost invariably taken to be of igneous origin. It varies in appearance, but consists essentially of weathered debris bound together by a limonitic cement. It has been formed in pools of stagnant water by the deposition, during evaporation, of the iron salts which were in solution. This process is repeated every year, and the loose debris which accumulates between the rainy seasons is thus cemented to a kind of bog-iron-ore. The thickness of the laterite varies, within short distances, from a few inches to several feet. Near the coast it contains much sand, but inland it is more homogeneous. In the Middelburg district of the Transvaal it often includes considerable beds of limonite and haematite,

Fig. 77.—Old Sand-dune Cliff near Struys Point, Bredasdorp.

which, in some instances, may be of economic importance in the future.

An interesting limonite deposit occurs around the hot spring at Caledon, Cape Colony, the iron having been deposited during the evaporation of the water.

Siliceous Deposits

The siliceous deposits are best known in the districts of Caledon, Bredasdorp, Swellendam and Riversdale in the south of Cape Colony, and also farther east in Komgha and Kentani, in the Transkei, where, in the form of compact quartzites and siliceous conglomerates, they form cappings to the hills and lie on all the formations up to and including the Uitenhage Series.

On the northern slopes of the Langebergen are to be seen peculiar platform-like terraces formed by the accumulation of gravel and sand more or less compacted together. On the tops of the kopjes, just north of the Zwartebergen, accumulations of quartzite boulders and pebbles are found. These have recently been described under the name "High-level Gravels of the Cape," by Schwarz,[1] who concludes that they are the result of past river action.

At Durban Road, near Cape Town, there is a peculiar ridge of rock, first mentioned by Bain, which in places is a hard quartzite, in others a sandstone. It appears to be an old sand-dune compacted by secondary silicification.

1 Schwarz, 1904. PAKT IV VOLCANIC ROCKS OF DOUBTFUL STRATI-GRAPHICAL POSITION

CHAPTER I THE BUSH VELD AMYGDALOID

The Springbok Flats extend as a remarkably even plain from near Warm Baths north to the southern declivities of the Chunie range south of Pietersburg. The surface of this plain is covered by a thick deposit of soil and calcareous tufa: it is only in the cuttings of the Pretoria-Pietersburg Railway, and in well-sinkings, that the subjacent igneous rock can be seen. It is a basic lava, characterised by a great number of amygdales of calcite, zeolites, agate and chalcedony.

Specimens of the Bushveld rock obtained from well-borings on Kortom on the Springbok Flats are of sage-green colour, and are spotted over with amygdales, which are filled sometimes with carbonate of lime (aragonite) and sometimes with a pinkish-white and opaque zeolite. A chemical analysis of the zeolite shows that it approximates to the composition of heulandite. Under the microscope the rock is seen to be made up of a fine plexus of lath-shaped felspar crystals and microlites, hi which are scattered small grains of a pale-brown augite. Green patches of chlorite show by their shape that they are derived from the decomposition of olivine. On the whole the rock, therefore, has the structure and composition of a typical olivine basalt. According to Mr. Holmes, a rock of similar charac-ter occurs on the Limpopo River near Rhodes' Drift.

Molengraaff[1] has expressed the view that the extrusion of these volcanic lavas marked the close of the period during which the intrusion of the Bushveld plutonic rocks took place. Passarge[2] suggests that they were erupted after the deposition of the Stormberg Beds, and connects them with the amygdaloids of Loale and with the Ngami diabases of the Kalahari.

1 Molengraaff, 1898 a. 2 Passarge, 1904, p. 179. CHAPTER II DIAMOND-BEARING DEPOSITS

At Kimberley and at several localities in Griqualand West, Cape Colony; in the Orange River Colony at Jagersfontein, at Koffyfontein near Kroonstad, and in the Smaldeel and Winburg districts; and north-east of Pretoria in the Transvaal occurs a remarkable diamond-bearing, serpentinous breccia. It is found in "pipes" penetrating the stratified rocks of these different localities (see Figs. 78 and 79). When a "diamond mine" is spoken of in South Africa, one of these more or less vertical pipes is meant, in contradistinction to a diamond-bearing wash or alluvial deposit.

The pipes are generally roughly circular in transverse section, and in the case of those in which mining operations have been carried to a considerable depth the diameter has been found to decrease somewhat. The wall-rock varies according to the particular occurrence, and pieces of it are included in the breccia filling the pipe. In the Kimberley and Orange River pipes which have been forced through the Ecca Series, for instance, many pieces of shale are found; whereas in the Pretoria pipes pieces of quartzite and felsitic rocks are common. According to the usage on the diamondfields the country rock of the pipes, whatever its nature, is known as "reef," and where masses of it are included in the breccia thev are termed "floating reef."

In essential characteristics the material filling the various pipes is identical, whether at Kimberley or at Pretoria. It is composed of a large number of minerals together with rock fragments or boulders imbedded in a serpentinous matrix. In the fresh condition it is known as "blue ground," in the weathered stages as "yellow ground." In some pipes, or in parts of the same pipe, the weathered and the fresh variety are sharply separated; in others, the "yellow" passes gradually into the "blue." Examination of the blue ground shows it to consist chiefly of fragments and crystals of the following minerals: olivine (sometimes fresh but generally weathered to serpentine), garnet, ilmenite, chrome-diopside, enstatite, bastite and biotite; and, in less quantity, of magnetite, chromite, picotite, perofskite (seen in abundance under the microscope in the Kimberley rocks), tourmaline, zircon, rutile, cyanite, corundum and diamond. Among the diamond miners some of these minerals have special names, as for example: "greenstone" for diopside and the greener varieties of olivine, "ruby" for garnet, "carbon" for ilmenite, which in the early mining days was mistaken for carbonado, and "Australian boart" for zircon.

Olivine is the chief of the individual minerals, as, in addition to the recognisable pieces always met with, much, recognisable, but many of the pieces are rounded. The crystals, or grains, may be as much as one centimetre in length. A good pinacoidal cleavage is often visible under the microscope, and the usual serpentisation is seen around the crystals or in the cracks.

The diopside is generally of a bright, emerald-green colour, and consequently is more conspicuous than the olivine. It has a very distinct cleavage. Large pieces are occasionally found with a smooth, rounded surface, as if abraded.

Garnet is a common mineral in the blue and also in the yellow ground; in the latter, however, it is sometimes reduced by weathering to a brownish-red powder or clay. It is usually the pyrope variety, and is characterised by a very dark colour. In the blue ground the larger as well as the microscopic grains generally show a brown alteration ring of the so-called kelyphite.

The biotite is also prominent, occurring in numerous small scales but also as crystals about a centimetre in diameter. Under the microscope, and sometimes to the naked eye, it shows a brownish, or black, corroded margin, frequently with a rounded outline. Its alteration product, "vaalite," is soft instead of elastic, and yellowish or bluish green in colour.

The perofskite is only visible under the microscope. It occurs abundantly in the blue ground from Kimberley, its high refractive index making the small crystals quite a prominent feature in thin sections.

The ilmenite is often very abundant, occurring in rounded grains; crystals are rare, however.

The diamond itself occurs in a great variety of crystal combinations. Many of the Kimberley stones are more or less complex combinations of octahedron, dodecahedron and hexakis-octahedron, but simple octahedra also occur. In colour and purity all varieties are found, from the purest "blue white" down to "black" and "spotted rubbish."

In size the diamonds vary greatly: some of over 100 carats are frequently found. The Cullinan stone, discovered on January 25, 1905, in the Premier mine, near Pretoria, weighs 3024f carats, or T37 lbs. avoirdupois. It is a portion of an original octahedral crystal, and measures 4 by 2 by 2 inches. It shows eight surfaces, four of which are faces of the original crystal and four are cleavage planes. Fig. 80, reproduced from a photograph by Mr. E. H. V. Melvill, shows the largest cleavage plane and the best-developed octahedral face in front view, while Fig. 81 is a diagrammatic representation of all the surfaces. For a large stone the crystal is of remarkable purity, and the colour approximates to "blue-white." *Petrographical Description of the Diamond-bearing Breccia*

In addition to the mineral fragments, the breccia contains numerous boulders and pieces of rock, recognisable as derived in some instances from the walls of the pipe, but in others from depths greater than the mining operations have yet reached. In the Kimberley mines the chief rocks present in the breccia of the upper part of the pipe were shale and amygdaloidal diabase, while on the lower levels, now being worked, quartzite, granite, quartz-porphyry and diabase chiefly occur. In the Jagersfontein mine the boulders now found consist chiefly of the dolerite which forms the greater portion of the wall of the pipe. In the Lace mine near Kroonstad, at its present stage of development, the chief boulders present are of amygdaloidal diabase and Karroo sandstone. In the upper beds of the Premier mine, near Pretoria, the boulders are largely composed of quartzite, some of which is recognisable as belonging to the Waterberg System, the remainder being from the Pretoria Beds; granite, felsite and diabase of various types also occur. The presence of boulders and large masses of Waterberg Sandstone indicates that in its upper portion the pipe must have penetrated that series (see Fig. 88).

In addition to these foreign boulders, there are in all the mines concretionary nodules or masses which were formed in the magma from which the breccia is derived. These will be described later.

In the yellow ground more or less of the minerals and boulders are always visible, but the mass of the rock has become disintegrated, the various minerals being reduced to clayey, sandy, or calcareous decomposition products. The minerals which, in varying proportion, almost always remain unaltered in the yellow ground are garnet, ilmenite, diopside, mica, and the diamond, while fragments of foreign rock enclosures are always recognisable. It is the three first-mentioned minerals which form the greater portion of the "deposit" obtained by the diamond prospector, after washing and sieving the crushed rock.

While the same minerals are to be found in all blue and yellow grounds, their proportion varies very much: in some mines garnet predominates, in others ilmenite; the diopside is always subordinate, but is sometimes more, sometimes less, abundant than the unweathered olivine.

The cementing material has generally a greenish rather than a blue tinge. It consists of serpentinous clayey matter; much calcite and other carbonates are present, and various zeolities have been recognised. In all mines there are portions of the blue ground known to the miners as "hardibank," which, unlike the normal rock, does not disintegrate on exposure: it is unworkable as a source of diamonds, at least by present methods.

Besides the pipes filled by diamond-bearing breccia, there are others in which the diamonds are apparently absent, although the breccia has all the remaining characteristics. At Britstown, in Cape Colony, there is an outcrop of typical soft blue, which has not yielded a single diamond. Recently Messrs. Rogers and du Toit have described certain pipes in the Sutherland district, Cape Colony, some filled with melilite basalt, others with agglomerates and tuffs, comparable in many respects to the diamond-bearing breccia, but which have been prospected in vain for diamonds.[1] Other pipes contain diamonds, but not in sufficient quantity to repay exploitation.

1 Rogers and du Toit, 1904 a. *The Discovery of Diamonds in South Africa*
The story of the discovery of diamonds in South Africa is not lacking in romance. Early in 1867 a Dutch farmer, Schalk van Niekerk, saw, on the banks of the Orange River near Hope Town, the children of another Boer named Daniel Jacob, or Jacobs, playing with some river pebbles. Attracted by the lustre of one of them, he got the mother to give it to him. Niekerk handed it to a Mr. John O'Reilly, who happened to be returning from a hunting and trading expedition, to have it examined. O'Reilly took the stone to Colesberg and showed it to Mr. Lorenzo Boyes, Clerk of the Peace for the District, who sent it, on March 12, in a letter to Dr. W. Guybon Atherstone in Graham's Town. Atherstone recognised it as a diamond, and wrote at once to the Colonial Secretary in Cape Town, the Hon. Richard Southey, to whom the stone was subsequently sent. Atherstone's determination having been confirmed by the French Consul, M. Henriette, the stone was forwarded to the Paris Exhibition and subsequently purchased for £500 by

Sir Philip Wodehouse, Governor of Cape Colony. Ten months elapsed before another stone was found; but in May 1869 Atherstone was able to give the following list of finds and localities: "Six along the Orange River in the Hope Town Division, six along the Vaal, three beyond the Vaal, two beyond the Orange River, two along the Riet River, one in Waterboer's country, and one on government land in the Colony." [1]

In March 1869 the "Star of South Africa," 83J carats, was found on the farm Zandfontein near the Orange River. Organised search in the river gravels was begun by a party [1] Atherstone, 1869, *Among the Diamonds*. of Natal prospectors at Hebron in November 1869, and their success gradually attracted a large and motley crowd to the valley of the Vaal in the neighbourhood of Klip Drift, now Barkly West, and of Pniel. The river-diggings stretched from Hebron, 20 miles north-east of Klip Drift, to Sofenells 60 miles west.[1] At the present day the river-diggings are owned by individual workers, each having his own claim,[2] in both the Cape and Orange River Colonies. In the latter Colony, during 1903-04, an average of seventy diggers were working. The river stones have a recognisable difference from those obtained in any of the mines: so far their original source has not been discovered.

The first "dry digging" appears to have been discovered on Bultfontein, then in the Jacobsdaal District, Orange Free State. On November 6, 1869,[8] a Boer named Cornelius Hendrik du Plooy brought into the village of Jacobsdaal some stones which he had picked up on his farm: amongst them was a diamond. In August 1870 diamonds were found on the farm Jagersfontein; a month later they were found at Dutoitspan, on the farm Dorstfontein, about 20 miles southeast of Pniel. In May 1871 diamonds were found at a place on De Beers' farm Vooruitzicht, about 2 miles from Dutoitspan, which has since become the De Beers mine; and two months later, on the same farm, another deposit, now the Kimberley

mine, was discovered.[4] In September 1890 the Wesselton mine, about 4 miles from Kimberley, was opened.

Neither the early diggers nor the Government realised at first the difference between the dry and the river diggings, the general idea being that the former were old alluvial [1] Gardner Williams, 1902, p. 158.
2 A diamond claim, whether alluvial or in a pipe, is 30 x 30 Cape feet. 3 See letters from David Draper and E. E. Hurley, *South African Mines,* February 4 and 11, 1904. Williams, 1904. deposits: in many cases, after working out the yellow ground, the claim-owners abandoned their holdings, under the mistaken idea that the harder blue ground was the bedrock of the deposit. *Characteristics of the Diamonds*
Though certain types of stones may be found in all the mines, there is a considerable individuality in the yield from any one mine, parcels being characterised by certain wellmarked features easily recognisable by the expert.[1]

The river stones are the finest in respect of brilliancy and colour, many of them being quite equal to the best Brazilian stones. They are distinguished from the produce of the mines by their water-worn appearance. Next to the river diamonds are the Jagersfontein stones, among which are " blue whites " of exceptionally fine quality and size. Fine "whites" also occur, but there is an almost entire absence of the ordinary yellow stones. The De Beers mine is noted for an abnormally large percentage of ordinary "yellows," and a very small percentage of dark "yellows" which are classed as "fancies." There is a limited proportion of fine "silver Capes," and of light brown "cleavage" of a rather delicate shade. There is an almost entire absence of really white diamonds, most of the so-called "whites" possessing a slight " Cape " tinge. The produce of the Kimberley mine, although most nearly resembling that of the De Beers mine, possesses, nevertheless, its own distinct characteristics. It shows a fair proportion of white "crystals" (octahedra) which are rarely met with in the De Beers mine, a good percentage of "white cleavage" and a comparatively high 1 The characteristics of the stones from the Cape and Orange River Colony mines:iic from notes by Mr. *A.* Brink in Lawn. 18!8.

percentage of large macles or flat twin stones. "Yellows" are found in fairly large proportion, generally lighter in colour than those from De Beers. Dutoitspan mine is noted for its very fine "silver Capes" (finer in quality than those from the De Beers mine), its fine quality of ordinary white stones and "cleavages" and its large "yellows." The proportion of large stones is high, and diminutive diamonds are comparatively few. The Bultfontein mine produces easily distinguished stones. They are white but much spotted, and the diamond-cutters generally dislike dealing in parcels of supposedly pure stones from this mine, as the spots often cannot be detected until the stones are cut and polished. Very few " yellows" are found, and the produce consists of comparatively small diamonds, ranging from two to three carats downwards. The Wesselton mine produces chiefly white and brown diamonds, the latter being of very inferior quality. The white stones form a big percentage, and are of a better quality than in any of the other mines in the Kimberley district. There is also a small percentage of blue whites.

A parcel of diamonds from the Premier mine. Pretoria, is characterised by the large proportion of macles and big cleavage pieces, the quantity of irregularly shaped crystals, the variety of fancy colours—comprising blue (ultramarine), brown, green and deep yellow—and by the small percentage of octahedral stones.1 *The diamond mines of the Cape Colony*

The principal mines are those of the De Beers Company. They are situated in and around Kimberley, and comprise the Kimberley, the De Beers, Bultfontein, Dutoitspan and 1 We have to thank Mr. Devenish, Valuer of the Premier Company, for the substance of the above paragraph.

Wesselton mines. As shown in the accompanying sections (Fig. 82) by Mr. Gardner Williams,1 the geological character of the country is uniform. The sections show Ecca Shales with intrusive dolerites underlaid by Dwyka Conglomerate resting on a thick sheet of amygdaloidal melaphyre, beneath which are beds of a dark compact quartzite, flows of quartzporphyry, and a coarse, highly indurated conglomerate—all belonging to the Ventersdorp System.

The Kimberley mine (see Fig. 79) has a surface area of 470 claims, or 10'37 acres, and is richer than the others in its vicinity. For the year ending June 1904, the levels worked were from 1640 feet to 2080 feet, the interval between successive levels being here, as in the other De Beers mines, 40 feet. The main shaft had reached a depth of 2599 feet. The open mine was 880 feet below the surface and 377 feet below the hard rock, its lowest point being 1000 feet. Both at Kimberley and De Beers, as the underground workings are carried on, the mass of debris lying in the open mine is constantly sinking and thus increasing the depth of the latter.

The De Beers mine has a surface area of 622 claims, or 1372 acres, and is next to the Kimberley mine in richness. It contains areas of blue ground that are very poor. At June 1904 the levels worked were from 1200 feet to 1600 feet. The "rock shaft" had reached a depth of 2076 feet, and the 2040-foot level had Leen opened.

The average yield per load 1 washed from the Kimberley and De Beers mines is-54 of a carat: in 1903-04, 930,511 loads were washed from Kimberley, and 1,470,588 loads from De Beers. The yield for the year ending June 30, 1904, was 1,303,525 carats, and its value, £3,192,798.

Bultfontein mine has an area of 1067 claims, or 23'54 1 Williams, 1904. 2 A load in diamond-mining is 16 cubic feet.

Fio. 82.—Sections showing the rocks cut in the shafts of the Kimberley mines. (After Gardner Williams.) acres. Both the value of the diamonds and the yield per load have increased as depth has been gained. Down to 440 feet the mine is an open working; at June 30, 1904, the shaft had been sunk to a depth of 600 feet.

Dutoitspan, the largest *af* the De Beers group of mines, has an area of 1441 claims, or 3179 acres. This mine was noted for the large size and excellent quality of its diamonds, but for some years it was shut down, being considered too poor to work. It has now, like Bultfontein, passed entirely into the ownership of the De Beers Company and is being re-opened. A shaft has been sunk 814 feet and a drive has intersected the blue on the 750-foot level at a distance of 796 feet from the shaft. During development 30,377 loads of blue ground from the 750-foot level were washed, yielding 4031 J; carats, Aalued at £6457, or an average of "13 of a carat per load.1

The Wesselton mine (see Fig. 83), formerly called the Premier, a name now relinquished in favour of its more fortunate Transvaal rival, is at present worked as an open mine down to a depth of 300 feet. The levels from 300 down to 500 feet are being developed for underground working. Owing to a large proportion of inferior stones, the product of this mine is less valuable than that of the others. The average yield for 1903-04 was-28 of a carat per load; and the number of carats found, 605,241, worth £1,055,269.

The Newlands mines2 are situated on the Harts River about 40 miles northwest of Kimberley. The country rock consists of sandstone, shale and amygdaloidal diabase exactly as at Kimberley. There are four mines, all of which are connected by, and appear to be enlargements of, a dyke, 3 to 8 feet wide, of typical diamond-bearing breccia quite 1 Report to June 30, 1904. 2 Graichen, 1903; Beck, 1898, 1899. similar to that of the Kimberley mines. The narrow portions of the dyke are pierced by numerous calcite and quartz veins, and are too hard and narrow for successful mining. The "blue" contains the usual minerals: pyrope in various colours, chrome-diopside, dark green enstatite, ilmenite, chromite, magnetite, numerous flakes of secondary mica, secondary barytes and pyrites, but no zircon. Numerous boulders and concretions occur: the latter, according to Graichen, may consist (1) of mica alone; (2) of enstatite and mica; (3) of garnet, diopside and enstatite in equal proportions. One of them, 10 centimetres in diameter, was found to contain as many as twenty small diamonds. Some of these masses have been examined by Professor Bonney,[1] who determined them as saxonite, garnet-bearing lherzolite, enstatite-eulysite, pegmatitic hornblendic gabbro and eclogite. He concludes from his researches, that as the diamond is associated with the minerals typical of an eclogite, that rock must have been the original matrix of the diamond. The matrix of the Newlands blue ground was analysed for Professor Bonney by Mr. C. James, with the following result:[2]—

About 12 miles north of Newlands there are two other mines connected by a vein or dyke of diamond-bearing 1 Bonney, 1899, 1901.
3 Bonney, 1901, p. 480. breccia 20 feet wide. The north-eastern portion forms the Frank Smith mine, and the southwest the Weltevrede mine, while the intervening dyke-like portion, which is rich in diamonds and contains exceptionally large pieces of ilmenite, is separately worked. *The diamond mines of the Orange River Colony*

The Jagersfontein mine lies 30 miles west of the main line of railway, and is consequently not so well known as the more accessible mines. Its area is 1124 claims, or 24-8 acres. Up to the present, exploitation has been entirely by open workings, the greatest depth reached being 510 feet from the surface. The pipe lies in the Ecca sandstones and shales, which are invaded by a dolerite sheet some 400 feet thick and inclined from north to south. The sedimentary rocks are laid bare on the southern rim of the pipe, but the dolerite forms about two-thirds of the circumference on the northern side, and practically the entire wall of the pipe as far as exposed by present workings. The yellow ground is still present in the eastern half of the mine, but in the western and part of the southern area it has been removed and the

blue has been worked to a depth of over 400 feet. At the south-eastern corner there is a dykelike extension of the breccia into the country rock. The breccia contains many of the concretions already referred to, and the usual minerals are often in large pieces. The mine is famous for its large diamonds, the largest found being the Excelsior, weighing 971 carats.

In 1904 the greater portion of the blue was won from the 450 and 410 foot levels, which yielded the best returns. During the year ending March 31, 1904, 1,836,834 loads were washed, yielding 167,597f carats, worth £555,695, or 66s. 3'75d. per carat, the highest value of any South African stones.

Thirty-five miles east of Jagersfontein is the Koffyfontein mine. This is a large pipe, comprising in all some 1450 claims, penetrating Ecca shales, which are overlaid by red sand and calctufa. The mine is at present worked open cast to a depth of 110 feet. The yield is not a high one, being from 5 to 6 carats per 100 loads, but the stones are of good quality.

Adjoining the Koffyfontein mine is the Ebenhaezer or Ebenezer, with a proclaimed area of 526 claims, extending in a north and south direction somewhat in the form of a human foot. The walls are of the same material as those of Koffyfontein.

A mile north of the Ebenezer is the abandoned Klipfontein mine. This pipe consists of two large circular areas united by a narrow dyke-like portion of the breccia through a dolerite sheet.

The Lace mine (see Fig. 85) lies about 16 miles northwest of Kroonstad, on the farm Driekopjes. It has an *fhuta 11. LuUman-Juhmon.*

Fig. 85.—The Lace mine, November 1904, showing the face of two levels and the beginning of a third.
area of some 400 claims. The formation penetrated by the pipe consists of sandstones belonging to the Karroo

System. In the neighbourhood there are outcrops of hard amygdaloidal diabase and diabase breccia, which were taken for blue ground by early prospectors. In the mine the blue ground is met

with at a depth of 40 to 45 feet from the surface; it shows a sharp line of demarcation from the

"yellow." The boulders consist almost exclusively of u various types of diabase. A little sandstone occurs as floating reef. The yield of the Lace mine is at present about 16 carats per 100 loads.

On the farm Bester's Kraal, west of the Lace mine, a pipe has been discovered, which, like those at Newlands in Griqualand West, appears to be a local enlargement of a dyke of diamondbearing breccia: it has been opened up and prospected for diamonds.

The Monastery mine (see Fig. 86) is situated on a farm of the same name, 36 miles south-east of Winburg, in the Orange River Colony. The two pipes, which have penetrated the Red Beds of the Stormberg Series, are in immediate proximity to the Cave Sandstone, which they probably also pierce. Passing through the pipes are two felsite dykes. 1 The blue ground is composed of the usual minerals, often in large pieces, the garnets having a distinct kelyphite rim. The boulders are chiefly of diabase and sandstone, but numerous 1 From information supplied by Mr. H. D. Griffiths, A.R.S.M., etc.

specimens of an interesting pegmatitic intergrowth of a green pyroxene with magnetite are also found.

In the neighbourhood of Smaldeel there are several places where diamond mining or prospecting is carried on, as for instance on the farm Kaal Valley, where the Robinson Diamond Mining Company has worked for some years past.

The diamond mines of the Transvaal

The first Transvaal diamond mine was discovered in 1897 on the farm Rietfontein (No. 501). It is known as the Schuller mine, and is situated 2 miles south-east of Van der Merwe station. There are two pipes penetrating the Pretoria Quartzites, which dip north-east at 18a. In shape No. 1 pipe is an irregular ellipse, some 240 feet long by 200 feet in breadth. The breccia contains a large proportion of hardibank, which outcrops in places. The second pipe was found in 1898 on the boundary of Rietfontein and Kaalfontein. The portion which lies in the latter farm is owned and worked by the Kaalfontein Company. In section it is an irregular ellipse measuring roughly 400 by 300 feet. The rock is weathered to yellow ground down to a depth of about 25 feet. At the edge of both pipes the sedimentary rocks are much broken; but the actual junction with the diamond-bearing ground is a very sharp one.

The matrix of the Schuller blue ground consists largely of serpentine, derived as usual from olivine, the other minerals being garnet, ilmenite, vaalite, bastite, augite, hypersthene and apatite, while the fragments of foreign rocks consist chiefly of diabase, quartzite and shale; calcite is present in some of the fragments. A chemical analysis of the rock from No. 1 pipe gave the following results 1:— 1 Kymurton and Hall, 1904.
100-444

Sp. gr. 2-757

According to the Report of the Sclmller Company the number of loads washed in 1903 was 3961 of yellow ground, yielding 8-4 carats per 100 loads, and 3687 loads of blue, yielding 6"2 carats per 100 loads. Up to the period covered by the first report, dated January 31, 1902, 38,015 loads had been washed, yielding 33"28 carats per 100 loads.

The most important mine in the Transvaal, the Premier, was opened towards the end of 1902 (see Figs. 87 and 89). It is situated on the farm Elandsfontein (No. 85), about 5 miles north of Van der Merwe station, on the PretoriaDelagoa Bay railway. The pipe has been forced through felsite and quartzite, which form a ridge around the area in which the diamond-bearing breccia occurs. The hollow in which the mine lies is, however, higher than the general level of the surrounding country; it is drained by two small streams which, flowing over the ground owned by the Pretoria District and the Byeneest Poort Diamond Companies, have carried thither the alluvium at present worked for diamonds by those companies.

The mine is now being exploited in two places by open workings—one at the south-east corner of the pipe, the other at the south-west. The section disclosed by the workings is: surface soil, red or white sand, yellow ground, followed by soft blue at a depth varying from 15 to 40 feet or more. In the boreholes put down by the company, the rock was not hard enough to form a core till a depth of 60 feet had been reached. The boulders consist chiefly of red or brown quartzite, conglomerate, felsite and various basic igneous rocks. In the south-east corner of the mine there *Photo A. Macco.*

Fig. 88.—Premier mine, Pretoria. A mass of Waterberg Conglomerate occurring as "floating reef." are large masses of " floating reef," composed of Waterberg sandstone and conglomerate (see Fig. 88). Two boreholes near the centre of the mine passed through an average of 180 feet of similar floating reef. In one of the holes a considerable thickness of an intrusive igneous rock was also pierced. The greatest depth reached in the blue by the boreholes was 1000 feet.

The blue of the Premier mine has a greenish tinge, and contains a large proportion of ilmenite.

The Premier mine is the largest in the world, having a surface area of about 3500 claims, and has recently produced the largest diamond hitherto found (see Fig. 80). The diamonds obtained for the year ending October 31, 1904, weighed 749,6532-carats, being an average per load of *Photo A. Atiuxo.*

Fig. 89.—Premier mine, Transvaal. View of the open working at the beginning of 190:1.
0"798 carats. In the previous year, 99,208 carats were obtained, this being an average of 1"29 carats per load.

The Montrose pipe, the second discovered in the Transvaal, is mainly on the farm Vryneb, but extends also to the north-west into Rooikopjes. The country rock is said to be an intrusive diabase passing into a reddish, more fine-grained rock resembling felsite.1 Recently on the farm Zonderwater a small pipe has also been discovered. Both

these localities are near Van der Merwe station. On the farm Franz Poort a sandy, calcareous, diamond-bearing breccia was worked for some time by the Eastern Diamond Mining Company. Blue ground outcrops on Byeneest Poort, in the bed of a small stream; but the workings of the Company, like those of the Pretoria District Company, are confined to the alluvial deposit already mentioned.
1 Kynaston and Hall, 1904.

It is remarkable that all the Transvaal pipes hitherto discovered lie within a comparatively small area of somewhat elevated ground between the Elands and the Pienaars Rivers.

The Origin of the Diamonds

No definite conclusion has yet been reached as tQ the mode of origin of the pipes. They have been variously regarded as necks marking the site of ordinary volcanic activity, or as the product of ancient mud volcanoes in which water played an important part. On either view, the absence of any trace of volcanic ejectamenta or of a flow of lava or mud-lava from any of the vents is difficult to explain. It is true that since the intrusion of the breccia the surface of the country has been enormously lowered by denudation, still it is remarkable that all evidence of such volcanic activity other than the vents themselves has disappeared.

Daubree has shown experimentally how similar pipes can be produced on a small scale: his deduction that the diamond-bearing necks were produced by violent explosions of gas or steam is the only one which appears tenable. If the explosions were largely due to steam, then the mudlike character of the contents of the pipes can be explained. Possibly the original condition was more like that of a modern geyser than any other known form of volcanic activity. There is evidence in the divergent nature of the blue ground in different parts of individual mines, especially of De Beers, Kimberley, and Jagersfontein, to show that the explosions took place at intervals: the material was probably consolidated as a breccia after a long period during which it had been in a state of motion as a semi-fluid mass.

Diverse views also prevail as to the source of the diamonds. In the early days of the Kimberley mines it was considered that the fusion of the carbonaceous shales forming the walls of the pipe had provided the material for the production of the diamond. Such an explanation became untenable when it was found that the diamonds were present in the "blue" found below the horizon of the shales, and even more so when the Transvaal diamond pipes, which cut through quartzites devoid of any carbonaceous material, were discovered.

Lately the view has been brought forward that the original matrix of the diamond is to be sought in the "boulders" of eclomte and similar rocks that occur in the blue ground. This conclusion has been arrived at by Professor T. G. Bonney, from a study of specimens from the Newlands mine.[1] Bonney suggests that the boulders were already waterworn before they entered the breccia, and regards the Dwyka Conglomerate as a possible source—a view which it is difficult to maintain. The occurrence of the diamond with or in garnet has long been known, specimens having been obtained at Kimberlev and Jagersfontein before the Newlands "eclogite" was discovered. Such boulders are known in all the mines, and recently Mr. Gardner Williams had twenty tons collected at Kimberley and separately crushed and jigged without recovering any [1] Bonney, 1899 a, 1900, and 1900 a. diamonds.[1] Professor Beck[2] regards the Newlands boulders as concretions in the magma from which the blue ground is derived, and this certainly is the explanation suggested by those from Jagersfontein and Kimberley. The very fact that the Newlands specimens as described by Bonney, show so much variation in mineral composition, suggests that they are original concretions or segregations rather than portions of independent rock masses which passed directly or by the medium of some underlying conglomerate into the breccia. The rounded appearance presented by many of the boulders is quite compara-

ble to that of the basic patches so common in many granites.

There is no question that the general character and composition of the breccia points to its derivation from a rock which existed originally as a very basic magma. Experiments carried out by W. Luzi of Leipzig show that the diamond is dissolved by fusion with the S.outh African breccia.[3] The basic character of the rock suggests comparison with the meteoric irons and stones which have been found to contain diamonds; and Moissan's[4] experiments in which he produced diamonds from carbon fused in iron have an important bearing on the question.

From the state of strain in which the diamonds are sometimes found—a condition which occasionally results in their destruction—and from the presence of cavities containing gas under enormous pressure it is certain that they were formed at great depths. Sir William Crookes[5] has suggested that the diamonds were separated out, during the

[1] Williams, 1904. [i] Beck, 1898, 1899.

[J] Quoted by Gardner Williams, 1904.
[4] Moissan, 1893, 1894, 1896.
[5] Lecture on Diamonds delivered at the Royal Institute, London, 1897. cooling of molten iron holding carbon in solution, at great pressure and high temperature. But the facts so far known do not in any way controvert the view that the blue ground, or the rock from which it was formed, is itself the original matrix of the diamond. The fragmental character of many of the diamonds is as explicable on the assumption that they were formed in the molten magma and broken during the movement which went on in the pipes, as it is by assuming that the diamonds are derived from some foreign rock. The fact that some occurrences of blue ground contain all the characteristic minerals except the diamond, points, if anything, in the same direction; for in such cases the chemical or physical conditions necessary for the production of diamonds may simply have been lacking in the magma. Again, the fact that the stones from the different mines have definite peculiarities points rather to their origin

in the individual pipes than to their derivation from an extraneous source.

The age of the various diamond-bearing pipes cannot be definitely ascertained; but as they all have the same main characteristics it is more than probable that they belong to the same period of geological time. The youngest rocks known to be penetrated by diamond-bearing or analogous necks belong to the Stormberg Series. The invasion of the strata by the breccias took place therefore at a later date than the close of this epoch, but no limit is obtainable so far as our present knowledge goes. The Sutherland melilite-basalt and agglomerate necks have, according to Messrs. Rogers and du Toit, a certain analogy with the diamond-bearing pipes. These authors conclude that, as those necks are younger than the Karroo dolerites, they are probably younger than the Stormberg. If they can be correlated with the intrusion of melilite basalt at Spiegel River their age is Lower Cretaceous or later; possibly the diamond-bearing pipes belong to the same epoch. The only definite fact established is that, as some of the diamond necks have pierced the Stormberg Beds, they are posterior to the Rhadtic.

PART V CORRELATION OF THE STRATA

Correlation of the Pre-Karroo formations that occur in the various parts of South Africa involves more than ordinary difficulties. These arise mainly from the surprising absence of fossils; but they are enhanced by the large development of quartzites and conglomerates of almost identical appearance throughout many of the series, and by the existence of many marked unconformities, whose relation to one another is not at once apparent.

The sparse occurrence of fossils is not easy to understand. Even in the formation in which organic remains are most abundant—namely, the Bokkeveld Series—their distribution is limited; and large areas covered by these beds have not yielded a single specimen. Further, although fossils are present in the Bokkeveld Series in sufficient variety and abundance for a safe correlation, this series is confined to the south and west of the Cape Colony, no evidence being yet forthcoming of its existence in the north. In the other formations, notably the Malmesbury Series, there are many fine-grained beds whose appearance warrants the expectation of organic remains, yet minute and careful search in numerous localities has, up to the present, been fruitless. The history of fossil discoveries, however, gives hope that, although unknown, fossils may still be there, which further search one day will bring to light. While the geologist has in South Africa the advantage of a greater abundance of natural outcrops than are afforded in European countries, he has less assistance from artificial cuttings and quarries. The help which may lie afforded by such excavations is well illustrated by the rich discoveries which Mr. T. N. Leslie has made in the quarries in the coal sandstone of Vereeniging; for in these a fossil flora, of which the outcrops afford little indication, has been revealed. It is possible that with the opening up of the older series similar fortunate results will ensue, and that material will lie found not only for a better comparison of the formations in the different parts of South Africa, but also for definite correlation with those of other countries.

The widespread occurrence of coarse quartzites in the older formations throughout the country is not only partly responsible for the absence of fossils, but is, in itself, an obstacle to easy correlation owing to want of individuality in the beds. In widely separated localities, and in formations known to be different, quartzites and conglomerates occur which, if petrographical similarity were alone to be considered, might appear capable of being correlated. Petrographical resemblance, however, affords a safe basis for correlation only where it is supported by stratigraphical evidence, and this, fortunately, is a condition which often prevails throughout South Africa. Such persistent petrographical characters and sequence of beds as is, for instance, afforded by the Black Reef, Dolomite and Pretoria Series can be held sufficient for the cor-

relation of distant outcrops. On the other hand, there are instances of the closest petrographical similarity, sometimes even in uncommon rock types, without any stratigraphical agreement: banded and contorted magnetite-quartzite slates occur, for example, in the Archaean System, in the Witwatersrand Series and in the Pretoria Series, which are so similar in appearance that hand-specimens, and even outcrops, may easily be confused.

Unconformities in the succession are not infrequent; but these, while useful as marking divisions in individual areas, are a source of danger when widely separated districts are under consideration.

However, in spite of such difficulties, it is possible to find material, in the facts now at our disposal, for a rational and connected view of the South African succession.

The most definite bench-march for correlation is afforded by the base of the Karroo System—the Ecca Series, and especially its basement conglomerate. Its widespread occurrence, its distinctive petrographical characteristics, and the fact that, while conformable in the south of the Cape Colony with the uppermost member of the Cape System, it shows a varying degree of unconformity elsewhere, make the Dwyka Conglomerate an excellent datum line.

As already pointed out, the glacial conglomerate in the south of the Karroo and in Natal differs considerably in appearance from that found in the north of the Cape Colony and in the Transvaal: there is therefore little cause for wonder that the stratigraphical identity of the various outcrops was long overlooked. The observations of Schmeisser, and especially the palaeo-botanical work of Seward, were the first steps towards a certain correlation of the beds above the conglomerate in the Transvaal with the Ecca shales of the Cape Colony; and the clue once having been obtained, there was no difficulty in correlating the whole of the Karroo formation of the Transvaal with that of the Cape.

Dunn, on his map of 1887, represented all the coalbearing area of the Trans-

vaal and Natal as of Stormberwage. For the Transvaal this correlation was adopted by Schenck in 1888 and by Molengraaff in 1890, being retained by the latter author until 1903, when he stated that the Transvaal coal was probably of Beaufort age. But Seward's plant determinations, together with the stratigraphical evidence obtained at Kroonstad and elsewhere in the Orange River Colony; at Vereeniging and on the Witwatersrand in the southern Transvaal; at Middelburg in the central, and in the Zoutpansberg in the northern, Transvaal; as well as from Vrvheid and Dundee in Natal—make it impossible to accept the coal-sandstones of the Transvaal as representing more than the basal division of the Karroo System. Boreholes on the East Rand show that the coal is, in many instances, interbedded with the glacial breccia, and the sandstones above are never more than a few hundred feet thick. In Vryheid the thickness is greater, but in that district the sandstones have been determined by Anderson to be of Ecca age. There is, therefore, in the Transvaal no representative of the Middle and Upper Karroo Series, nor of the coastal Cretaceous rocks known as the Uitenhage and Umtamvuna Series. Above the Ecca Beds there are no accumulations, except such surface deposits as laterite and calc-tufa, to represent the long period that has elapsed since Permocarboniferous times — a period during which the greater portion of South Africa has been a land surface.

It follows, therefore, that in any given area, or throughout the entire country, the Pre-Karroo formations as a whole can be easily identified: difficulty only arises when an attempt is made to arrange them in relation to one another. For this purpose the evidence obtained in the southern Karroo is of special importance: there the base of the Karroo lies, as already mentioned, conformably on the uppermost member of the Cape System—the Witteberg Series—thus constituting a perfectly conformable succession downward to the base of the Table Mountain Series; these formations must therefore represent a continuous period of geological time, and no other formation found elsewhere can be intercalated.

In the north, and in Natal, the Dwyka is always unconformable to its underlying rocks. The passage from conformable to unconformable relationship is seen in the west of the Cape Colony in the Calvinia and Clanwilliam divisions, where the conglomerate loses its conformable position on the Witteberg and is found resting unconformably on the denuded lower beds of the same series; still farther north it rests on the Bokkeveld Series; and so on in succession downward till it is found lying directly on the Archaean schists and granite. In the lower part of the Orange River valley the same conditions prevail; but in the Prieska and Hope Town districts, and in Griqualand West, rocks unknown in the south appear from beneath the conglomerate. These include, in ascending order, a great variety of igneous rocks, both acid and basic, mainly of volcanic origin, the Keis quartzites, the Campbell Rand limestones, the Griqua Town quartzites and the Matsap Series of quartzites and conglomerates. The volcanic series, the oldest of these, is separated by an unconformity from the Keis, the Campbell Rand, and the Griqua Town Series; while the Matsap Series, the youngest Pre-Karroo representative, lies unconformably above the latter.

In the Transvaal the glacial conglomerate is unconformable to all the formations up to and including the Waterberg Series; while in Natal it commonly rests on the Archaean schists and granite or on a denuded surface of the quartzites, which have been correlated with the Cape Table Mountain Series.

In the different areas enumerated the relationships are as given in the following table:— 1. In the South and West of Cape Colony:—

A conformable succession from the
DWYKA CONGLOMERATE
through the WITTEBERG and
BOKKEVELD SERIES, to the
base of the
TABLE MOUNTAIN SERIES
which is unconfoimable on the

CANGO
BEDS
anil 2. In the No.h of Cape Colony: —
An unconformity beneath the DWYKA
CONGLOMERATE
unconformably beneath which is the
MATSAP SERIES
unconformable on the
GRIQUA TOWN
CAMPBELL RAND and
KEIS SERIES
the latter being unconformable on the
VOLCANIC SERIES
which is unconformable ou the
MALMESBURY SERIES.
NAMAQUALAND SERIES.
An uncomformity beneath the
DWYKA CONGLOMERATE
which may rest upon the
WATERBERG SERIES
which is unconformable on the
PRETORIA SERIES
DOLOMITE and
BLACK REEF SERIES
tlie latter being unconformable ou the
VENTERSDORP SERIES
which is unconformable with the
WITWATERSRAND SERIES
which lies unconformably on the
SWAZILAND SERIES.

Recent work in the Transvaal has proved that the old rocks described, in Chapter I. Section II. of Part I., as the Archaean System are a distinct group, older than the lowest Witwatersrand beds; and observations made in Natal and in Rhodesia, Bechuanaland, northern Cape Colony, Namaqualand and southern Cape Colony tend to show that the same series of old rocks extends throughout the country. It seems reasonable to include in this group the Malmesbury Beds of southern Cape Colony, though they are less metamorphosed than the Swaziland and Namaqualand series in the north. The difference may be due to the fact that the Malmesbury Beds represent the upper portion of the Archaean, which has, in the south, been more protected by subsequent deposits. Denudation has been longer at work in the north: the land surface is older, and the basal portion of the old granite intrusion has been laid bare. It is noteworthy, in support of this, that

at no place in southern Cape Colony are there such extensive granite areas as prevail in the north.

The base of the Karroo being accepted as the upper limit and the Archaean schists and slates as the lower, the problem resolves itself into finding a correct arrangement of the intervening members occurring in the northern and in the southern regions.

In the south the most striking features are (1) the great gap beneath the Table Mountain Series, which is only filled locally in the Oudtshoorn division, south of the Zwartebergen, by the Cango Series, and in the Clanwilliam and Van Rhyn's Dorp divisions by the Ibiquas Series; and (2) the conformable succession from the Cape to the Karroo Systems. In the north, on the other hand, there is no conformable succession from the Pre-Karroo rocks upward, and the latter show the following marked unconformities:— below the Matsap or Waterberg Series, below the Keis or Black Reef Series, below the Ventersdorp System, and, finally, the great gap between the Witwatersrand System and the Archaean.

The first question for solution is— What northern horizon corresponds to the base of the Table Mountain Series? If this can be satisfactorily answered, the rest is comparatively easy. The lowest Witwatersrand beds have been frequently put forward as the answer to this question — a solution first suggested by Schenck. The basis for such a correlation has doubtless been the petrographical resemblance between portions of the two series, and the similar relation which they show to the old granite. On this assumption, the Witwatersrand System, from the Orange Grove Quartzites to the Elsburg Beds, must represent the entire Cape System of the south; and the Ventersdorp, the Potchefstroom and the Waterberg Systems must then be younger than the Witteberg Series, that is to say, they must come between the Witteberg and the Dwyka, a position made impossible by the stratigraphical conditions prevailing both in the north and in the south.

The threefold sequence of Black

Reef, Dolomite and Pretoria beds led Molengraaff, while State Geologist, to suggest a correlation of these formations with the three conformable members of the Cape System in the south. This correlation would mean that the base of the Table Mountain Series and the base of the Black Reef are identical, a view which their unconformable relation to the older rocks might seem to justify. It does not, however, provide a position for the Waterberg and Matsap Series, the youngest rocks beneath the Dwyka in the north, for the conformable sequence in the south from the Dwyka downward to the base of the Table Mountain Series makes it impossible to intercalate these northern beds.

If, on the other hand, the Waterberg and Matsap beds are regarded as the northern representatives of the Table Mountain Series, the difficulties disappear. In general character the rocks agree with the Table Mountain Series—as developed in Natal, more perhaps than with the formation in the Cape Colony. Only the basal portion of the Cape System is present in Natal: and on the west side of the Cape Colony its upper members successively disappear northward until the Dwyka comes to lie directly on Table Mountain Sandstone. Moreover, it is difficult to suppose that the entire Cape System could be present in the north without the occurrence of Bokkeveld or Witteberg fossils: these being wanting, it is reasonable to assume that only the non-fossiliferous basal member is present both in Natal and in the Transvaal.

If then, as the evidence certainly appears to indicate, the base of the Waterberg System of the Transvaal represents the base of the Table Mountain Series of southern Cape Colony, it follows that the Transvaal formations, from the top of the Pretoria Series down to the base of the Witwatersrand System, are only partially represented in the Cape Colony. Correlatives of the Pretoria, Dolomite, Black Reef and Ventersdorp beds are present, but none of the Witwatersrand. The first three are represented by the Griqua Town, Campbell Rand, and Keis Series, in the north of the Cape Colony. The continuity of the Dolomite from the Transvaal into Bechuanaland has been proved, and this formation has been traced, by the recent work of Mr. G. G. Holmes, close enough to the localities described by Stow to enable the whole to be viewed as on the same horizon.

The volcanic rocks of the Ventersdorp System pass from the south-western Transvaal along the basin of the Vaal River into Bechuanaland and Griqualand West. The amygdaloids over which the river flows for a considerable portion of its course are undoubtedly a part of this system, as are also the felsites and associated rocks described by Messrs. Rogers and Schwarz from Beer Vley, Hope Town, and the amygdaloid and other rocks beneath the Dwyka at Kimberley.

Further, it is not unlikely that the heterogeneous rocks hitherto grouped together as the Cango Series of southern Cape Colony represent both the Ventersdorp and the Potchefstroom Systems. The beds at Cango described on p. 65 are inverted; but there can be no doubt that they are older than the Table Mountain Series and younger than the Malmesbury. The presence in the Cango Series of a dolomitic limestone exactly similar to that of the northern regions at once suggests inquiry as to the possibility of finding a similar succession to that existing beneath and above the northern Dolomite. Though the region is much folded, the Cango limestone is doubtless overlaid by dark slates resembling the flagstones of the Pretoria Series, but, by virtue of their position on the flanks of a mountain chain, more crumpled and cleaved than the latter. Beneath the limestone there are beds of quartz-felspar-grit not unlike the arkose quartzite so often found at the base of the Black Reef. These peculiar grits, together with more normal quartzites, rest, with apparent conformity, on sheared conglomerates which, to follow this argument to its conclusion, would represent the Ventersdorp System. Between the latter and the Black Reef Series the unconformity is not always apparent, even in the north, and it might easily have been obliterated in such a disturbed region as the Cango.

There remains, then, only one doubtful formation—the Ibiquas Series. From the observations made by Messrs. Rogers and Schwarz, this appears to be an independent subdivision between the Table Mountain and Malmesbury Series. To some extent, petrographically, it resembles the Cango Series; and if that series represents both the Ventersdorp and Potchefstroom Systems of the north, then the Ibiquas may well be a western representative of one or the other, most probably of the latter.

In tabular form, the correlation of the Pre-Karroo rocks given above is as follows:—

Southern Cape Colony
: Base of the Karroo System
  Cape System—
Witteberg Series
Bokkeveld Scries
Table Mountain Series
  Cango Series—
Slates
Dolomite
Grits
  Cango Conglomerate
  Ibiquas Series (?)
  Archiean System— Malmesbury Series and Granite

There remains the question of finding the European equivalents of the South African strata: The oldest fossils known, those of the Bokkeveld Series, are Devonian, but the most recent work done on them leaves it uncertain to which portion of the system they belong.[1] The Table Mountain Series, which lies conformably beneath the Bokkeveld, is possibly also Devonian; but the beds older than that series cannot be placed with any degree of certainty. The geological position of the Potchefstroom System remains quite unknown, there being so far no data available to show 1 Reed, 1903. whether its members correspond to the Ordovician, Silurian, Cambrian, or even Pre-Cambrian of Europe.

The oldest schists and granites have,

in this book, been styled Archaean, but there is of course no proof of actual contemporaneity with the Archaean rocks of Europe and America. The term Pre-Cambrian cannot be applied to them— no Cambrian having been recognised; and, until more definite information is available, the name Archaean may be used as implying that they are the oldest rocks of the country.

The few plant fossils from the Witteberg Series hitherto determined, point to a correlation of that series with the Carboniferous System of the Northern Hemisphere; and the flora of the Ecca beds confirms this. The complete succession in the Cape Colony shows that there was a gradual passage from Palaeozoic to Mesozoic forms of life. As Seward has pointed out in dealing with the flora, there is a commingling of types; and the faunistic evidence demonstrates the continuance of allied reptilian forms from the base of the Ecca to the top of the Stormberg Series— that is,.from Carboniferous to Rhaetic times.

The Stormberg Beds having now been determined as Rhaetic, they, with the Beaufort Series, may be taken as representing the Triassic. No Jurassic representatives occur; the original Lower Cretaceous correlation of the Uitenhage Series having been confirmed by the recent work of Seward.

Tertiary rocks are not definitely known, for no fossils typical of that epoch have as yet been found. As already stated, South Africa has, with the exception of a few small areas round the coast, been a land surface since the close of the Trias: consequently there are, in the interior of the country, only terrestrial deposits to represent that long interval of time.

APPENDIX LIST OF LITERATURE1

Abel, Clarke— 1818. *Narrative of a Journey into the Interior of China, and of a Voyage to and from that Country in the Years 1816 and 1817*. London, 1818 pp. 285-312 give a geological description of the Cape Peninsula. Alford, Charles J.— 1890. *The Geology of the Witwatersrand District*—Wit. Min. and Met. Rev. I. 1, pp. 1-6. Johannesburg, 1890.

— *a. The Geological Features of the De Kaap Gold-fields*—Ibid. I. 2, pp. 1-4.

Johannesburg, 1890.

— *b. The Geology of the Sheba Mine*—Ibid. I. 5, p. 7. Johannesburg, 1890.

— *c. Notes of a Salt Deposit about Twenty-five Miles North of Pretoria, Transvaal, South Africa*—Ibid. I. 6, pp. 1-2. Johannesburg, 1890.

— *Notes on an Expedition to Zoutpansberg*—Ibid. I. 10, pp. 1-5. Johannesburg, 1890.

1891. *Geological Features of the Transvaal, South Africa*—8vo, pp. vi. and 69. London, 1891. 1894. *On Auriferous Rocks from Mashonaland*—Quart. Journ. Geol. Soc. Lond., 1894, Proc. pp. 8-9.-Alison, M. S.— 1898. *Un the Origin and Formation of Pans*—Trans. Geol. Soc. S. A. vol. iv. pp. 159-161. Johannesburg, Dec. 1898. Ammon, L. v.— 1893. *Devonische Vertteinerungen von Lagoinka in Mato Grosso Brasiliens*— Zeitschr. d. Gesellsch. f. Erdkunde zu Berlin, 1893, Bd. xxviii. Anderson, William— 1901. *First Report Geol. Survey Natal and Zululand*—Introduction, pp. 7-20. Pieterinaritzburg, 1901.

— *a. Historical Sketch of Natal Geology*—Ibid. pp. 23-27.

— *b. Report on a Reconnaissance Geological Survey of the Eastern Half of Zululand*—Ibid. p. 39. — *c. Report on the Geology of the Lower Tugela District, Victoria Co., Natal*— Ibid. p. 79.

1904. *Further Notes on the Reconnaissance Geological Survey of Zululand* — Second Report Geol. Survey Natal, p. 39. London, 1904. 1 This list includes only the more important papers and those referred to in the text. 1904 *a. Preliminary Report on the Geology of Durban, etc.*—Ibid. p. 107.

— *b. Geological Traverse from Pietermaritzburg via Richmond to the Umzinto District*—Ibid. p. 121.

— *c. The Geology of the Melmoth District, Zululand*—Ibid. p. 131.

— *d. Report on the Stormberg Coalmeasures to the West of Molteno, Cape Colony*—Ibid. p. 141.

Andrews, A. J.— 1898. *Discovery of Fossil Beds at the Witkopje Pan*—Trans. Geol. Soc. S. A. iii. p. 146. Johannesburg, 1898.

Atherstone, W. G.— 1857. *Geology of Uitenhage* — East. Prov. Mon. Mag. vol. i. No. 10, pp. 518-532, and No. 11, pp. 580-595. Grahamstown, 1857. 1869. *The Discovery of Diamonds at the Cape of Gooii Hope*—Geol. Mag. vi., May 1869, pp. 208-213. 1896. *Kimberley and Us Diamonds*—Trans. Geol. Soc. S. A. i. pp. 76-82. Johannesburg, 1896.

Baily, William H.— 1855. *Description of some Cretaceous Fossils from South Africa, collected by Capt. Garden of the 45th Regt.*—Quart. Journ. Geol. Soc. vol. xi. pp. 454-463. London, 1855. (See also Garden.)

Bain, A. G.— 1842. *On the Dead of an Ox found in the Alluvial Banks of the Modder, South Africa*—Proa Geol. Soc. iii., 1838-42, p. 152. London, 1842. 1856. *On the Discovery of the Fossil Remains of Bidental and other Reptiles in South Africa*—Trana Geol. Soc. Lond. sec. ser. vol. vii. pp. 53-59. London, 1856.

— *a. On the Geology of South Africa*—Trans. Geol. Soc. Lond. sec. ser. vol. vii. pp. 175-192. London, 1856. With Map and'Sections. 1897. *Reminiscences and Anecdotes connected with the History of Geology in South Africa, or the Pursuit of Knowledge under Difficulties*--Reprinted in the Trans. Geol. Soc. of S. A. vol. ii. part v. pp. 60-75. Johannesburg, 1897.

Bain, T.— 1886. *Report on the Recent Gold Discoveries in the Division of Knysna, tcith Description of the Goldfields by C. F. Osborne*—Pari. Report. Cape Town, 1886.

1891. *Report upon the Discovery of Gold in the Division of Prince Albert*—Pari. Report. Cape Town, 1891.

— *a. Report of the Geological and Irrigation Surveyor upon his Recent Investigations into the Gold Discoveries upon the Farms Spreeuwfontein and Klein Waterval, Prinre Albert*—Pari. Report. Cape Town, 1891. ballot, J.— 1888. *The Banket Formation: its Probable*

Origin and its Present Position. Johannesburg, 1888.

Barrow, John— 1806. *Travels in Southern Africa.* London, 1806, 4to, 2 vols. Bauer, Max— 1896. "*Vorkommen des Diamants in Siid-Afribi,*" pp. 208-280, being part ii. section b, 3, of the work on *Edelsteinkunde.* Leipzig, 1896. English translation by L. J. Spencer, under the title *Gems and Precious Stones.* London, 1904.

Bawden, F. W.— 1897. *A Short Description of the Klerksdorp Gold-fields, with a Map and Section*—Trans. Geol. Soc. S. A. vol. iii. p. 12. Johannesburg, March 1897.

Beck, R.— 1898 *Die Diamantlagerstiitte von Newlands in Griqualand lVest*—Zeit. prak. Geol., 1898, pp. 163-164. 1899. *Neues von dm Afrikanischen Diamantlagerstiitten*—Zeit. prak. Geol., 1899, pp. 417-419. Becker, G. F.— 1897. *The H'itwatersrand Banket, with Note on oiher Gold-beariny Puddingstones.*— 18th Ann. Rep. U.S. Geol. Survey, part v. p. 153. Washington, 1897.

Bell, Chas. D.— 1855. *Reports on the Copper-fields of Little Namaqualand*— Pari. Report. Cape Town, 1855.

Blanfohd, H. F.— 1875. *On the Age and Correlations of the Plant-hearing Series of India and the Former Existence of an Indo-Oceanic Continent*— Quart. Journ. Geol. Soc. xxxi. pp. 519, 540-542. 1875. 1877. *Note on the Question of the Glacial or Volcanic Origin of the Talchir Boulder-bed of India and the Karroo Boulder-bed of South Africa*— Quart. Journ. Geol. Soc. xxxiii. Proc. p. 7. 1877.

Bleloch, W.— 1899. *Sand Conglomerates*—Trans. Geol. Soc. S. A. vol. iv. p. 175. Johannesburg, Jan. 1899.

Bonney, T. G.— 1897. *On some Rock-specimens from Kimberley, South Africa*—Geol. Mag. iv., 1897, pp. 448-453 and 497-502. 1899. *The Original Rock of the South African Diamond*—Nat. Sci. xv. p. 173. 1899.

— *a. Thy Parent Rock of the Diamond in South Africa*—Proc. Roy. Soc. lxv., 1899, pp. 223-236.

1900. *The Parent Rock of the Diamond: Reply to a Criticism*—Geol. Mag. vii., 1900, pp. 246-248.

— *a. Additional Notes on Boulders and other Rock-specimens from the New lands Diamond Mines, Griqualand West*—Proc. Roy. Soc. lxvii., 1900, pp. 475-484. See also Lewis, Henry Carvill.

Bonney, T. G., and Raisin, C. A.— 1891. *Report an some Rock-specimens from the Kimberley Diamond Mines*— Geol. Mag. viii., 1891, pp. 412-415.

Bonney, T. G., Raisin, C. A., and Stone, J. B.— 1895. *Notes on the Diamond-bearing Rock of Kimberley*— I. Stone, J. B.— *The Kimberley Diamond Mines, South Africa* — Geol. Mag. ii., 1895, pp. 492-495.' 1895. II. Bonney, T. G., and Raisin, C. A.—*On the Rock and other Specimens from the Kimberley Mine*—Geol. Mag. ii., 1895, pp. 496-502. Bordeaux, A.— 1897. *Etudes sur les champs auriferes de Lydenburg, De Kaap et du Charterland (Afrique du Snd)*—Annales d. Mines, xi. pp. 273-349. Paris, 1897. 1898. *Le Murchison Range et ses champs auriferes*—Annales d. Mines, xiv., 1898, p. 95.

— *a. Les Mines de V Afrique du Slid, Transvaal, Rhodesia, etc.*—8vo. pp. viii. and 211. Paris, 1898.

BORNHARDT, W. 1900. *Zur Oberfliichungsgestaltung und Geologic Deutsch-Ostafrikas. Ergebnisse der von in den Jahren 1895-1897 in Ost-Afrika unternommenen Reisen* —Deut.xch-Ost-Afrika, Bd. vii. Berlin, 1900. Bousqubt, J. G.— 1897. *The present Condition of the Gold-mining Industry in the De Kaap Formation of the Lydenburg Gold-fields*—Report State Min. Eng. for 1896, p. 38." Pretoria, 1897. Boutan, M. E.— 1886. *Le Diamant* (extrait de l'Encyclopcdie chimique de M. Fremy). Paris, 1886. Bowman, H. L.— 1900. *Communications from the Osford Mineralogical Laboratory: On a Rhombic Pyroxene from South Africa*—Min. Mag. xii. pp. 349-353. London, 1900. Bright, Richard— 1855. *Lecture on Namaqualand and its Mines.* Cape Town, Said Solomon and Co., 1855, pp. 1-23.

Broom, R— 1897. *On the Occurrence of an apparently llutincl Prevomer in Gomphognathus*—Journ. Anat. and Phys. xxxi. pp. 277-282. 1897. 1899. *On two New Species of Dicynodonts*—Annals S. A. Mus. i. 3, pp. 452-456. Cape Town, 1899. 1901. *On the Structure and Affinities of Udenodon*—Proc. Zool. Soc. vii., 1901, pp. 162-190.

— *a. On the Structure of the Palate in Dicynodon and its Allies*—Trans. S. A. PhiL Soc. xi. 3, pp. 169-176. Cape Town, 1901.

— *b. On Ictidosuchus 1trimwvus*— Trans. S. A. Phil. Soc. xi. 3, pp. 177-184.

Cape Town, 1901.

1902. *The Leg and Toe Bones of Ptychosiagum*—Trans. S. A. Phil. Soc. vol. xi. pp. 233-235. Cape Town, 1902. 1903. *On an almost Perfect Skeleton oj Pareiasaurus serridens*—Annals S. A. Mus. vol. iv. p. 123. Cape Town, 1903.

— *a. On the Structure of the Shoulder Girdle in Lystrosaurus*—Ibid. p. 139.

— *On Evidence of a New Species oj Titanosuchus (T. cloctei)*—Ibid. p. 142.

— *c On some new Primitive Theriodonts in the South African Museum*— Ibid. p. 147.

— *d. On a New Reptile from the Karroo Beds of Tarkastadt, South Africa*— Ibid. l. 159.

— *e. On an almost Perfect Skull of a new Primitive Theriodont (Lycosuchus vanderrieti)*—Trans. S. A. PhiL Soc. vol. xiv. p. 197. Cape Town, 1903.

1904. *On two New Therocephalian Reptiles (Glanosuchus macrops and Pristerognathus baini)*—Trans. S. A. Phil. Soc. voL xv. pp. 85-88. Cape Town, 1904.

— *a. Tfie Origin of the Mammalian Carpus and Tarsus*—Trans. S. A. Phil. Soc. pp. 89-94. Cape Town, 1904.

— *b. Observations on the Structure of Mesosaurus*—Trans. S. A. Phil. Soc. pp. 103-112. Cape Town, 1904.

Brown, Nicol— 1896. *The Succession of the Rocks in the Pilgrim's Rest District, with Section* —Trans. Geol. Soc. S. A. ii., 1896, pp. 3-4.

Bunkell, H. B.— 1896. *Notes on the Venterskroon Gold-fields, South African*

Republic—Trans.

Fed. Inst. Min. Eng. xii., 1896, p. 186. 1902. *Geology of the Krugersdorp District*—Trans. Geol. Soc. S. A. vol. v. pt. iv. p. 75. Johannesburg, Dec. 1902.

Burchell, W. J.— 1822. *Travels into the Interior of Southern Africa. With an entirely New Map, and numerous Engravings*—2 vols. 4to. London, 1822-24.

Chalmers, J. A., and Hatch, F. H.— 1895. *Notes on the Geology of Mashonaland and Matabeleland*—Geol. Mag., 1895, pp. 193-203. *See also* under Hatch and Chalmers.

Chaper, Mai1Rice— 1880. *Note sur la region diamantifere de vAfrigue australe, suivie d'un tableau resumant les etudes faites par M. Fouque' et M. Michel-Levy sur les roches rapporte'es de vAfrique australe par Fauteur.* Paris, 1880. Chapman, Frederick 1901. *Notes on the Olifant Klip from Natal, the Transvaal and Lydenburg*—

GeoL Mag. viii., 1901, pp. 552-555. 1904. *Foraminifera and Ostracoda from the Cretaceous of East Pondoland*— Annals S. A. Mus. voL iv. p. 221. Cape Town, 1904. Churchill, F. F. — 1899. *Notes on the Geology of the Drakensbergen, Natal*—Trans. S. A. Phil. Soc. x. 3, pp. 419-426. Cape Town, 1899. Clarke, W. B.— 1842. *On the Geological Phenomena in the Vicinity of Cape Tovyn, South Africa*—Proc. GeoL Soc. iii., 1838-42, pp. 418-423. London, 1842. Cohen, E.— 1874. *Geognostisch-petrographische Skizzen aus Swl-Afrika*—Pt. I.—Neues Jahrb. f. Min., 1874, pp. 460-505.

1887. Pt. II.—*Die Karr oof or motion nebst einigen Bemerkungen iiber das palaeozoisehe Gebiet im siidlichen Capland*—N. Jahrb. BeiL Bd. v., 1887, pp. 195-274. 1875. *Erliiuternde Bemerkungen zu der Routenkarte einer Reise von Lydenburg nach den Goblfeldern und von Lydenburg nach der Delagoa Bai im ostlichen Siid-Afrika*—L. Friederichsen's zweit. JahreslxT. d. geog. Ges. in Hamburg. 1875. 1877. *Titaneisen von den Diamantfeldern in Siid-Afrika*— Neues Jahrb. f. Min., 1877. 1887. *Uber Speckstein, Pseudophit und dichten*

Muscovit aus Slid-Afrika— Neues Jahrb. f. Min., 1887, Bd. i. 1888. *Uber den Granat der siidafrikanischen Diamantfelder und Uber den Chromgehult der Pyrope*—Mitt. d. liaturw. V. fur Neuvorpommem u. Riigen, 20. Jahrg. 1888. 1891. *See* Dahms, P. H. 1894. *Melilithaugitgestein und caleitfiihrender Aplit aus Siid-Afrika*—Tschermak's Min. u. petr. Mitt. xiv. Hft, 2, pp. 188-190. Vienna, 1894. 1895. *Tiber eine nordlich von Pretoria (Transvaal Republik) in Granit gelegene Sahpfanne*—Tschermak's Min. u. petr. Mitt. xv. Vienna, 1895. 1900. *The Meteoric Irons from Griqualand East, South Africa* -Annals S. A. Mus. vol. ii. p. 9. Cape Town, 1900.

— a. *TTie Meteoric Iron from Bethany, Great Xamaqualand*—Ibid. p. 21.

CORSTORPHINk, GEO. S. 1897. *Geologist's Report for 1896*—Annual Report of the Geol. Comm. for 1896. Cape Town, 1897.

— a. *The Cango Cave*—Annual Report Geol. Comm., 189fi, pp. 34-36.

Cape Town, 1897.

1898. *Geologist's Report for 1897*—Annual Report of the GeoL Comm. for 1897. Cape Town, 1898. 1900. *Geologist's Report for 1898*—Annual Report of the GeoL Comm. for 1898. Cape Town, 1900.

—a. *Geologist's Report for 1899*—Annual Report of the Geol. Comm. for 1899. Cape Town, 1900.

1901. *Report of the Director of the Survey for 1900*—Annual Report Geol. Comm. for 1900, p. vii. Cape Town, 1901. 1903. *Note on the Age of the Central South African Coal-field*—Trans. Geol. Soc. S. A. vol. vi. pp. 16-19. Johannesburg, 1903. 1904. *The Volca nic. Series underlying the Black Reef*—Trans. of the GeoL Soc. of South Africa, vol. vi. part v. p. 99. Johannesburg, 1904.

— a. *The Geological Relation of the Old Granite to the Witwatersrand Series*

—Geol. Soc. of South Africa, vol. vii. part i. pp. 9-12. Johannesburg, 1904.

— b. *The History of Stratiyraphical Inrestiyation in South Africa*—Report S. Air. Assoc. Adv. Sc., 1904, pp.

145-181. Johannesburg, 1904. *See also* Hatch and Corstorphine.

Crookes, William— 1897. *Diamonds*—A Lecture delivered at the Royal Institution, June 11, 1897— Journ. Roy. Inst. London, 1897. Curtis, J. S.— 1890. *The Banket Deposits of the iritwatersrand*—Eng. and Min. Journ. of New York, Feb. 15, 1890.

Czyszkowski, Stephen— 1896. *La venue aurifere de vAfrique du Sud et considerations sur les Thalwegs et Niveaux Metalliferes*—Paris, 1896. 1896. 77c *Deposition of Gold in South Africa* (translation of the above by H. V. Yvinchell)—The Amer. Geologist, May 1896, p. 306. Dahmk, P. H.— 1891. *Uber einige Eruptivgesteine aus Transvaal in Siid-Afrika*—Xeuea Jahrb. f. Min., 1891, B. Bd. xiv. pp. 90-131.

Dale, Langham— 1872. *On a Collection of Stone Implements and Pottery from the Cape of Good Hope*—Journ. Anthrop. Inst. i. pp. 345-348. London, 1872. Darwin, Charles— 1844. *Geological Observations on the Vulcanic Islands visited during the Voyage of H. M.S. "Beagle" together with some Brief Notices on the Geology of Australia and the Cape of Good Hope.* 8vo. London, 1844. Delesse, M.— 1855. *Notice sur les mines de cuivrc du Cap de Bonne Espe'rance*—Ann. d. Mines, 5 ser., 1855, Tome viii. pp. 186-212. Paris, 1855. Demaret, Dr. Leon— 1896. *On the Extension of the Main Reef Eastwards beyond Vogelfuntein, and the Nature of the Rietfontein Reef*—Trans. Geol. Sou. S. A. vol. ii. part x. No. 2, pp. 143-14 4. Johannesburg, 1896.

Denny, G. A.— 1897. *The Klerksdorp Goldfields.* London, 1897. Desdemaines-hugon— 1874. *Les Mines des Diamants du Cap*—Rev. d. deux Mondes, Juin 1874, p. 569. Dorpfel, D.— 1904. *The Balmoral Cobalt Lodes*— Trans. Geol. Soc. S. A. vol. vi. part v. p. 93. Johannesburg, 1904.

— a. *The Kromdraai Quartz Reef and its Geological Association*—Trans. Geol. Soc. S. A. voL vi. part v. pp. 101-103. Johannesburg, 1904.

— b. *Note on the Geological Position of the Basement Granite*—Trans. Geol. Soc. S. A. vol. vi. part v. p. 104. Johannesburg, 1904.

— c. The Relation of the Buffelsdoorn Series to the Lower Witwatersrand Beds in the Klerksdorp District—Trans. Geol. Sou. S. A. vol. vii. pp. 7-8. Johannesburg, 1904. Draper, David—1894. Notes on the Geology of South-Eastern Africa—Quart. Journ. Geol. Soc. voL 1. p. 548. London, 1894.

— a. The Occurrence of Dolomite in South Africa—Ibid. p. 561.

1895. The Marble Beds of Natal—Ibid. vol. li., 1895, p. 51. 1896. The Primary Systems of South Africa, with special Reference to the Conglomerate Beds of the Witwatersrand—Trans. Geol. Soc. S. A. vol. i. pp. 12-26. Johannesburg, 1896.

— a. The Dwyka Conglomerate—Trans. Geol. Soc. S. A. vol. i. part v. pp. 90-103. Johannesburg, 1896.

— b. The Auriferous Conglomerates of South Africa—(Read at the Imp. Inst.
, Oct. 26). London, 1896.

1897. The Extension of the Main Reef Westward on the Farm IVitpoortje—Trans. Geol. Soc. S. A. vol. ii. part i. pp. 5-14. Johannesburg, 1897.

— «. On the Connection between the Conglomerate Beds of the Witwatersrand and those situated in the Districts of Potchefstroom and Klerksdorp—Trans. Geol. Soc. S. A. vol. ii. part iv. pp. 47-51. Johannesburg, 1897

— b. A Ramble through the Geology of Southern Africa—Trans. Geol. Soc. S. A. vol. iii. parts ii. and iii. Johannesburg, 1897.

— c. Notes on Vertebraria and Glossopteris—Trans. Geol. Soc. S. A. vol. iii. part iv. p. 48. Johannesburg, 1897. 1897. d. 1h'amonds at Rietfontein—Trans. Geol. Sot S. A. vol. iii. p. 87. Johannesburg, 1897.

— e. On the Coal Deposits of South Africa—Trans. Geol. Soc. S. A. vol. iii. p. 128. Johannesburg, 1897. 1898. On the Diamond Pipes of the South African Republic—Trans. Geol. Soc. S. A. vol. iv. p. 5. Johannesburg, Feb. 1898.

— «. Notes on the Zuurbekom Basin as a source of Water Supply for Johannesburg—Trans. Geol. Sue. S. A. vol. iv. p.

11. Johannesburg, 1898.

Draper, D., and Frames, Minktt E.—1898. The Diamond—8vo, pp. 40. Johannesburg, 1898.

Dunn, E. J.— 1873. Geological Reports nn a Gold Prospecting Expedition, 1872, and on the Stormberg Coalfields—Parl. Report. Cape Town, 1873.

— a. Geological Sketch Map of Cape Colony—E. Stanford, London, 1873. 1874. On the Mode of Occurrence of Diamonds in South Africa—Quart. Journ. Geol. Soc vol. xxx. p. 54, 1874. 1875. Geological Sketch Map of South Africa. 1875. 1877. Further Notes on the Diamond Fields of South Africa, with Observations on the Gold Mines and Cobalt Mine in the Transvaal—Quart. Journ. Geol. Soc. Lond. xxxiii. pp. 879-883. London, 1877. 1878. Report on the Stormberg Coal-fields—Parl. Report. Cape Town, 1878. 1879. Report on the Camdeboo and Nieuwveldt Coal.—Cape Town, 1879. 1880. Report on the Occurrence of Gold in the Knysnit District—Parl. Report. Cape Town, 1880. 1883. Re-port upon recent Coal-borings in the Camdeboo and Stormberg—Parl. Report. Cape Town, 1883. 1886. Report on a Supposed Extensive Deposit of Coal underlging the Central Districts of the Colony—Parl. Report. Cape Town, 1886. 1887. Geological Sketch Map of South Africa—Sands and M'Dougall, Melbourne, 1887. 1898. On Sub-Karroo Coal—Trans. GeoL Soc. S. A. vol. iv. p. 115. Johannesburg, 1898. 1899. Notes on the Differences between the Stormberg and Vereeniging Coalmeasures—Trans. Geol. Soc. S. A. vol. v. part iii. p. 61. Johannesburg, 1899. 1900. Notes on the Dwyka Coal-measures at Vereeniging, Transvaal, etc.—Trans. S. A. Phil. Soc. vol. xi. p. 67. Cape Town, 1900.

Du ToiT, A. L. See Toit, A. L du.

Etheriihsk, Junr., R—

1900. Notes on Fossil Plants from the St. Lucia Bay Coal-field, Enseleni River, Zululand—First Report GeoL Survey, Natal. Pietermaritzburg, 1900, p. 69. 1904. Cretaceous Fossils of Natal—Part I.—The Umkwelane Hill Deposit—Second Report Geol. Survey Natal.

London, 1904, p. 69. Evans, Sir John—1900. Paleolithic Man in Africa—Proc. Roy. Soc. vol. Ixvi. No. 43:5, pp. 486-488. London, Aug. 1900. Exton, H.—1897. Some Evidence bearing upon the relation of the Stormberg Beds of South Africa to the Triassic System—Trans. Geol. Soc. S. A. vol. iii. pp. 123127. Johannesburg, 1897. 1901. Geological Notes Oh the Neighbourhood of Ladysmith, Natal—Geol. Mag. dec. iv. voL viii. pp. 509-510, 549-552. London, Nov. and Dec. 1901.

Farrar, Sidney H.— 1886. Note on the Gold-fields of South Africa—Min. of Pro. of the Inst, of Civil Engineers, vol. lxxxvi. London, 1886.

Feiktmantel, Ottokar.— 1887. Ucber die Pflanzen mid kohlenfiihrenden Schichten in Indian (beziehnngsio. Asien), Afrika und Australian und darin vorkommende ylaciale Krsclieinungen—Sitzungsb. d. k. bohm. Ges. d. Wiss. Prag, 1887, pp. 1-102. Nachtrag, pp. 570-576.

1889. Uebersichtliche Darstellung der geologisch-paliiontologischen Verliiiltnisse Slid-Afrikas. I. Theil. — Die Karrooformation und die dieselbe unterlagernden Schichten—Abh. der kon. bohni. Ges. d. Wiss. VII. Folge, 3. Bd. pp. 6-89. Prag, 1889.

Flight, W. See Maskelyne, Story X., and Flight, W.

Frames, Minett E.— 1897. A few Observations on the Potehefstroom and Klerksdorp Districts— Trans. Geol. Soc. S. A. vol. ii. part vi. No. 3, pp. 87-90. Johannesburg, 1897.

— a. Notes on the Coal-fields of the Transvaal—Trans. GeoL Soc. S. A. vol. ii. part xi. Xo. 2, pp. 150-157. Johannesburg, 1897.

1899. Sub-Karroo Coal—Trans. Geol. Soc. S. A. vol. v. pp. 63-65. Johannesburg, May 1899. 1905. Some Notes on the Geology of the Amsterdam Valley and the Surrounding Neighbourhood — Trans. Geol. Soc. S. A. vol. vii. pp. 123-129. Johannesburg, 1905. Fdtterer, Karl.— 1895. Africa in seiner Bedeutung fiir die Gold-Production, etc. 8vo, pp. 191. Berlin, 1895. Galloway, W.—1890. The South African Coal-field—Proc. South Wales lust, of Engineers,

vol. xvii. pp. 67-84. London, 1890.
Gamble, John G.— 1886. *Altitudes above Sea Level in South Africa.* Cape Town, 1886. Garden, R. J. — 1855. *Notice of some Cretaceous Bocks near Natal, South Africa*—Quart. Journ. Geol. Soc. vol. xi. p. 453. London, 1855. (See aLso Baily.) Garnier, Jules.— 1897. *Gold and Diamonds in the Transvaal and the Cape*—Trans. Geol. Soc. S. A. vol. ii. part vii. pp. 91-103. Johannesburg, 1897—Continuation in part viii. pp. 109-120. Gibson, Walcot.— 1892. *The Geology of the Gold-bearing and Associated Rocks of the Southern Transvaal*—Quart. Journ. Geol. Soc. vol. xlviii. pp. 404-435. London, 1892. 1893. *Geology of the Southern Transvaal*—Trans. Fed. Inst. Min. Eng. vol. vi. London, 1893. 1890. *The Geology of Africa in Relation to its Mineral Wealth*—Trans. of Fed. Inst. of Min. Eng. vol. xii. London, 1896. 1902. *On the Correlation of the Palceozoic Roelts of South Africa*—Geol. Mag., N.S., Dec. 4, vol. ix. p. 210, 1902. GOLDMANN, C. S. 1899. *Map of the Witwatersrand Gold-fields,* 1899—Stanford's Geog. Establishment, London. Scale, 100 roods= 1 in. Gotz, Joseph.— 1886. *Untersuchung einer Gesteinssuite a us der Gejend der Goldf elder. on Marabastad im nordlichen Transvaal, Siid-Afrika*—Nenes Jahrb. f. Min., 1886, B. Bd. iv. pp. 110-177. Stuttgart, 1886. Graichen, W.— 1903. *Die Newlands Diamantminen, Siid-Afrika*—Zeit. fur prakt. Geol. xi., 1903, p. 448.

Green, A. H.— 1883. *Report on the Coals of the Cape Colony.* London, 1883. 1888. *A Contribution to the Geology and Physical Geography of the Cape Colony.* Quart. Journ. Geol. Soc. vol. xliv. pp. 239-269. London, 1888.

Gregory, J. B 1868. *Diamonds from the Cape of Good Hope*—Geol. Mag. vol. v., 1868, pp. 558-561.

1869. *The Lignite Bed near Cape Town, South Africa*—Geol. Mag. vol. vi. No. 1, Jan. 1869.

Griesbach, Carl Ludolf— 1870. *Geologischer Durchschnitt durch Siid-Afrika*—Jahrb. d. geol. Beichsaustalt, 1870, 20. Bd. pp. 501-504.

1871. *On the Geology of Natal, in South Africa*—Quart. Journ. Geol. Soc. vol. xxvii. pp. 53-72. London, 1871. 1880. *Geological Notes*— Becords Geol. Survey India, xiii. pt. 2, 1880, pp. 83-93. 1885. *African Field Notes*—Becords Geol. Survey India, xviiL, 1885, pp. 57-64.

Gurich, Georg— 1887. *Ueberblick iiber den geologischen Bau des Afrikanischen Kontinents.*

—Peterm. Mitt., 1887, pp. 257-265. 1890. *Geologisch-mineralogische Mittheihmgen aus Sudwest-Afrika—* 1. *Mineralien aus den deutschen Schutagebiet in Siidwest-Afrika* —

Nenes Jahrb., 1890, Bd. i. pp. 103-117. — a. *Zur Altersbestimmung der unteren Grenze der Karrooformatioii—* Neues

Jahrb., 1890, Bd. i. pp. 283-285. 1897. *Zur Theorie der Diainantlagerstatten in Siid-Afrika*—Zeit. fur prakt. Geol., 1897, p. 143. 1902. *Cambrium (?) in Deutsch-SiidwestafrikaCenl* f. Min., 1902, No. 3, pp. 65-69. Hall, A. L. — 1904. *On the Area to the North of the Mayaliesberg Range and to the East of the Pietersburg Railway Line*—Beport Geol. Survey Transvaal, 1903. pp. 28-35, Append. pp. 36-38. Pretoria, 1904. -a. *On the Geological Features of the Pienaars River Valley South of tht Magaliesberg Range (Pretoria District)*—Report Geol. Survey Transvaal, 1903, pp. 39-42. Pretoria, 1904. *See also* Kynaston and Hall, and Hall and Steart.

Hall, A. L., and Steart, F. A.— 1905. *On Folding and Faulting in the Pretoria Series and the Dolomite*— Trans. Geol. Soc. S. A. vol. viii. pp. 7-15. Johannesburg, 1905. Harger, H. S.— 1897. *On the Occurrence of Red Sandstone in the Pretoria District*—Trans. Geol. Soc. S. A. vol. iii. pt. ix. p. 107. Johannesburg, Nov. 1897. Hatch, F. H.— 1897. *A Geological Map of the Southern Transvaal.* Stanford, London, 1897.

1898. *A Geological Surrey of the lVitwatersrand and other Districts in the Southern Transvaal*—Quart. Journ. Geol. Soc. voL liv. pp. 73-100. Loudon, 1898. 1903. *A Geological Map of the Southern Transvaal*—2nd edit. Stanford, London, 1903.

— a. *Notes on the lVitwatersrand Gold Deposits and their Associated Rocks—*

Trans. South African Assoc. of Engineers, Johannesburg, 1903, *and* Geol. Mag., Dec 4, vol. x. pp. 543-547. London, 1903.

— b. *A Description of Two Geological Sections taken through the Potchefstroom District*—Trans. Geol. Soc. S. A. vol. vi. pt. iii. pp. 50-51. Johannesburg, 1903.

— c. *Note on an Unusual Basal Development of the Black Reef Series in the Orange River Colony*—Trans. Geol. Soc. S. A. vol. vi. pt. iv. p. 69. Johannesburg, 1903.

1904. *The Boulder Beds of Ventersdorp, Transvaal*—Trans. GeoL Soc. S. A. vol. vi. pt, v. pp. 95-97. Johannesburg, 1904.

— a. *The Geology of the Marico District, Transvaul*—Trans. Geol. Soc. S. A. vol. vii. pt. i. pp. 1-6. Johannesburg, 1904.

— 6. *The Extension of the lVitwatersrand Beds Eastwards under the Dolomite and the Ecca Series of the Southern Transvaal*—Trans. Geol. Soc. S. A. voL vii. pp. 57-69. Johannesburg, 1904.

1905. *The Oldest Sedimentary Rocks of the Transvaal*—Trans. Geol. Soc. S. A. voL vii. pp. 147-150. Johannesburg, 1905. *See also* under Leggett and Hatch, and under Chalmers and Hatch.

Hatch, F. H, and Chalmers, J. A.— 1895. *The Gold Mines of the Rand*—8vo, pp. 306. London, 1895.

Hatch, F. H., and Corntorphine, G. S. — 1904. *The Geology of the Bezuidenhout Valley and the District East of Johannesburg*—Trans. Geol. Soc. S. A. vol. vii. p. 97. Johannesburg, 1904. 1905. 77k; *Petrography of the lVitwatersrand Conglomerates, with special reference to the Origin of the Gold*—Trans. Geol. Soc. S. A. vol. vii. pt. iii. pp. 140-145. Johannesburg, 1905.

— a. *The Cullinan Diamond*—Trans. Geol. Soc. S. A. voL viii. pp. 26-27, 1905, *and* Geol. Mag., April 1905. Hausmann— 1837. *Beytriige zur Kunde der geognostischeu Constitution von Siid-Africa*— Gdtt. Gelehrte Auz. pp. 1449-1462. Gottingen, 14th Sept. 1837.

Henderson, J. A. Leo— 1898. *Pet-*

rographical and Geological Investigations of certain Transvaal Norites, Gahbrns, and Pgroxenitcs and other South African Rocks—8vo, pp. 56. London, Dulau and Co., 1898.

Heneage and Holford— 1905. Notes on the Occurrence of Gold in Primary Formations—Trans. S. A. Assoc. Eng. Johannesburg, 1905. Heslop, W. T.— 1897. Later Volcanic Eruptions on the Witwatersrand—Trans. Geol. Soc. S. A. vol. iii. pt. iv. pp. 49-52. Johannesburg, June 1897.

HOCHSTETTEH, F. VON 1866. Beitrilge zur Geologic des Caplandes—Kovara Expedition, Geologischer Theil. II. Band, I. Abth. pp. 19-38. Wien, 1866.

Holmes, (!. G.— 1904. Some Notes on the Geology of the Northern Transvaal—Trans. Geol. Soc. S. A. vol. viL pp. 51-56. Johannesburg, 1904.

—-a. The Geology of u part oj Bechuanalavd West of Vryburg — Ibid. vol. vii. p. 130. Johannesburg, 1904. 1905. The Geology of a Part of the Rustenburg District—Ibid. vol. viii. pp. 1-6. Johannesburg, 1905.

Holub, E., and M. Neumayr— 1881. Ueber einige Fossilien am der Uitenhage-Formation in Siid-Afrika—

Bd. XLIV. d. Denkschr. d. math.-naturwiss. Classe der kais. Akad. der Wiss. Wien, 1881. Horwood, C. B.— 1904. The Red Granite of Balmoral and its relation to the Cobalt Lodes— Trans. Geol. Soc. S. A. vol. vii. p. 110. Johannesburg, 1904.

Hubner, Adolf— 1872. Geognostische Skizzen aus Siidost-Afrika—Pet. Mitt. Band 18, pp. 422431. Gotha, 1872. Huhdleston, W. H.— 1883. Notes on the Diamond Rock of South Africa—Proc. Geol. Asfoc. vol. viii. pp. 05-81, 1883.

Huxley, T. H.— 1867. On some remains of large Dinosaurian Reptiles from the Stormberg Mountains, South Africa—Quart. Journ. Geol. Soc. Lond. vol. xxiiL pp. 1-6. London, 1867.

Itier, Jules— 1848. Notice sur la constitution geologique du cap de Bonne-Esptrance—In "Journal d'un voyage en Chine, etc." 3 vols. 8vo. Paris, 1848.

Jacobs and Chatrian— 1884. Le Diamant. Paris, 1884. Johnson, H.

Luttman— 1905. Notes on the Geology of the Fortuna Valley, Heidelberg, Transvaal— Trans. Geol. Soc. S. A. vol. vii. pp. 136-139. Johannesburg, 1905.

Johnson, J. P.— 1903. Notes on Sections at Shark River and the Creek, Algoa Bay—Trans.

Geol. Soc. S. A. vol. vi. pp. 9-11. Johannesburg, 1903.—— «. On the Discovery of Implement-bearing Deposits in the neighbourhood of Johannesburg; their relative Age, and bearing on the question of the Antiquity of Man in South Africa. Trans. Geol. Soc, S. A. vol. vi. pp. 60-66. Johannesburg, 1903. 1904. Stone Implements from beneath and abore the Alluvium of the Taaibosch Spruit—Trans. Geol. Soc. S. A. vol. vii. pp. 95-96. Johannesburg, 1904. 1905. Notes on a Section through the Witwatersrand Beds—Trans. Geol. Soc. S. A. vol. vii. pp. 117-122. Johannesburg, 1905.

— a. Note on the Stone Implements from Elandsfontein—No. 1, Trans. Geol.

Soc. S. A. vol. vii. p. 146. Johannesburg, 1905. Jones, T. Rupert— 1884. On the Geology of South Africa—Report Brit. Assoc. at Montreal, 1884, pp. 736-738, London, 1885, and Nature, xxx. pp. 553-554, London, 1884. 1899. The Great Glacial Moraine of Permian Age in South Africa—Xat. Sci. p. 199. March 1899.

— a. Notes on the Geology of West Swaziland—Geol. Mag. N.S., Dec. iv. vol.

vi. p. 105. March 1899. 1901. The Enon Conglomerate and its fossil Estheriie—Geol. Mag. N.S., Dec. iv. vol. viii. p. 350. August 1901. JORISSEN, E.— 1904. On the Occurrence of the Dolomite and Chert Series in the North-Eastern Part of the Rustenburg District.—Trans. Geol. Soc. S. A. vol. vii. pp. 30-38. Johannesburg, 1904. 1905. Notes on Some Intrusiva Granites in the Transvaal, the Orange River Colony, and in Swaziland—Trans. Geol. Soc. S. A. vol. vii. pp. 151-160. Johannesburg, 1905. Koch. See Schiueisser, 1895. Kossmat, Franz— 1894. Die Bedeutung der siidindischen

Kreide-Formation fiir die Reurtheilung der geographischen Verhaltnisse wahrend der s)titeren Kreidezeit—Jahrb.

d. k.-k. geol. Reichsanstalt, Wien, 1894, xliv. Pts. 3 and 4. K Hau.se, P. R.— 1897. Ueber den Einfluss der Eruptivgesteine auf die Erzfidirung der Witwatersrand Conglomerate und der im dolomitischen Kalkgebirge vorn Lydenberg auftretenden Quarzfliitze, nebst einer kurzen Schilderung der Grubenbezirke von Pilgrimsrest und De Kaap—Zeitechr. fur prakt. Geol., 1897, pp. 12-30. Krauss, Ferd.— 1843. Ueber die geologischen Verhaltnisse der ostlichen Kii.tc dis Kaplandes —Ber. iiber d. 20ste Versamml. d. ties. deut. Xaturf. u. Aeizte, pp. 126131. Mainz, 1843. 1850. Ueber einige Petrefacten aus der untern Kreide des Kaplandes—Nov. Act. Acad. C'aes. Leop.-Car. Nat. Cur. vol. xxii. pp. 441-446. 1850.

KuBALE, G.

1897. Un the Geology of the Klerksdorp Goldfields of the South African Republic—Report of the Slate Min. Engineer for 1896, p. 50. Pretoria, 1897.

KuNTZ, J.

1896. The Rand Conglomerates: How they were formed—Trans. Geol. Soc. of S. A. vol. i. part vi. pp. 113-122. Johannesburg, 1896. 1903. Pseudomorphosis of Quarts Pebbles into Calcite—Trans. Geol. Soc. S. A. vol. vi. p. 74. Johannesburg, 1903. 1904. Copper Ore in South-West Africa—Trans. Geol. Soc S. A. vol. vii. p. 70. Johannesburg, 1904. KYNASTON, H. 1904 Report on the Area lging to the North-East of Hatherley, and between the Pienaan and Elands Rivers—Report Geol. Survey Transvaal, 1903, pp. 3-6. Pretoria, 1904. Kynaston, H., and Hall, A. L.— 1904. The Geological Eeatures of the Diamond Pipes of the Pretoria District—

Report S. A. Assoc. Adv. Science, pp. 182-196. Johannesburg, 1904. — a. Diamondif rous Deposits—Report Geol. Survey Transvaal, 1903, pp. 43-48. Pretoria, 1904.

Lake, Philip— 1904. The Trilobites of the Bokkeveld Beds—Annals S. A. Museum, voL iv. pp. 2(il-220. Cape Town, 1904.

Launay, L. De— 1896. *Les mines d'or da Transvaal*—Paris, 1896.
1897. *Les diamants du Cap*—Paris, 1897. 1903. *Les richesses mine'rales de VAfrique*—Paris, 1903. Lawn, J. G.— 1898. *Thf Story of the Diamond Mines* — Diamond Fields Advertiser, Christmas Number. Kimbi-rley, Dec. 1898.

Legkktt, T. H., and Hatch, F. H.— 1902. *An Estimate of the Gold Production and Life of the Main Reef Series, Witnxitersrand, down to 6000 feet*— Trans. of the Institution of Mining and Metallurgy, vol. x. (1901-1902). London.

Leslie, T. N.— 1904. *The Fossil Flora of Vereeniging*—Trans. Geol. Soc. S. A. vol. vi. pp. 82-88. Johannesburg, 1904.

Lewis, Henry Carvill— 1897. *Papers and Notes on the Genesis and Matrix of the Diamond*. London, 1897. (Edited by T. G. Bonney.)

Lichtknstkin, Henry— 1812. *Travels in Southern Africa in the gears* 1803, 1804, 1805, and 1806— 4to. 2 vols. London, 1812. Lyddeker, R.— 1898. *The Tertiary Connection of South America irith South Africa*—Trans. Geol. Soc. S. A. vol. iii. p. 151. Johannesburg, Jan. 1898.

Marriott, H. F.— 1904. *Notes on the Chemical Composition of the Hospital Hill Shales*—Trans. (ieol. Soc. S. A. vol. vii. pp. 27-29. Johannesburg, 1904.

Maskelyne, Story X., and Flight, W. — 1874. *On the Character of the Diamantiferous Rock of South Africa*— Quart. Joum. GeoL Soc. vol. xxx. pp. 406-408. London, 1874.

Maucft, Carl— 1872. *Carl Mauch's Reisen im Inneren von Siid-Afrika*, 1865-1872, Pet. Mitt, Gotha, 1872—Erganzimgsband VII.

Mellor, E. T.— 1904. *On some Glaciated Land Surfaces occurring in the District between Pretoria and Balmoral, with Notes on the Extent and Distribution of the Glacial Conglomerate in the same Area*—Trans. Geol. Soc. S. A. vol. vii. pp. 18-26. Johannesburg, 1904.

——*a. The Waterberg Sandstone Formation, etc.* — Trans. Geol. Soe. S. A. vol. vii. p. 39. Johannesburg, 1904.

— 6. *Report on Portions of the Pretoria and Middelburg Districts between the Elands River Valley and Balmoral*— Report Geol. Survey Transvaal, 1903, pp. 7-27. Pretoria, 1904.

1905. *Outliers of the Karroo System near the junction of the Elands and Olifants Rivers in the Transvaal*—Tram. Geol. Soc. S. A. vol. vii. p. 133. Johannesburg, 1905.

— a. *The Sandstones of Buiskop and the Springbok Flats.*—Ibid. voL viii. pp. 33-37. Johannesburg, 1905.

— b. *Evidence of Contemporaneous Volcanic Action of the Lower Portion of the Waterberg Formation*—Ibid. vol. viii. pp. 38-41. Johannesburg, 1905. Mennell, F. P.— 1902. *The Geology of the Country round BuUixcayo*—First Annual Report Rhodesia Musenm for 1902, pp. 9-11.

1904. *The Geology of Southern Rhodesia*—Rhodesian Musenm Special Report No. 2, 1904, 8vo, pp. 42.

Merensky, Hans— 1905. *The Gold Deposits of the Murchison Range in the North-Eastern Transvaal*—Trans. Geol. Soc. S. A. vol. viii. pp. 4 2-46. Johannesburg, 1905.

Meunier, Stanislas— 1893. *Recherches mine'ralogiques sur les Gisements diamantiferes de VAfrique australe*—Bull. Soc. d'hist. nat. d'Autun, tome 6me, 1893.

Moissan, Henri— 1893. *Etude de la m/teorite de Canon Diablo*—Comptes rendus Acad. Sci. Paris, tome cxvi. (1893), pp. 228-295.

1 894. *Nouvelles experiences sur la reproduction du diamant*—Ibid. tome cxviii. (1894), pp. 320-326. 1896. *Sur quelqnes experiences nouvelles relatives d la preparation du diamant* — Ibid. tome exxiii. pp. 206-210.

Moi.EXGRAAFF, G. A. F. 1 890. *Schets van de Bodemgesteldheid van de Zuid-Afrikaan sche Republiek*— Tijdschrift van het Koninklijk Nederlandsch Aardrijkskundig Genootschap, Jaargang, 1890. Leiden. 1891. *Voordracht over de geologische gesteldheid van de goudvelden op het Hoogereld in de Transvaal, Gehouden op de algemeene vergadering van het derde Natuur-en Scheikundig Congres te Utrecht, 3*

April 1891. 1894. *Beitrag zur Geologie der Umgegend der Goldfeldern auf dem Hoogeveld in der Süd-Afrikanischen Republik*—Nenes Jahrb. f. Min., Beil. Bd. ix. pp. 174-290. Stuttgart, 1894.

1897. *Diamonds at Rietfontein*—Trans. Geol. Soc. S. A. vol. iii. pt. 9, pp. 122-123. Johannesburg, Nov. 1897. 1898. *The Glacial Origin of the Diryka Conglomerate*—Trans. Geol. Soc. S. A. vol. iv. p. 103. Johannesburg, Oct. 1898.

1898 a. *Report of the Shite Geologist of the South African Republic for the gear* 1897. Trans. GeoL Soc. S. A. vol. iv. pt. 6, pp. 119-147. Johannesburg, 1898.

1899. *Rapport over het jaar* 1898 *van den Staats geoloog aan HEd. Reegering der Zuid Afrikaansche Republiek, Pretoria*, 1899—English Translation. Pretoria, 1902. 1900. *Die Reihenfolge and Correlation der geologischen Formationen in Siid*

Neues Jahrb. f. Miu., 1900, Bd. i. pp. 113-119.

1901. *Ge'ologie de la Republique Sud-Africaine du Transvaal*—Bull, de la Soc. Geol. de. France, 4 Serie, Tome i., 1901, pp. 13-92. 1902. *Geological Sketch Map of the Transvaal*, 1902— (With explanatory note.)

— a. *Address by Vice-President*— Trans. Geol. Soc. S. A. vol. v. pp. 69-75,

Nov. 1902. Johannesburg, 1902.

1903. *Remarks on the Vredefart Mountain-Land*—Trans. Geol. Soc. S. A. vol. vi. pp. 20-26. Johannesburg, 1903.

—-«. *Preliminary Note on a hitherto unrecognised Formation underlging the Black Reef Series* — Trans. Geol. Soc. S. A. vol. vi. part iv. p. 68. Johannesburg, 1903.

1904. *Notes on our Present Knowledge of the Occurrence of Nepheline Sgenite and allied Rocks in the Transvaal*— Trans. Geol. Soc. S. A. vol. vi. pp. 89-90. Johannesburg, 1904.

— a. *The Vredefort Mountain-land*— Trans. Geol. Soc. S. A. voL vii. pp. 110-116. Johannesburg, 1904.

— b. *Geology of the Transvaal.* Translation by J. H. Ronaldson of 1901, with additions by the author. Edinburgh and Johannesburg, 1904.

1905. *Note on the Geology of a Portion*

of the Klerksdorp District, with Special Reference to th. Development of the Lower Witwatersrand Beds and the Vaal River System—Trans. Geol. S. A. vol. viii. pp. 16-25. Johannesburg, 1905.

MolYNEUx, A. J. C.— 1903. 77k Sedimentary Deposits of Rhodesia—Q.J.G. S. voL lix. pp. 266-291. 1903.

Molyneox, William— 1881. Report on the Geology of the Karroo and Stormberg—Parl. Report. Cape Town, 1881. Moore, C. Wilson— 1896. The Economic Importance of the Murchison Range—Trans. Geol. Soe. S. A. pp. 51-62, vol. i. part. iii. Johannesburg, 1896. 1897. Some Observations on the Geology of the Sabie Valley—Trans. Geol. Soc. S. A. vol. ii. part ix. pp. 131-140. Johannesburg, 1897. MOUllk, A. 1885. Memoire sur la ge'ologie generate et sur les mines de diamants de vAfrique du Sud—Ann. des Mines, 8 serie, tome vii., Paris, 1885, pp. 178-344. Newton, R Billen— 1896. On the Occurrence of Alectryonia ungulata in S.E. Africa, with a Notice of Previous Researches on the Cretaceous Cunchology of Southern Africa—Journ. of Conch, vol. viii. pp. 136-151. London, 1896. North, Frederic W.— 1878. Colonial Mining Engineer's Report on the Coalfield of the Stormbergen —Parliamentary Report. Cape Town, 1878. 1881. Report upon the Coalfields of Klip Rirer, Weenan, Umvoti, and Victoria Counties, Natal—Dept. of Mines Report, 1881.

Osborne, C. F. See Bain, T.

Owen, Richard— 1856. Pt, L Description of Certain Fossil Crania, discovered by A. G. Bain, Esq., in Sandstone Rocks at the South-Eastern Extremity of Africa, referable to Different Species of an Extinct Genus of Reptilia (Dicynodon, and indicative of a New Tribe or Sub-Order of Sauna — Trans. Geol. Soc. 2nd ser. vol. vii. p. 59. London, 1856.

— Pt, II. Ibid. p. 233.

— Pt. III. Ibid. p. 241.

1862. On the Dicynodont Reptilia, etc—Phil. Trans. Roy. Soc. MDCCCLXII. Passargk, S.— 1901. Beitrag zur Kenntnis der Geologic von Brituch Betschnanaland—Zeit. der Ges. fur Erdk. zu Berlin. Bd. xxxvi. 1901, pp.

20-68. Berlin, 1901. 1904. Die klimatischen Verhiiltnisse Siid-Afrikas seit dem mittlerm Mcsozoicum —Zeitschrift der Gesellschaft fur Erdkunde zu Berlin. Jalirgang 1904, No. 3, pp. 176-193.

— a. Die Inselsberglandschaften im tropuchen Afrika—Naturw. Wochensch.

Jena, July 17, p. 657. 1904.

Penning, W. H.— 1884. A Sketch of the High-level Coalfields of South Africa—Quart. Journ. Geol. Soc. vol. xL pp. 658-662. London, 1884.

1885. A Sketch of the Gold Fields of Lydenburg and De Kaap, in the Transvaal, South Africa—Quart. Journ. Geol. Soc. vol. xli. p. 569. London, 1885. 1888. The South African Gulofields—J our. Soc. Arts, xxxvi. pp. 433-444. 1888. 1891. A Contribution to the Geology of the Southern Transvaal—Quart. Journ. GeoL Soc. vol. xlvii. pp. 451-461. London, 1891.

PlNCHIN, R.

1875. A Short Description of the Geology of part of the Eastern Province of the Colony of the Cape of Good Hope—Quart, Journ. Geol. Soc. vol. xxxi. pp. 106-108. London, 1875.

Prister, August— 1898. Notes on the Origin and Formation of the Witwatersrand Auriferous Deposits—Trans. Geol. Soc. S. A. vol. iv. p. 19. Johannesburg, May 1898.

Raisin, C. A. See under Bonney, Raisin, and Stone.

Redmayne, R. A. G.— 1893. The Geology and Coal-Deposits of Natal—Trans. Fed. Inst. Min. Eng. London, 1893.

Reed, F. R. C— 1903. Brachiopoda from the Bokkerehl Beds—Annals S. A. Mus. vol. iv. p. 165. Cape Town, 1903. 1904. Mollusca from the Bokkeveld Beds—Annals S. A. Mus. vol. iv. p. 239. Cape Town, 1904.

Rogers, A. W.— 1897. Summary of the llrork done in the South-lVestern Districts—Annual Report Geol. Comm. for 1896, pp. 13-14. Cape Town, 1897. 1898. Survey of the Stellenboseh District—-Annual Report Geol. Comm. for 1897, p. 47. Cape Town, 1898. 1902. On a Glacial Conglomerate-in the Table Mountain Sandstone—Trans.

S. A. Phil. Soc. vol. xi. pp. 236-242. Cape Town, 1902. 1903. Report of the Acting Geologist for the Year 1902—Annual Report Geol. Comm. for 1902, p. 3. Cape Town, 1903.

— a. The Geological History of the Gouritz Rirer System—Trans. S. A. PhiL

Soc. vol. xiv. p. 375. Cape Town, 1903.

1904. Geological Surrey of Parts of the Divisions of Piquetberg, Clanmlliam, and Van Rhyn's Dorp. Annual Report Geol. Comm. for 1903, p. 141. Cape Town, 1904. 190". An Introduction to the Geology of Cape Colony—8vo, pp. 463. Iiomlon, 1805.

Rogers, A. W., and Schwarz, E. H. L. — 1898. Summary of Work done during 1897 between the Karroo and tin; Langebergen—Annual Report Geol. Comm. for 1897, p. 61. Cape Town, 1898.

1899. Notes on-the Recent Limestones on Parts of the South and ll'est Coasts of Cape Colony—Trans. South African Phil. Soc. vol. x. part iii. pp. 427435. Cape Town, 1899. 1900. Report on Caledon, Bredasdorp, Swellendam, and Southern Part of Worcester—Annual Report Geol. Comm. for 1898, p. 39. Cape Town, 1900.

— a. Report on the Southern Districts between Breede River and George—

Annual Report GeoL Comm. for 1898, p. 57. Cape Town, 1900.

— 6. Report on Oudtshoorn—Annual Report of the Geol. Comm. for 1898, pp. 67-69. Cape Town, 1900.

— c. Notes on the Geology round Worcester—Annual Report Geol. Comm.

for 1898, p. 83. Cape Town, 1900.

— d. Geology of the Orange River Valley in the Hope Town and Prieska Districts—Annual Report of the Geol. Comm. for 1899, pp. 67-97. Cape Town, 1900.

— e. The Orange Rirer Ground Moraine—Trans. S. A. Phil. Soc. voL xi. part ii. pp. 113-120. Cape Town, 1900. 1901. Report on the Survey of Parts of the Uitenhage and Port Elizabeth Divisions—Annual Report Geol. Comm. for 1900, pp. 3-18. Cape Town, 1901.

— *a. Report on the Survey of Parts of the Clanwilliam, Van Rhyn's Dorp, and Calvinia Divisions*—Annual Report Geol. Comm. for 1900, p. 21. Cape Town, 1901.

— *ft. Report on a Geological Route Survey from Beaufort West to Calvinia*—
Annual Report Geol. Comm. for 1900, p. 57. Cape Town, 1901.

— *c. Belort on th« Geology of the Cederbergen and adjoining Country*—
Annual Report Geol. Comm. for 1900, p. 67. Cale Town, 1901.

1902. *Report on a Journey from Swellendam to Mossel Bay*—Annual Report Geol. Com. for 1901, p. 8. Cape Town, 1902.

— *a. General Survey of the Rocks in the Southern Parts of the Transkei and Pondoland, including a Description of the Cretaceous Rocks of Eastern Pondoland*—Annual Report of the Geol. Comm. for 1901, pp. 25-46.
Cape Town, 1902.

1902 *b. Geological Survey of the Division ofKentani*— Annual Report Geol. Comm. for 1901, p. 49. Cape Town, 1902.

1903. *lteport on a Survey of Parts of the Beaufort West, Prince Albert, and Sutherland Divisions*—Annual Report Geol. Comm. for 1902, p. 98. Cape Town, 1903.

— *a. The Transkei Gap*—Trans. S. A. Phil. Soc. vol. xiv. p 66. Cape Town, 1903.

Rogers, A. W., and Du Toit, A. L.
— 1904. *Geological Survey of Ports of the Divisions of Ceres, Sutherland, and Calvinia*—Annual Report Geol. Comm. for 1903, p. 11. Cape Town, 1904.

— *a. The Sutherland Volcanic Pipes and their Relationship to other Vents in South Africa*—Trans. S. A. Phil. Soc. vol. xv. p. 61. Cape Town, 1904.

RtJRIDGk, R. X.
1856. *Notes on the Geology of Some Parts of South Africa*—Quart. Journ. Geol. Soc. vol. xii. pp. 237-238. London, 1856. 1859. *Some Points in the Geology of South Africa*—Quart. Journ. GeoL Soc.
vol. xv. p. 195. London, 1859. 1865. *On the Changes rendered Necessary in*

thr Geological Map of South Africa by Recent Discoveries of Fossils—Quart. Journ. Geol. Soc. vol. xxi. pp. 437-439. London, 1865.
Salter, J. W.— 1856. *Description of Palaeozoic Crustacea and Radiata from South Africa* —
Trans. GeoL Soc. Lond., Second Ser. vol. vii. pp. 215-225. London, 1856.
SaNDBERfiEH, F.
1852. *Vber einige yalUozoische Versteinerungen des Cap-Landes*—Neues Jahrb. f. Min., 1852, pp. 581-585.
Sawyer, A. R— 1889. *The Witwatersrand Gold-field: Mining at Johannesburg*—Trans. N. Staff. Inst, of Min. and Mech. Eng. vol. x. 1889.

— *a. Coal-mining in South Africa*—Trans. N. Staff. Inst, of Min. and Mech. Eng. vol. x. 1889.

— *6. Diamonds in South Africa: Mining at Kimberley* —Trans. N. Staff. Inst, of Min. and Mech. Eng. vol. x. 1889. 1893. *Report npnu the Geology and Mineral Resources of the Division of Prince Albert and Surrounding Districts*—Parliamentary Report. Cape Town, 1893.
1897. *Notes on the Extension of the Alain Reef Westwards of li'itpoortje*—Trans. Geol. Soc. S. A. vol. ii. part iii. No. 1, pp. 35-36. Johannesburg, 1897.
— *a. Notes on the Bezuidenville Borehole*—Trans. Geol. Soc. S. A. vol. ii. part iii. p. 38. Johannesburg, 1897.
1898. *The South Rand Coal-field*—Trans. Fed. Inst. Min. Eng. London, 1898. 1899. *Remarks on the Anticlinal Theory in Connection with Rand Deposits*— Trans. Geol. Soc. S. A., vol. v. pp. 45-52. Johannesburg, April 1899.
1901. *The Portuguese Manica Gold-field*—Trans. Inst. Min. Eng. voL xix. (1900), pp. 265-278. London, 1901.
1903. *Remarks on some Granite Masses of the Transvaal*—Trans. GeoL Soc. S. A. vol. vi. pp. 47-49. Johannesburg, 1903.
— *«. The Origin of the Slates occurring on the Rand and in other African Gold fields*—Trans. Geol. Soc. S. A. vol. vii. pp. 70-72. Johannesburg, 1903.
— *6. Remarks on the South-Eastern Extension of the Vredefort Granite Mass*—Trans. Geol. Soc. S. A. vol. vi. pp.

75-76. Johannesburg, 1903.
— *c. Further Remarks on the Portuguese Manica Gold-field*—Trans. Inst. Min. Eng. vol. xxv. pp. 637-642. London, 1903. Schellwiejj, E.— 1901. *Uber Semionotus Ay.*—Schrift. d. phys. -6kon. Ges. zu Konigsberg, i. Pr. 1901.
Schenck, Adolf— 1888. *Die geologische Entwickelung Siidafrikas*—Pet. Mitt, 34. Band, pp. 225-232. Gotha, 1888.
1889. *Vorkommen des Goldes in Transvaal*—Zeit. dor deut. geol. (Jos. Jahrg.) 1889.
— *«. Ueber GUicialerscheinungen in Siidafrika*— Abd. d. VIII. deut. Geo graphentages, pp. 145-161. Berlin, 1889. 1893. *Gebirgsbau und fiodengestaltung von Deatsch-SudweM-Afrika* —Verb. d. X. deut. geogr. Tagus in Stuttgart, 1893, pp. 155-172.
1896. *On Glacial Phenomena in South Africa*—Traus. Geol. Soc. S. A. vol. i. part vii. pp. 129-141. Johannesburg, 1896. 1901. *Deutsch-Siidwest-Afrika im Vergleich zum ubrigen Siid-afrika*— Alxl. d. XIII. deut. Georalihentages, in Breslau, 1901. Schmeisseh— 1895. *Ueber Vorkommen und Gewinnung der nutzbaren Mineralien in der Siidafrikanischen Republik (Transvaal) unter besonderer Berucksichtigung d.cs Goldhergbaues*, pp. 1-151. Berlin, 1895. SCHMITZ-DUMONT 1897. *Explanation of the Geological Map of Pretoria and the Section running South and North from Vereeniging to Pretoria*—Report State Mining Engineer, 1896, p. 14. Pretoria, 1897.
Schwarz, E. H. L.— 1897. *Geological Survey of the Beaufort lVest District*—Annual Report Geol. Com., 1896, pp. 15-26. Cape Town, 1897.
— *a. Summary of the Work done in the Tullwyh Area and Worcester District*—Annual Report Geol. Com., 1896, pp. 27-29. Cape Town, 1897.
1898. *Summary of Work done in the Robertson, Lady Grey, and Eastern Parts of the Swelkndam District*—Annual Report Geol. Com. for 1897, p. 53. Cape Town, 1898. 1900. *Report on the Country round Vogelvlei, Piquetberg Road, and Saron*— Annual Report Ge-

ol. Com. for 1898, p. 25. Cape Town, 1900.

— *a. The Country round French Hock and Pniel*—Annual Report Geol. Com. for 1898, p. 29. Cape Town, 1900.

— *b. Detailed Description of lite Bokkeveld Beds at the Gamka Poort, Prince Albert*—Annual Report GeoL Com. 1899, p. 33. Cape Town, 1900.

— *c. Knysna, between the Gouwkamma (Homtini) and the Blue Krantz Rivers*
—Annual Report Geol. Com. for 1899, pp. 53-63. Cape Town, 1900.

1903. *Geological Survey of Parts of the Matatiele Division, Griqualand East* — Annual Report Geol. Com. for 1902, p. 13. Cape Town, 1903.

— *a. The Volcanoes of Griqualand East*—Trans. S. A. Phil. Soc., vol. xiv p. 98. Cape Town, 1903.

1904. *High-level Gravels of the Cape and the Problem of the Karroo Gold*—Tram S. A. Phil. Soc. vol. xv. p. 43. Cape Town, 1904.

— *a. Geological Survey of Parts of Prince Albert, Willowmore and Uniondale*
—Annual Report Geol. Com. for 1903, p. 73. Cape Town, 1904. *See also* Rogers and Schwarz.

Seeley, H. G.— 1878. *On New Species of Procolophon from the Cape Colony, preserved in Dr. Grierson's Museum, Thornhill, Dumfriesshire, with some Remarks on the Affinities of the Genus*—Quart. Journ. Geol. Soc. Lond. xxxiv. pp. 797807. London, 1878.

1887. *Researches on the Structure, Organisation, and Classification of the Fossil Reptilia. I. On Proterosaurus speneri* (von Meyer)—Phil. Trans. Roy. Soc. Lond. vol. clxxviii. (1887), B, pp. 187-213. London, 1887. 1888. *Ditto.* II. On *Pareiasaurus bombidens* (Owen) *and the Significance of its Affinities to Amphibians, Reptiles and Mammals*— Ibid. vol. clxxix. (1888), B, pp. 59-109. London, 1888.

— *a. Ditto.* III. *On Parts of the Skeleton of a Mammal from Triassic Rocks of Klipfontein, Fraserburg, South. Africa (Theriodesmus phxjlarchus, Seeley), illustrating the Reptilian Inheritance in the Mammalian Hand* —Ibid. vol.

clxxix. (1888), B, pp. 141-155. London, 1888.

— *h. Ditto.* V. *On Associated Bones of a Small Anomodont Reptile, Keiro gnathus cordylus (Seeley), showing the Relative Dimensions of the Anterior Parts of the Skeleton and Structure of the Fore-limb and Shoulder Girdle* — Ibid. vol. clxxix. (1888), B, pp. 487-501 London, 1888.

1889. *Ditto.* VI. *On the Anomodont Reptilia and their Allies*—Ibid. vol. clxxx. (1889), B, pp. 215-296. London, 1889.

— *a. Lecture on the Resources of the Cape Colony*—8vo, pp. 24. Cape Town, 1889.

1890. *Some Scientific Results of a Mission to South Africa*—-Trans. S. A. Phil. Soc. vol. vi. part i. pp. 1-16. Cape Town, 1890. 1891. *On Bubalus baini*— Geol. Mag. decade 3, viii. pp. 199-201. London, 1891. 1892. *a. On Delphinognathus conocephalus (Seeley) from the Middle Karroo Beds, Cape Colony, preserved in the South African Museum, Cape Town*— Quart. Journ. Geol. Soc. Lond. xlviii. pp. 469-475. London, 1892.

— *b. On some further Evidence of Endothiodon bathystoma (Owen) from Oude Kloof in the Nieuwveldt Mountains, Cape Colony*—Quart. Journ. Geol. Soc. Lond. xlviii. pp. 476-480. London, 1892.

— *c On a New Reptile from Weltevreden, Beaufort West, Eunotosaurus africanus* (Seeley) — Quart. Journ. Geol. Soc. Lond. xlviii. pp. 583585. London, 1892.

— *d. The Mesosauria of South Africa*—Quart. Journ. Geol. Soc. Lond. vol. xlviii. pp. 586-604. London, 1892.

— *e. Researches on the Structure, Organisation, and Classification of the Fossil Reptilia.* VII. *Further Observations on Pareiasaurus* — Phil. Trans. Roy. Soc. vol. clxxxiii. (1892), B, pp. 311-370. London, 1892. 1894. *Ditto.* VIII. *Further Evidences of the Skeleton in Deuterosaurus and Blwpalodon froni the Permian Rocks of Russia*—Ibid. vol. clxxxv. (1894;,
B, pp. 663-717. London, 1894. 1894 *a. Ditto. On Euskelesaurus brownii*

(Huxley)—Ann. and Mag. Nat. Hist. series 6, voL xiv., 1894, pp. 317-340. 1895. *Ditto.* IX. Sect. 1. *On the Therosuchia*— PhiL Trans. vol. clxxxv. (1894), B, pp. 987-1018. London, 1895.

—. *a. Ditto.* Part IX. Sect. 2. *The Reputed Mammals from the Karroo Formation of Cape Colony* — Ibid. vol. clxxxv. (1894), B, pp. 10191028. London, 1895.

— 6. *Ditto.* Part IX Sect. 3. *On Diademodon*—Ibid. vol. clxxxv. (1894), B, pp. 1029-1041. London, 1895.

— *c. Ditto.* Part IX. Sect. 4. *On the Gomphodontia*—. Ibid. voL clxxxvL (1895), B, pp. 1-57. London; 1895.

— /. *Ditto.* Part IX. Sect. 5. *On the Skeleton in New Vynodontia from the Karroo Rocks*—Ibid. voL clxxxvi. (1895), B, pp. 59-148. London, 1895.

— *e. Ditto.* Part IX. Sect. 6. *Associated Remains of Two Small Skeletons from Klipfontein, Fraserburg*—Ibid. vol. clxxxvi. (1895), B, pp. 149162. London, 1895.

— /. *Ditto. On the Type of the Genus Masospondylus and on Some Vertebra: and Limb-Rones of M. (?) brownii*— Aim. and Mag. of Nat. Hist, series 6, xv. pp. 102-125. London, 1895.

— *g. Ditto. Note on the Skeleton of Pareiasaurus baini*—Geol. Mag. dec. 4, voL ii., 1895, pp. 1-3. London, 1895. 1897. *On Ceratodus kannemegeri*—Geol. Mag. dec. 4, 1897, pp. 543-544. 1898. *On the Skull of Mochlorhinus platyceps from Bethulie, O.F.S., preserved in the Albany Museum, Grahamstown*—Ann. and Mag. Nat. Hist. series 7, vol. i., 1898, pp. 164-171.

— *a. On Oudenodon (Aulacephalus) pithecops from the Dicynodon Beds of East London, Cape Colony*—Geol. Mag. dec. 4, vol. v. pp. 107-110. 1898. 1900. *On the Skeleton of a Theriodont Reptile from the Baviaans River (Cape Colony)*—Dicranozygoma leptoscelus, gen. et sp. nov., Quart. Journ. Geol. Soc. voL lvi. p. 646. London, 1900. Seward, A. C.— 1897. *On the Association of Sigillaria and Glussopteris in South Africa*— Quart. Journ. Geol. Soc. vol. liii. pp. 315-340. London, 1897. 1898. *Notes on the Plant-Remains (from Vereeniging) in Dr. Hatch's Paper*—

Quart, Journ. Geol. Soc. vol. liv. pp. 92-93. London, 1898. 1903. *Fossil Floras of Cape Colony* —Annals of the South African Museum, vol. IV. Gape Town, 1903. 1904. *Report on Collections of Natal Fossil Plants from (1) The Ecca Coal Series of Umhlali on the North-East Coast of Natal; (2) The Drakensbery Range in West Natal*—Second Report Geol. Survey Natal, p. 97. London, 1904.

Shakpf., Daniki,— 1856. *Description of Fossils from the Secondary Rocks of Sunday River and Zwartkop River, South Africa, collected by Dr. Atherstone and A. G. Haiti, Esq.*—Trans. Geol. Soc. second series, vol. vii. pp. 193-203. London, 1856.

— a. *Description of Palceozoic Mollusca from South Africa*—Trans. GeoL Soc.

second series, vol. vii. pp. 206-215. London, 1856. 1856 b. *Notes on some Fossils from the Karroo Desert and its Vicinity*— Trans. Geol. Soc. second series, vol. vii. p. 225. London, 1856.

— c. *Description of some Remains of Mollusca from near Graaf Reinet*—

Trans. Geol. Soc. second series, vol. vii. pp. 225-226. London, 1856. Shaw, F. G.— 1896. *The Gold-fields of Matabeleland*—Trans. Fed. Inst. Min. Eng. London, 1896.

Stapff, F. M.— 1889. *Das "glaziale" Dwykakonglomerat Siidafrikas*— Naturw. Wochenschrift. Berlin, 1889.

— a. *Enigegnung auf den Vortrag des Herrn Dr. A. Schenck: "Ueber Glacialer scheinungen in SUd-Afrika"*—Abh. des 8ten dent. Geographentages, pp. 16-21. Berlin, 1889.

Steart, F. A. *See* Hall, A. K, and Steart, F. A.

Stelzner, A. W.— 1894. *Die Diamantgruben im Kimberley*—Zeit. fiir prakt. Geol., 1894, p. 153.

Stewart, D. S.-S.— 1899. *The Mineral Wealth of the Zoutpansberg: the Murchison Range Goldbelt*—Trans. Inst. Min. Eng. London, 1899.

Stone, J. B. *See under* Bonney, Raisin and Stone.

Stonbstreet, G. D.— 1897. *Notes on the Black Reef at Natal Spruit*—Trans. Geol. Soc. S. A. vol. ii. pt. iii. pp. 53-55.

Johannesburg, 1897.

Stow, G. W.— 1859. *On some Fossils from South Africa*—Quart. Journ. Geol. Soc. vol. xv. pp. 193-5. London, 1859. 1861. *Note on the Geology of Sunday River*—The Geologist, vol. iv. p. 238. London, June 1861. 1 871. *On some Points in South African Geology*—Quart-Journ. Geol. Soc. vol. xxvii. pp. 497-548. London, 1871. 1 874. *Geological Notes upon Griqualand West, with descriptions of the Specimens by T. Rupert Jones*—Quart. Journ. Geol. Soc. vol. xxx. pp. 581-680. London, 1874. 1878. *Report of the Geological Surveyor.* Bloemfontein, 1878. 1879. *Report of the Geological Survey of the Orange Free State from the ltfih April to 17th December 1878.* Bloemfontein, 1879. 1881. *Correspondence "between the Griqualand West Government and Mr. Geo. W. Stow on the subject of the Geological Survey of Griqualand West*— Pari. Paper. Cape Town, 1881.

Sutherland, P. C.— 1855. *Notes on the Geology of Natal, South Africa*—Quart. Journ. Geol. Soc. vol. xi. pp. 465-468. London, 1855. 1868. *On the Geology of Natal.* Pietermaritzburg, 1868.

Tate, Ralph— 1867. *On Some Secondary Fossils from South Africa*— Quart. Journ. Geol. Soc. vol. xxiii. pp. 139-175. London, 1867.

Toit, A. L. DC— 1904. *Geological Survey of Elliot and Xalanga*—Annual Report Gcol. Com. for 1903, p. 171. Cape Town, 1904. *See also* Rogers, A. W., and Toit, A. L. do.

Truscott, S. J.— 1902. *The Witwatersrand Gold-fields Banket and Mining Practice.* London, 1902. Uleich, Arnold— 1893. *Paliiozoische Versteinerungen a us llolivien*— Xeues Jahrb. Reil. R. viii. pp. 5-115. Stuttgart, 1893. Voit, F. W.— 1904. *A Contribution to the Geology of German South-West Africa*—Trans. Oeol. Soe. S. A. voL vii. Johannesburg, 1904. Watermeyer, J. C.— 1898. *Deutsch SM-West Afrika*—Berlin, 1898. 1900. *Notes on a Journey in German South-West Africa*—Trans. S. A. Phil. Soc. vol. xi.

pt. i. p. 19. Cape Town, 1900. Williams, Gardner F.— 1902. *The Diamond Mines of South Africa,* 8vo, pp. 681. London, 1902. 1904. 77k; *Genesis of the Diamond* — Trans. Anier. Inst. Min. Eng. Read at the Lake Superior Meeting in Sept. 1904. Woodward, Henry— 1873. *Oh a New Trilobite from the Cape of Good Hcrpe* —Quart. Journ. Geo!. Soc. vol. xxix. pp. 31-33. London, 1873.

Wclf, Heinrich— 1887. *Reitrag zur Petrographie des Hercrolandes in Siid-West Afrika*—Inailg. Diss. Wien, 1887. WOLFINg, E. A.— 1888. *Untersuchuny eines Nephelinsgenit aus dem mittleren Transvaal, SudAfrika*—Neues Jahrb., 1888, Bd. ii. pp. 16-34.

Wyley, Andrew— 1856. *Provisional Report upon the Nature and General Character of the Copper Districts of South Namaqualand* — Parliamentary Report (C. 35-56). Cape Town, 1856. 1858. *Report of the Geological Surveyor upon a Journey made by him, mainly during the gear 1858, in two directions across the Colony, and its results.* (Detailed report to follow as Appendix.) 1859. *Notes of a Journey in two directions across the Colony, made in the Years 1857-58, with a view to determine the Character and Order of the various Geological Formations*—being the Appendix to the above report. Cape Town, 1859..

Zeiller, R— 1896. *Etude sur quelques plantes fosriles, en particulier vertehraria et glossopteris, des environs de Johannesburg (Transvaal).* Bull. Soc. Geol. France, 3 sir, tome xxiv. pp. 349-378. Lille, 1896.

CPSIA information can be obtained at www.ICGtesting.com
Printed in the USA
LVOW05s1021111113

360737LV00028B/799/P